PARROTS

PARROTS

David Alderton

Photography by Cyril Laubscher

No. 16070

ISBN 1-56465-100-2
Library of Congress catalog card no. 91-67676

The author

David Alderton has kept and bred a wide variety of birds for
nearly 30 years and has travelled extensively in pursuit of this
interest, visiting other enthusiasts in various parts of the
world. He has written a number of books on avicultural subjects,
and contributes regularly to general and specialist publications
in the UK and overseas. David studied veterinary medicine at
Cambridge University, and now, in addition to writing, runs a
highly respected international service that offers advice on the
needs of animals kept in both domestic and commercial
environments. He is presently both a Council Member of the
Avicultural Society and the Chairman of the National Council for
Aviculture – the umbrella organisation for birdkeeping
societies in the UK.

The photographer

Cyril Laubscher has been interested in aviculture and
ornithology for more than 35 years and has travelled extensively
in Europe, Australia and Southern Africa photographing wildlife.
When he left England for Australia in 1966 as an enthusiastic
birdkeeper this fascination found expression as he began to
portray birds photographically.
Since then, special techniques have been developed by him for
photographing birds and animals under studio conditions – to
augment his photography in the wild – and his photographs have met
with considerable international acclaim. Solo photographic
exhibitions of his work at the NEC Birmingham, have further
enhanced his reputation. During the last five years, Cyril has
completed 12 books as sole photographer and has been a major
photographic contributor to numerous others.
Cyril is currently working with Dr Karl-L Schuchmann on 'The
Anchicaya Rainforest Project', preparing text and photographs for
a series of books and lectures on the importance of rainforests
and how birds, in particular, have a crucial role
to play in their regeneration.

*Endpapers: **Red-masked Conures***
*Half-title page: **Nyassa Lovebird***
*Title page: **Hawk-headed Parrot***
*Page 5: **Fairy Lorikeet***
*Pages 6-7: **Celestial Parrotlets***

Credits

Editor: Anne McDowall
Designer: John Heritage
Colour reproductions: P & W Graphics Pte Ltd.
Filmset: SX Composing Ltd.
Index: Stuart Craik
Printed in Hong Kong

CONTENTS

INTRODUCTION

Most people, even if they have no particular interest in birds, will recognize a parrot without any difficulty. The reasons for the popularity of parrots as pets are well known: the majority of species are quite easy to maintain, and few other pets will become as responsive to their owners, displaying unrivalled powers of mimicry. In addition, their potentially long lifespan is almost legendary; many live for 50 years or more, and even the smaller members of the group will breed in their twenties.

The 330 or so parrot species are found in the tropical areas of the world, where they have been kept for centuries. In Central America, for example, it is clear from archaeological evidence that macaws and other parrots were being kept and bred successfully in aviary surroundings as long ago as the

1400s. It was at about this time, too, that parrots from the New World were first introduced to Europe, where they soon became very popular as companion birds. (King Henry VIII is just one monarch to have owned a pet parrot, which possessed a large vocabulary) — and even before this, Asiatic species were known here.

Until comparatively recently, most parrots were kept as pet birds, and relatively little emphasis was placed on breeding them. Since the early 1980s, however, this situation has changed, as knowledge about the nutritional and reproductive needs of parrots has advanced. At least 243 species have now been bred successfully in captivity.

This book gives indispensable advice on all aspects of keeping parrots, from selecting a pet through to housing and breeding these birds. In the second part of the book (from page 76) you can find more specific information about the requirements of the individual species in a detailed survey of all the main groups represented in aviculture, including the Budgerigar, the Cockatiel, lovebirds, parrotlets, conures, lories and lorikeets, parakeets, amazons, macaws, cockatoos, and more.

CHOOSING PARROTS

The parrots featured in the second part of this book have a wide range of requirements, which you will need to consider carefully before choosing a particular species. This section details some of the more general points that you should bear in mind when choosing a parrot, in particular how to tell if a bird is healthy. While some species can be kept quite happily in the home – budgerigars and cockatiels make good family pets, and amazons, macaws and cockatoos are suitable for the more ambitious – others, such as parrotlets and parakeets, really need to be kept in an aviary.

Which birds make the best pets?

While the Budgerigar remains unchallenged as the most widely kept pet bird, many other birds in the parrot family are also highly valued as companions. Unfortunately, however, a significant number of the larger species, such as the cockatoos, can be very noisy in the home, and

tend to screech regularly as they mature. They are also destructive by nature, and their powerful beaks also mean that they can be difficult to handle.

Cockatiels are similar in appearance to cockatoos, but are much quieter birds, with an attractive warbling song, and more placid than cockatoos, making them

ideal for a home where there are young children who may want to become involved in the bird's care. Like budgerigars they often prove talented mimics, too.

The African Grey Parrot is accepted as being the best talking parrot, and amazons are also talented in this respect, although they are noisier, too. Macaws can also learn to talk, and become very devoted to their owners, but the large multi-coloured species can be difficult to house successfully in the home as they require considerable space, and again, their natural calls are quite raucous.

Sadly, the feeding habits of the lories and lorikeets create problems in the home; their fluid droppings are likely to be scattered onto nearby furniture through the sides of their quarters, unless these are adequately screened, and their desire to bathe means that water will also inevitably splash about. However, if you are prepared to tolerate such difficulties (and the use of dry nectar mixes has helped with regard to their droppings), these colourful birds will make delightful pets, and surprisingly talented mimics.

You may also want to consider the likely lifespan of a bird when selecting a pet. Budgerigars live perhaps seven or eight years on average, whereas cockatiels and most parakeets should live well into their twenties. The larger parrots can make lifelong companions as they frequently live for 50 years or more. These birds rarely show signs of ageing, although towards the end of their lives moulting may be prolonged and feathers not replaced.

Keeping parrots outdoors

Other factors are likely to apply if you are intending to keep parrots in an aviary. Your interest may lie in exhibiting them or in colour-breeding, in which case, consider the Budgerigar, the Cockatiel and the Peach-faced Lovebird. Or you may want to choose parrots that can be bred without too much difficulty, in which case

Left: Cockatiels are ideal as family pets: a young bird should become quite tame (though it may be nervous at first) and will live for many years.

Above: Australian parakeets, such as these Bourke's Grass Parakeets, are ideal for the aviary and breed readily. Try to start with young birds.

kakarikis, and Australian species, such as the Red-rumped Parakeet, are recommended; they will usually breed twice during the summer in temperate climes.

From a practical standpoint, you should think about the noise factor, especially if you live in a fairly urban area. While you may not object to the raucous calls of your Amazon parrots echoing through the neighbourhood at first light on a summer's morning, other people are unlikely to be so enthusiastic or tolerant! Most of the larger parrots prove quite noisy, and you may need to sound-proof their quarters, which will entail extra expense.

The destructive nature of larger parrots means that building them suitable accommodation is likely to be a costly exercise — and, of course, such birds are expensive to buy, particularly if you want a pair.

Thankfully, there are many parrots that can be housed and bred in suburban areas, without a vast investment; the grass parakeets (*Neophema* species), and other related Australian parakeets, lovebirds, kakarikis, parrotlets and hanging parrots all fit into this category. Conures and the psittaculid parakeets are also popular choices, although they can prove rather more noisy and destructive.

Finding a supplier
It is important to try to define your aims at the outset; if you are planning to exhibit budgerigars, for example, then you should buy exhibition rather than pet-type stock. You can contact established breeders through a local society, details of which are likely to be available from your library, or in the advertisement columns of one of the birdkeeping periodicals available from good newsagents.

The same information sources can be useful for tracking down suppliers of other parrots, too, if pet shops in your area cannot help you. Having found a potential supplier, and ascertained that he or she has the birds you are seeking, there are a number of questions that you should ask before arranging a visit. Firstly, you will need to know the age of the bird, particularly if you are seeking a pet, and its sex, which is obviously vital if you are seeking to make up a pair. You may also want to know whether the bird has bred before, whether it has been placed at any shows, and whether it is acclimatized, if it has been imported.

Although it may be possible to have the bird sent to you, it is a good idea to visit the vendor's premises if you can. This gives you the opportunity to see the parrot's surroundings, and ask any more

Above: The Grey Parrot, one of the most popular pet birds, is often stocked by pet shops. Check the bird's condition carefully before you decide to buy it.

specific questions about the diet and general care that the bird has been receiving. As the cost of larger parrots has climbed steeply during recent years, some breeders are now selling these more expensive birds with veterinary certificates of health. This will give you some assurance of the bird's present state, but can provide no absolute long-term health guarantee.

CHOOSING PARROTS

Budgerigars and cockatiels	Popular pet and aviary birds, which can be kept and bred together in groups.
Australian parakeets, parrotlets and lovebirds	Attractive aviary occupants, generally keen to nest. Colour mutations are becoming more widespread, and are attracting great interest. Australian species are not really suitable pets.
Psittaculid parakeets and conures	Many more of these birds are now being bred in aviaries, and young hand-raised conures develop into good companions.
Hanging parrots, lories and lorikets	The specialist dietary needs of these parrots make their care more demanding, but pairs usually nest readily. Hanging parrots will live in harmony alongside other birds.
Amazon and *Pionus* parrots and caiques	Amazons are particularly vocal in the early morning and late afternoon. They are intelligent birds and youngsters can prove good mimics.
Vasa and fig parrots	These recent introductions to aviculture should not be kept as pets in the home.
Macaws	Tame birds may form a very strong bond with their owners, but accommodation for the large species can be a problem. Limited talking ability, with natural calls being rather raucous.
Grey Parrot and *Poicephalus* parrots	Young Greys settle well as pets, and prove talented mimics, as may *Poicephalus* parrots, whereas untame adults are nervous in comparison and must be housed in aviaries. Both groups are relatively quiet. Greys are susceptible to feather-plucking, which may result from boredom, a poor diet, sexual frustration or lack of bathing facilites.
Eclectus and *Tanygnathus* parrots	Eclectus, especially, may attempt to breed at any stage of the year. Recently imported birds of both species are often in poor feather condition and need careful management.

Buying imported birds

It is important to ascertain whether parrots you are thinking of buying have been imported recently, or whether they are home-bred. Although they may be cheaper, imported parrots (whether or not they were wild-caught) will be more demanding to manage until they are properly established in their new surroundings, which may take a year or so. Bear in mind that although such birds will have been quarantined, they will not be fully acclimatized, and so cannot be transferred outside until the summer.

In addition you may need to move recently imported parrots back into heated accommodation over their first winter, especially if they have not moulted completely during their period of time outdoors. This can present difficulties, and will inevitably mean extra expenditure. It is best to buy imported parrots in the early summer, when the risk of frost has passed. You can then house them outdoors immediately, (although you may prefer to confine them to the shelter of their aviary at first).

Imported parrots will take time to adjust to their new environment, and will not breed immediately; it can take three or four years for them to settle sufficiently to show signs of breeding activity. Parrots that are already established tend to breed much more quickly; many parakeets will go to nest the year after being set up in their new quarters.

The importation of birds is a controversial subject, but there is no doubt that many parrots do cause serious damage to growing crops by feeding on them. In Argentina, the losses caused by Blue-fronted Amazons in citrus plantations alone run into millions of dollars. By allowing the export of a limited number of these birds under a quota system, it is possible to prevent their widespread destruction, and allow the local people to benefit from this trade. The environment is also protected, because the nesting sites where the parrot chicks are collected

Above: Allow yourself plenty of time to choose a bird. Home-bred birds, though slightly more expensive than imported ones, will be easier to manage.

by the local people are left intact. In addition, only a proportion of the youngsters are removed, so that the adult birds will return to nest here again in the following year. (This means too, of course, that the trees themselves are worth more money to the native people if they are left standing than if they are sold for lumber and charcoal.) The need to destroy thousands of birds by non-selective and environmentally damaging means, such as the use of poisons and napalm, is also reduced.

There are strict international controls relating both to welfare and conservation concerns surrounding trade in parrots. Movement of parrots between most countries is carried out in accordance with the requirements of the Convention of

International Trade in Endangered Species (CITES), which regulates the movement of both wild and captive-bred parrots, through a permit system, rare species being subject to much tighter controls. Advice on quarantine matters is usually the responsibility of the agricultural department in your country, while the government department responsible for conservation matters normally administers CITES. On arrival in the country of import, the birds undergo a period of quarantine before being released for sale.

Australia is one country that presently bans the movement of native birds overseas, in spite of the fact that plagues of cockatoos can cause great damage to farmers' crops. This prohibition extends even to those birds that have been bred legally in captivity. However, because Australian parakeets have proved to be so prolific in aviary surroundings in other countries, large numbers of captive birds are traded internationally each year. Again, they are quarantined in the importing country, under official control, before they can be transferred to new aviaries.

Even if you are taking a pet parrot from one country to another, such controls will affect you. Contact the relevant authorities well in advance of your likely departure date to ascertain the current position, and so that all the necessary arrangements can be made. The International Air Transportation Association (IATA) produce information about the necessary shipping boxes for these birds, and, of course, the airline should be able to advise you.

Catching and handling parrots

The larger parrots, such as cockatoos, need to be handled with caution, and if you are not used to catching birds yourself, you should ask the dealer to do this for you. From outside the aviary, you will also be able to keep a close watch on the birds in which you are interested.

All the bigger parrots, including

Below: When you enter the aviary, the bird is likely to fly onto the mesh. You should find it relatively easy to catch it here using a net.

Below: A deep net that is well padded around the rim is ideal for catching larger parrots as it will prevent them from escaping or injuring themselves.

Below: Once the bird is within the net, you can transfer it to a secure travelling box. Take care not to be bitten; strong gloves are advisable.

Above: It is a good idea to wear a strong glove (avoid knitted fabrics) when handling larger parrots, as their powerful beaks can inflict painful bites.

Below: Hold the bird's head between the first and second fingers of your hand (but don't grip its neck), restraining its back and wings in your palm.

amazons, macaws and the African Grey, have powerful beaks, and can easily draw blood from an exposed finger. While they will not normally bite without provocation, they usually resent being restrained, and you should safeguard your hands with a pair of thick gloves before attempting to handle them. Avoid knitted gloves, as these afford little protection, and the parrot's sharp claws can easily become caught up in the threads. Leather gardening gloves are stronger, and the birds cannot become ensnared in the fabric. You may decide to wear a thinner pair beneath these, as a further protection.

Within the confines of a small enclosure or cage you may be able to restrain the parrot while it climbs around the wire mesh. Start by placing your hands on each side of its shoulders, and free the bird's toes from the mesh. Then slide the fingers of one hand round the side of the bird's body to dislodge one foot from the mesh. You can tuck this back against the bird's body while you repeat the procedure with the other hand. Finally, restraining the parrot by keeping its neck carefully between your first and second fingers, so that it will be less able to bite you, move it out from its quarters.

You may find it easier to let the parrot fly down to the floor of its quarters, where it will have nothing to grip onto. (As always, be careful not to grip tightly around the bird's neck.)

A deep catching net, which is well-padded around the edges, provides the simplest means of catching aviary birds, and the padded rim will help to protect them from injury. Parakeets and cockatiels, in particular, are very quick in flight, and can be difficult to catch. Start by lowering or removing all the perches in the aviary so that you can move around unhindered, and then shut off the entrance to the aviary shelter, confining the birds in the flight. You will probably find it easier to catch the birds in the net when they are resting on the aviary mesh, rather than in flight. As soon as you have the bird inside the net, place one hand over the top to prevent the bird escaping, and gently lower the net to the ground. Then, with the same hand, reach in and restrain the parrot carefully, placing your fingers either side of its head. As you draw the parrot out of the net, you will probably find that it has clinched its feet in the material of the net. Using your other hand, you will need to prize the claws gently away from the net to free the bird. Provided that the wings are adequately restrained in the palm of your hand, it will not attempt to struggle unduly. You can inspect its body easily while it is in this position in your hand to ensure that it is in good condition.

CHOOSING A HEALTHY BIRD

A healthy bird, irrespective of its species (this is a Crimson Rosella), should appear alert and lively. Examine a bird carefully before you decide to buy it.

Check that the nostrils are unblocked and of equal size

Eyes should be open and clear with no sign of discharge

Check that all the flight feathers are present and that there is no sign of French moult or feather-plucking

Check that the beak is not malformed in any way; the upper bill should extend slightly over the lower

The bird should be reasonably plump with no distinct hollows on either side of the breastbone

Check the feet and claws for any signs of past injury or frostbite

Tail feathers may sometimes be soiled or damaged, but they will be replaced at the next moult

Choosing a healthy bird

The plumage Always start by looking at the parrot's feathering. This is especially critical in the case of cockatoos, which are prone to the feathering ailment known as PBFD (Psittacine Beak and Feather Disease). This is now known to be a viral infection, and young birds can become infected while they are still in the nest. It is usually chronic; the symptoms become evident over some months and the illness can be difficult to recognize in its early stages. There is presently no cure for PBFD, and the outcome is inevitably fatal. Much still remains to be learnt about this disease, but over 30 different species of parrot are now known to have been infected, including Vasa parrots and African Greys, young birds being most at risk.

Avoid buying a cockatoo if you have any doubts about the condition of its feathering; abnormal – twisted or stunted – plumage will be noticeable first over the breast, worsening as the new feathers start to emerge following a moult. Another indicator may be a change in coloration of the beak, which often takes on a brownish rather than black hue, and grows excessively. In most instances, the beak is not affected until the feather loss is quite widespread, but you may be able to detect the characteristic changes here early on. You should also avoid buying breeding stock from a group of birds where one or more is showing signs of the disease. Some apparently healthy birds may be suffering from the infection, though not yet displaying clinical signs.

Another feather ailment to watch for, especially if you are buying budgerigars, is French moult. It results in a variable loss of flight and tail feathers, and becomes evident around the time that the chicks leave the nestbox. In a mild case, these may regrow, but often a badly affected budgerigar will never be able to fly properly. A similar disease has been recorded in Peach-faced Lovebirds, but is relatively uncommon at present.

Such loss of feathers may not be a problem if you are looking for a pet – in fact, you may prefer to have a budgerigar whose flight is handicapped, so that it will be easier to catch when at liberty in the room, and cannot escape – but birds suffering from French moult may represent a threat to others if used for breeding purposes. The moulting period may bring a problem, however, as the new flight feathers can prove brittle and may break at their bases. If you have a budgerigar afflicted with French moult, have a styptic pencil available to stop any blood loss.

If you are buying adult stock, you will find it more difficult to spot the effects of French moult; where a budgerigar has been affected with a mild case as a youngster, the flight and tail feathers are likely to have regrown, making the symptoms almost undetectable, yet it could transmit the infection to its offspring. You may be able to identify such budgies by opening each wing in turn, and looking closely a short distance up from the bases of the primary flight feathers. In a bird that has been affected, you may notice a reddish brown area in the shaft. The tail feathers may be similarly affected.

Lutino cockatiels often display a bald patch of variable size on the head behind the crest. This is not the result of an infection, but a genetic flaw. Young birds of this colour are also susceptible to feather-plucking. Although the plumage should regrow normally, affected cockatiels are more likely to pluck their youngsters. This vice is also quite common in budgerigars. You are most likely to pick up signs of feather-plucking in chicks at the base of the neck and at the top of the wings.

Feather-plucking can be a particular problem in the larger parrots, notably cockatoos and the African Grey. Areas of sparse plumage, especially in the vicinity of the breast will usually be clearly evident. It is a difficult problem to overcome, as it rapidly becomes habitual, and the birds will remove new feathers almost as soon as they emerge through the skin.

Finally, there is no need to worry if the parrot's plumage is simply less sleek than that of others you have seen housed in aviary surroundings; this may simply reflect a lack of bathing opportunities, and can be corrected in due course by regular spraying, as described later (see page 27).

The eyes In healthy birds, the eyes should be clear and bright, with no signs of swelling or discharge, which could indicate an active infection. Cloudiness, or a white sheen over the eye, described as corneal opacity, is indicative of a previous injury or infection that has affected the bird's vision.

The nostrils Check that the nostrils are even in size and free of any discharge. A parrot that has one nostril much larger than the other is likely to be suffering from a long-standing, but usually minor, infection of the upper part of the respiratory tract. The same applies if the bird has one or both nostrils blocked, but otherwise appears healthy. Such infections are often caused by micro-organisms called mycoplasmas, which you may be able to eliminate with a specific antibiotic treatment. However, the damage caused to the nostril will remain apparent throughout the bird's life, and if it is stressed – by being moved to a new environment, for example – the infection may well flare up again, resulting typically in a clear discharge from the affected nostril. In general, it is the larger parrots that seem most prone to this problem.

The beak The shape of the beak varies naturally, depending on the species concerned. In the case of the Slender-billed Conure, for example, the upper mandible is relatively long and pointed; the budgerigar, in contrast, has a much more compact beak. The parrot's beak continues growing throughout its life, and if the bird has been denied access to wood for gnawing, then its beak will become overgrown. This is especially true of the various fig parrots and the Blue-rumped Parrot, whose beaks appear to grow at a faster rate than those of other species. The provision of adequate branches, perhaps coupled with judicious trimming, will help to correct this problem.

Birds with obvious beak deformities or injuries are likely to require regular shaping of their beaks throughout their lives, so that they can continue eating without difficulty. Check your budgerigars closely; the upper part of the beak should overlap the lower. In some cases, however, the beak can become undershot, with the upper mandible failing to make contact with the lower and curling round inside the bill, under the tongue. The lower part of the beak will then start to grow excessively and must be cut back regularly with a stout pair of clippers. Sometimes this problem is of genetic origin, although dirty nesting conditions are often the cause; droppings stuck under the tongue at the front of the lower beak may be responsible. (The upper mandible may also be malformed for the same reason, but this is less common.) Unfortunately, unless the accumulation of dirt is spotted at an early stage, before it distorts the tissue, there is nothing that can be done to remedy this problem.

Another ailment that frequently affects the beaks of budgerigars, particularly in older birds, is scaly face. Look carefully for any trace of snail-like tracks across the upper beak, which is an early sign of this disease, caused by *Cnemidocoptes* mites.

Above: This Lesser Sulphur-crested Cockatoo is suffering from PBFD. The feathers haemorrhage easily and will eventually fall out. There is no cure.

Above: This Eclectus hen shows severe signs of feather-plucking. Such abnormal behaviour may be a sign of sexual frustration in an adult bird.

Above: Signs of French moult first appear around the time that the chicks leave the nestbox. Badly affected birds may never be able to fly properly.

In more advanced cases, coral-like encrustations around the sides of the beak may be apparent; these can spread around the cere and even over the body and legs. Scaly face can lead to permanent malformation of the beak if left untreated, but in a mild case, treatment is straightforward, and the budgerigar will not suffer any permanent disfigurement. Kakarikis are also prone to this ailment.

The mouth Imported lories and lorikeets, as well as Eclectus, *Tanygnathus* parrots and the Philippine Red-vented Cockatoo can all suffer from candidiasis, usually resulting from a deficiency of Vitamin A in their diet. Affected birds often toy with their food rather than eating it readily, and some weight loss will be noticeable. You may want to check the inside of the mouth for any signs of this infection, which causes whitish, rather slimy patches here. Provided that the bird is not too seriously affected, candidiasis is treatable, but it can be a recurrent problem in some of the more unusual small nectar-feeding parrots, such as the Fairy Lorikeet (*Charmosyna pulchella*).

The breast You can gain a good indication of a parrot's overall state of health by locating its breastbone. This is normally evident as a slightly raised prominence running vertically in the midline, on the underside of the body, from the vicinity of the lower chest. The bird should feel reasonably plump, with no discernible hollows on either side of the breastbone.

Muscle wasting here – sometimes described as 'going light' – may be indicative of a chronic and progressive disease. This may be coupled with other signs, such as faecal staining around the vent. Alternatively, it could be indicative of a heavy burden of parasites, such as intestinal roundworms, particularly in Australian parakeets.

Conversely, in the case of the Galah Cockatoo and budgerigars, you should check for a slight swelling of the body. This is likely to be indicative of lipomas (fatty tumours). Surgical removal may be required to prevent loss of flying ability, but recurrences are not uncommon.

The feet Look carefully at the chick's feet; parrots normally perch with two toes gripping the front of the perch, and two providing support behind. However, sometimes, especially if the bird has been kept on a slippery surface or unsuitable bedding during the rearing period, one toe may have slipped forward. This problem, sometimes described as slipped toe, will be virtually impossible to correct in a weaned youngster and the bird will be handicapped to some extent throughout its life. It need not prevent the chick from settling well as a pet, however, and in time it should adapt to its situation, but you will have to trim the nail of the affected toe at regular intervals.

You should also check that none of the toes are swollen, particularly in Grey and Eclectus Parrots. The precise cause of this condition is unclear; it may be a local infection, or the result of a shortage of B vitamins in the rearing food. Sometimes the swelling is associated with a joint, or it may be close to the nail of one or more

13

Above: This budgerigar is suffering from scaly face, caused by a parasitic infestation. If left untreated, the beak will become permanently malformed.

Right: Note how this budgerigar's upper beak has curved inside the lower. It will need regular trimming with clippers.

digits. Affected birds show no apparent signs of discomfort, and seem to be healthy in other respects. Unfortunately, the swelling usually interferes with the blood supply to the toes, causing gangrene, so that the lower part of the digit, including the nail shrivels up (usually over weeks) before breaking off, with little if any blood loss. Further problems are then unlikely and the stub should heal rapidly.

It is not uncommon for lovebirds, in particular, to have odd missing claws, which may be the result of fighting. Provided that there is no accompanying sign of injury, this will not be a problem, unless you want to exhibit the bird. Psittaculid species are particularly at risk from frostbite, which can lead to not only loss of claws, but in severe cases, part of a toe as well. The bird may show little discomfort, but it may encounter difficulty in mating.

In other cases, especially with cockatiels, a claw may project at an abnormal angle, often in the vertical plane. A past injury or accumulation of nest dirt on the affected toe may be the cause, and the claw will require regular trimming.

Breathing The parrot's tail movements give a clear indication of its respiratory rate. Its breathing should not be laboured in any way or noisy. Some parrots, notably the Philippine Red-vented Cockatoo and *Pionus* species, are prone to the fungal disease aspergillosis. They may have become infected in the wild, by inhaling fungal spores present in their nest litter, which then develop in their airways hindering their respiration. Unfortunately, aspergillosis is very difficult to detect merely by an external examination, but after a period of exertion, affected parrots usually breathe in a very laboured fashion, and may wheeze as well. In the latter stages of this chronic disease, they are likely to be dull and depressed, and show weight loss over the breast.

Left: Double wire adjoining aviaries to prevent loss of claws through fighting.

Insurance schemes
Having decided on your purchase, you may want to consider one of the avian health insurance schemes that are now available. This will give you some reassurance, should your bird fall sick once you have taken it home and may also cover you if you are unfortunate enough to lose birds through vandalism or other causes of damage to your aviary. Although the cost of policies of this nature can be fairly high, the cover they give to imported stock especially, where the age of the adult bird is unknown, is worth the investment. Compare policy details carefully to ensure that the cover provided is suitable for your needs.

Choosing a pet bird
If you are looking for a bird to keep as a pet, it is vital to choose a young bird; at this stage birds have little fear of people, and so are much easier to tame. Since many more parrot chicks are now being raised by hand, you should be able to obtain a genuine youngster quite easily.

Be sure to obtain a diet sheet and follow this closely for a week or so, before in-

troducing any significant changes to the parrot's feeding routine. This should help to prevent any digestive upsets during its first critical days with you. Incidentally, do not be tempted to buy a young parrot that has been raised by hand but is not yet independent. Especially if you are not used to hand-feeding birds, this can prove, at the very least, a worrying period, and more serious complications may arise.

There are certain specific points to consider when choosing a young, hand-reared parrot. Start by looking at the plumage; most young parrots are duller in overall coloration than adults and their plumage may not be as sleek. Furthermore, especially around the mouth, deposits of food may have stuck the feathers together. To some extent, this is unavoidable, particularly as chicks at the weaning stage are likely to toy with the food on offer, rather than swallowing it. But if the plumage is fluffed up and the parrot appears depressed, then it could be ill.

Owning a pet parrot could turn into a life-long commitment, so do not be seduced simply by the cuddly appearance of a young bird. Hand-raised birds need a great deal of attention, even after they are independent. If you suspect that you could be away from home for much of the day, do seriously consider obtaining two birds. They will provide company for each other (irrespective of their gender) and there is no reason why both should not develop into tame companions.

If you think that you may want to breed parrots at a later stage, you would do better to start off with a young pair, than to try to pair up a single pet bird later in life. Attempting to introduce a companion alongside an established pet can be very difficult; the newcomer is likely to arouse jealousy in your bird, and even overt aggression. In view of the powerful beaks of most parrots, it can be very dangerous to place unfamiliar birds together in the confines of a cage when one is already well-settled as a member of the family. If

Right: Macaws make great companions, but avoid buying a bird that has been kept for a long time as a shop pet, as it will be used to constant attention.

you select two young birds from the outset, they will grow up as equals, sharing your attention, and there is unlikely to be any serious friction. However, some amazon cocks and cockatoos can become aggressive for a period while in breeding condition, and may turn on their partners; separating the birds for a while should hopefully solve the problem.

Alternatively, you can, of course, purchase a parrot that is already tame and talking. This may be less satisfactory in the longer term, however: it will take longer to win the confidence of the bird; it may display a preference for either a male or female, depending on its past experience; or it may have learnt some undesirable phrases. It can be especially difficult to integrate a parrot that has spent several years living in a pet store into domestic surroundings. Having become used to the constant stream of people and attention in the shop, where it may well have been the focal point, such a bird will often pine when first introduced to the relative tranquility of a home with an unfamiliar owner.

Hand-rearing is very labour-intensive, and hence very costly, and this expense will obviously be reflected in the price of the birds. Most budgerigars and cockatiels are not hand-reared and a parent-reared chick that has fledged and is feeding itself will soon settle with you.

The best selection of young budgerigars and cockatiels will be available in the late summer and young Peach-faced Lovebirds can also be acquired in the widest range of colours at this stage.

(Although more usually kept in aviaries in Europe and North America, the latter are popular pets in Australia; young birds will settle well in the home, and can learn to say a few words.)

Most young budgerigars are already finger-tame by the time they leave the nest, sitting quite readily on a finger extended parallel with the perch, as long as they are not disturbed. You can recognize youngsters by the purplish colour of the cere – the fleshy area above the beak, encircling the nostrils. You still may be able to sex them if there are a number of chicks – to compare young cocks have slightly

Below left and right: If you are looking for a pet budgerigar, choose a young bird; eyes, cere and markings should all provide an indication of its immaturity. Compare the young normal cobalt (left) with the adult (right).

more prominent and deeper purplish ceres than young hens.

Traditionally, it has been accepted that cock birds make the best pets, proving more talented talkers than hens. These observations may be true to a certain extent, but hens can prove quite reliable mimics and are great characters.

If you are buying a budgerigar, choose a chick around six weeks old. It may still be showing some dark markings on its upper beak at this stage, and its eyes will be dark (as in most fledgling parrots), showing no trace of the white iris that becomes evident around the perimeter when the youngster is about three months old.

The head markings of a young bird are also distinctive, especially in the so-called 'normal' varieties, such as the sky blue. At this stage, the darker wavy pattern of banding in the plumage extends right up to the cere, giving rise to the description of 'barhead' for young budgerigars. This pattern is lost at the first moult. The spots that form the so-called 'mask' on the head are relatively thin and elongated in youngsters, but will become much more prominent once the birds become older. (The paler varieties, including lutinos and recessive pieds, lack these markings.)

Young cockatiels are normally obtained at a slightly older age than budgerigars, around seven weeks old. They resemble young hens at this stage, but can be distinguished by the pinkish skin around the cere, (in the case of most varieties), and by their shorter tails.

Lovebirds should also be obtained as soon as possible after fledging, once they are known to be feeding independently. If you are buying from a breeder, you may be able to choose a chick before it has left the nest, and the breeder will contact you once it is feeding itself.

Choosing breeding stock

In general terms, certainly with cockatiels, lovebirds, budgerigars and most parakeets, it is better to start with young stock. Since they should breed in the following year, you will not be losing any time by choosing young birds, and you will be acquiring birds with a long reproductive life, rather than those which could already be elderly, or have developed a vice such as feather-plucking.

It is virtually impossible to age parrots once they have moulted into adult plumage, at least by visual means, though heavy scaling on the legs may indicate a more elderly bird. It is, of course, impossible to know the age of imported birds, and even with home-bred birds you may need to rely on the vendor's honesty. The only way that you can be certain of a bird's age is if it is wearing a closed ring. This is fitted while the bird is a young chick, still in the nest, and so provides a reliable means of ageing it; after this early stage, the parrot's toes are too large for the ring

to be slid over them. These rings are circular bands of metal, made either of aluminium, or tougher stainless steel for larger parrots. The information coded on the ring is likely to include the year in which the chick hatched, such as '92', a ring number identifying the bird in the breeder's register, and, possibly, the breeder's initials or code number, if he or she is using society rings. Celluloid split rings will not confirm a bird's age; they are used mainly on budgerigars as an auxiliary means of identification.

Sexing young birds can be a problem; the only reliable method is chromosomal karyotyping (see page 61), although if you are working with a particular sex-linked mutation, the colours of the chicks may be equally reliable (see page 74).

In the case of most larger parrots, such as cockatoos, amazons and macaws, as well as the Grey Parrot, compatability — the birds must agree well together — is a significant factor in obtaining breeding results. Obtaining two birds of opposite

sexes does not necessarily guarantee that they will attempt to go to nest. This has become clearly apparent during recent years with the establishment of large-scale breeding units, where pairs are housed and fed under identical conditions. Here it has been demonstrated that changing partners, when pairs fail to nest, can result in almost instant success.

If you buy a proven pair, you should have the reassurance that the birds are compatible. An alternative, though expensive, solution is to buy a number of larger parrots of species where compatibility can be a problem. House six together in a large aviary, and observe them carefully to see which birds are compatible; you can then transfer these to separate breeding accommodation.

If you have more limited resources and

Below: Most amazons are not sexually dimorphic and you will need to buy reliably sexed birds if you want to start with a potential breeding pair.

Left: A cardboard box may be strong enough for moving a budgerigar. Remember to provide ventilation holes and secure the lid with tape.

can buy only two birds from a dealer, you may be able to recognize pair-bonded individuals by watching the birds very closely from a distance away. Such birds will tend to follow each other around, at times pausing to preen each other, and they are also likely to perch together. Much still remains to be learnt about pair-bonding. It seems likely to occur around the time that the birds reach maturity; clearly, if two parrots of opposite sexes have been kept together up to this stage, then they are much more likely to accept each other as mates. A few of the larger parrots, notably the Eclectus and Great-bill, do not form a strong pair bond, and will be far less choosy about a partner.

You may want to consider obtaining young birds for breeding purposes. Although this may appear a more lengthy process, there are several advantages: you should end up with a bonded pair, which, hopefully, will breed consistently for a decade or more; and you will know their background. You can be certain of none of these points with a pair of imported birds, and the change of environment means that they will still take three years or more to become established in their new quarters – probably as long as a pair of youngsters will take to mature.

It is important to obtain the parrots from unrelated pairs and, if possible, to set up two pairs of a species yourself. This will enable you to continue breeding unrelated birds to the second generation, and, at the same time, to offer fellow breeders unrelated pairs. (Take care when moving young parrots to an outside aviary for the first time; check that they are eating properly and do not become chilled.)

Travelling boxes

Make sure that you take a suitable box with you when you are planning to buy a parrot. A box will provide a more suitable environment than a cage, because travelling in semi-darkness is less disturbing for the parrot. In a cage, the bird is likely to cling onto the sides, and could injure

itself, and parakeets, for example, may flap around and suffer minor abrasions around the cere, or possibly to the wings.

The most suitable type of container will depend to some extent on the bird, but wooden boxes are always preferable to cardboard ones. You can make a suitable carrying box from plywood, with a sliding hatch on top and ventilation holes around the sides. Position these holes fairly near to the roof of the container, where they

will be less accessible to the birds. As larger parrots, in particular, are very adept at finding any weakness in a box of this type, and may be able to slide open a hatch, fix a hasp and padlock on the outside to ensure that the lid remains closed.

You may prefer to buy a suitable travelling box, which will be useful at a later date to take your parrot to a veterinarian for example. In an emergency, you can use a cat basket, but make sure that you disinfect it thoroughly first, as some bacteria normally associated with cats can prove harmful to birds. Avoid wicker baskets, which will be no match for a parrot's beak, and check the door fastening carefully.

Line the box or basket with newspaper. There is no need to worry about providing food or water, except on a very long journey, although you can offer a little seed or pieces of cut apple if you wish. It is vital, however, never to leave the parrot alone in a car during hot weather; the temperature inside can rise to a fatal level within minutes. Nor should you transport the birds in the car boot, where they will be in danger from exhaust fumes.

Below: A wooden travelling box is ideal for transferring most parrots (even those with very strong beaks) between flights or for bringing new stock home.

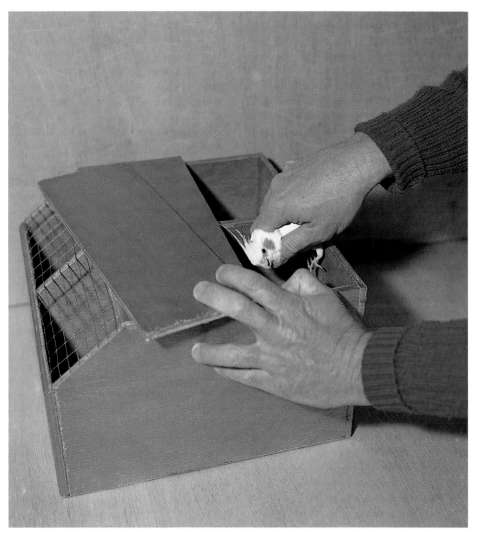

KEEPING PARROTS IN THE HOME

There are many different designs of cages and indoor flights marketed for budgerigars, cockatiels and other parrots. The traditional bird cage is formed entirely of wire mesh, whereas a breeding cage for budgerigars and other smaller parrots, such as parrotlets, usually has solid walls and a wire mesh front. In this section we look at vital points to consider when selecting and equipping (with floor coverings, perches and toys) a cage or indoor flight (which offers more space) for a parrot, as well as at how to care for birds in the home, including how to successfully tame your parrot and teach it to talk.

Above: Choose a spacious cage for your budgerigar. You may want a stand, and a cover to fit around the base to catch seed husks. Position it at eye level.

Cages for budgerigars

You can easily obtain a cage suitable for a pet budgerigar from your local pet store; if possible, try to see a wide selection of the types available before you decide on one. Choose a design that will allow the budgerigar as much flying space as possible, as you may not always be able to let your pet out into the room. For this reason, rectangular-shaped cages are preferable to tall ones.

The colour of the bars is not really significant and although a silver-type finish is traditional, a much wider range of colours is now available. Some designs have bars covered with a white epoxy resin to prolong the lifespan of the cage and facilitate cleaning; you can easily wipe any dirt or droppings from this surface with a damp paper towel. Avoid a cage that shows signs of damage, such as chipped coating, as rust may develop and spoil the appearance of the cage as well as pose a potential health hazard.

Older style cages tend to incorporate more wire mesh in their design and the lower sides are enclosed with lengths of glass or plastic to prevent husks being scattered into the room. These cages are potentially more difficult to clean, but, if treated carefully, should prove as durable as more modern designs. (The cage you choose should last for the whole of your budgerigar's life.)

Door fastenings are a weakness in the design of some cages: those that swing shut on their own may harm the budgerigar if it attempts to escape as you close the door. Choose a cage that has a clip to hold the door closed in preference to one with a spring.

Cages for cockatiels and parakeets

Many cages are not suitable for cockatiels and parakeets; most of the Australian species, in particular, are too nervous and their tails are too easily damaged for them to be kept satisfactorily in confined surroundings, even as recently fledged youngsters, and they are therefore less popular as pets than as aviary birds.

But there are cage designs that are satisfactory for cockatiels and the neotropical *Brotogeris* species. Choose a large model for these active birds, and check that the gap between the bars is not too great, or the birds could become caught up. (They will also be more at risk from a pet cat, especially when you are out of the room.) A metal cage is most suitable, since these parakeets are surprisingly destructive. A budgerigar flight cage is ideal for them, especially if you choose one of the modular systems, which you can enlarge by connecting additional units of the same basic design to the original one. Some cages may have plastic bases, but these are usually positioned so that the parakeets do not gnaw at them, and you can distract their attention from the base by providing wooden branches as perches, which they can gnaw, and which you can replace easily.

Alternatively, you may wish to obtain a small indoor aviary. An increasing number of stylish designs are being produced, some of which are mounted on castors, which facilitates cleaning. Because these units are invariably taller than traditional cages, they are quite suitable for long-tailed parakeets, such as the Alexandrine or Ring-necked species. An indoor aviary of this type is also useful for accommodating recently imported birds over the winter period, or for housing young birds when they first become independent.

Preparing the cage

You should always wash a new cage thoroughly before placing the bird inside (even if you have bought your pets quarters new). Never use metal polish of any kind on the bars or elsewhere in the cage as this may be harmful; parrots often spend long periods of time, even in a spacious aviary, climbing around on the mesh of their quarters and so can easily ingest the remains of polish or other substances. Scrub the cage with a disinfectant solution that is safe for use with pets, and then rinse it thoroughly. (It is best to do this outdoors, rinsing it with a hose to ensure that it is really clean.)

Dry the various parts of the cage with paper towelling, taking care that no droplets of water remain, especially on the plastic. (If the cage is allowed to dry naturally, stubborn water marks will remain on the surface and may be hard to remove.) You can then reassemble the cage in readiness for the bird. Preparing its quarters can take some time, so, if possible, only obtain your new pet once everything is ready, so that it is able to settle in quickly when you arrive home.

Perches

Most cages are supplied complete with perches. If these are of plastic, replace them straight away. The trend towards plastic rather than wooden dowelling perchs can perhaps be justified on grounds of hygiene, but plastic perches simply do not seem comfortable for most parrots; birds in cages with plastic perches usually prefer to cling to the sides of their cage after a short period.

Wooden dowelling is commonly used for perches; 12.5mm (½in) diameter is best for budgerigars as it is narrow enough for the birds to grip easily, yet wide enough to prevent their claws touching underneath the perch. The main disadvantage with dowelling is that it is of an even diameter and, over a period of time,

Above left: A typical cage for a cockatiel. The plastic base clips to the wire-mesh top at either end. To clean the cage thoroughly separate the two parts.

the parts of the bird's feet that are in contact with the dowelling are likely to develop into pronounced pressure points, particularly in obese budgerigars. Apart from causing discomfort, these can also be a focus of infection, which may develop into bumblefoot, a condition best recognized in birds of prey.

The best material for perches is natural wood. Branches can be cut from a variety of trees – sycamore and apple are particularly good, but avoid using any poisonous plants, such as lilac (*Syringa*), yew (*Taxus*) and laburnum (*Laburnum*). You

Above: Gnawing on fresh, clean branches will keep parrots' beaks in trim. Most large parrots are destructive, so you will need a good supply.

may have access to fruit trees, but don't use any that may have been recently sprayed with chemicals, in case the residue proves harmful. Wash all branches thoroughly to remove any droppings of wild birds or excessive algal growth, using clean water and a scrubbing brush (but avoid detergent or disinfectant), before placing them in the parrot's quarters.

Dead branches may be easier to acquire, but are likely to be a source of fungal spores, which could harm your parrot. Dried wood is also more likely to

AN INDOOR FLIGHT FOR SMALL PARROTS

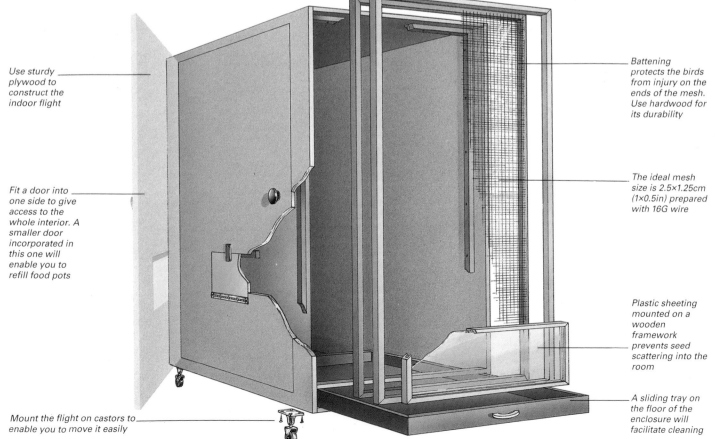

Use sturdy plywood to construct the indoor flight

Fit a door into one side to give access to the whole interior. A smaller door incorporated in this one will enable you to refill food pots

Mount the flight on castors to enable you to move it easily

Battening protects the birds from injury on the ends of the mesh. Use hardwood for its durability

The ideal mesh size is 2.5×1.25cm (1×0.5in) prepared with 16G wire

Plastic sheeting mounted on a wooden framework prevents seed scattering into the room

A sliding tray on the floor of the enclosure will facilitate cleaning

FITTING PERCHES IN THE CAGE

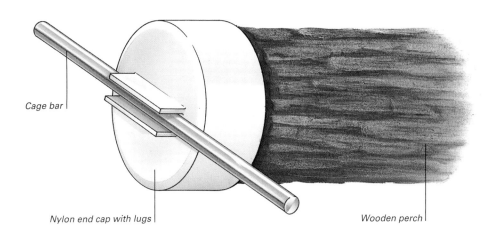

Cage bar

Nylon end cap with lugs

Wooden perch

split as it is gnawed. The fleshy cheek patches of macaws are vulnerable to sharp splinters, which may become lodged here from inside the mouth, a pronounced swelling appearing where the splinter entered the flesh.

Natural branches, being of variable diameter, will enable the bird to alter its grip, thus preventing the development of pressure sores on the underside of its feet. The birds will also be able to gnaw at the natural wood perches, thus helping to prevent their beaks becoming overgrown.

You will probably be able to fit only two perches in the cage, as you will need to ensure that they do not overhang seed or water containers. Cut the branches so that they fit comfortably within the cage, and avoid distorting the bars. Ideally, the perches should extend in a virtually straight line across the cage. If branches are crowded at either end, a parakeet's long tail is likely to rub repeatedly on the bars, causing the individual feathers to become frayed.

Most parrots start to gnaw their branches from the ends. If you cut the perch so that it is just wider than the flight, and fix it at a slight angle, you should not have to replace it so frequently, as you can simply slide it into a straighter position once your pet has worn it down. Once it becomes too short to fit across the width of the cage, you may be able to place the perch diagonally at one end, where it will provide a valuable gnawing block.

To secure the perches firmly in place, you can twist a stout strand of wire around each end, loop it through the sides of the cage and secure it on the outside of the flight, keeping the cut ends out of the bird's reach. You may be able to use the tips normally fitted to dowel perches, which slot into the bars of the cage, to hold natural branches in place. Alternatively, you can cut a notch into the wood and fit it directly onto the cage bars.

Some cages are also equipped with a swing, but, as only budgerigars seem to use a swing with any regularity, you may decide to remove it and replace it with a higher perch. (Most birds prefer to roost at a high level.)

Above: These plastic ends enable you to attach perches easily and directly to the sides of the cage without having to distort the bars.

Cleaning and floor coverings

Good hygiene is obviously important in ensuring that your bird does not fall ill, and as most of the dirt will accumulate on the floor of the cage, one with a detachable base that you can remove, will make washing the floor regularly an easier task. Avoid clear plastic bases because scratches will soon show, and young budgerigars, in particular, may fail to appreciate the presence of this plastic barrier and run repeatedly up and down the sides of the cage in an attempt to find an exit.

Sandsheets are an ideal way to line the floor and are available in various sizes to fit most standard cages. They are easy to change and tend to be less messy than loose bird sand; you can simply scrape off the droppings every day, and replace the sheet itself once or twice a week. This will restrict scattering of seed and feathers into the room and ensure that the cage remains clean. Some adult hen budgerigars in breeding condition have a tendency to chew sandsheets, however.

Sand has the advantage of being relatively cheap and may provide useful grit and minerals, but it is heavy to carry and it does not give such a good covering as a sandsheet. You will probably need to replace a thick layer of sand on the floor of the cage each day and you may have to wash the tray every time you clean the cage. It is inadvisable to use sand for cages housing laying hens as they have a tendency to scratch around the floor and the sand may become introduced into the vent and cause considerable irritation. Newspaper is a cheap and practical alternative but is unsightly. As a compromise, you can camouflage it with a light sprinkling of sand. Irrespective of whether or not you choose a stand (see page 25), it is useful to fit a flexible plastic cover around the base of the cage to help prevent seed husks and feathers from being scattered in the room.

Below: The panels of flight cages suitable for large parrots can be purchased separately, enabling you to build an enclosure to your chosen dimensions and expand it easily.

AN INDOOR FLIGHT FOR LARGE PARROTS

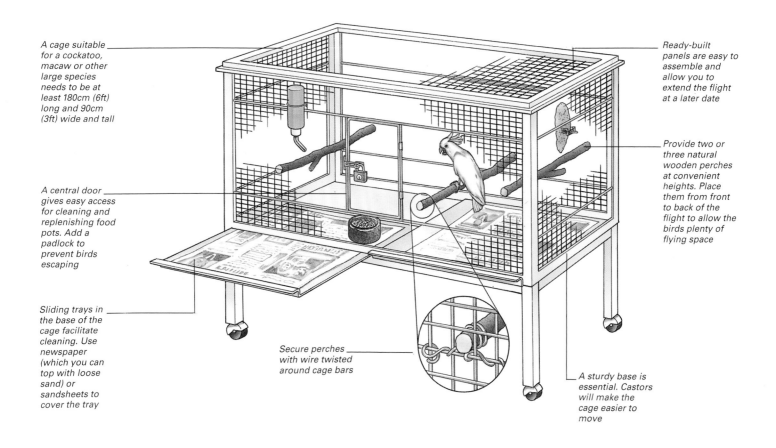

A cage suitable for a cockatoo, macaw or other large species needs to be at least 180cm (6ft) long and 90cm (3ft) wide and tall

A central door gives easy access for cleaning and replenishing food pots. Add a padlock to prevent birds escaping

Sliding trays in the base of the cage facilitate cleaning. Use newspaper (which you can top with loose sand) or sandsheets to cover the tray

Secure perches with wire twisted around cage bars

Ready-built panels are easy to assemble and allow you to extend the flight at a later date

Provide two or three natural wooden perches at convenient heights. Place them from front to back of the flight to allow the birds plenty of flying space

A sturdy base is essential. Castors will make the cage easier to move

Housing larger parrots

Don't try to economize on the size or the design of housing for your bird. Although a baby macaw may appear a rather innocent bundle of feathers, it will soon develop into a robust adolescent bird, eager to exercise both its wings and beak. If frustrated in its attempts, it is likely to end up plucking its feathers, or calling loudly.

Cages for budgerigars may be suitable for other smaller parrots, but macaws, Amazons and cockatoos, for example, require much larger and more robust structures to withstand their powerful beaks. The gauge of the mesh used on their enclosure is important – thick, 12G (gauge) is ideal for the large macaws and cockatoos, although thinner mesh (up to 16G) may be satisfactory. The size of mesh is also important; a macaw will be able to slip its beak easily through mesh that is more than 2.5cm (1in) square, gaining leverage and exerting great pressure on the individual strands. Parrots often do not break through mesh at the first attempt, but play with the strands, bending them back and forth with their powerful beaks and muscular tongues. Over a period of time, this weakens the mesh, which will eventually snap, and the sharp ends then easily injure the parrot's tongue. If the bird swallows a small piece, this may impact in the wall of the gizzard, or elsewhere in the digestive tract, with potentially fatal consequences.

The traditional square design of many parrot cages is really unsuitable for the active nature of such birds, allowing them very little space for exercise, and circular cages are even less satisfactory. Fortunately, an increasingly wide range of other housing options is now available.

Rather than buy a rigid design, you can plan the bird's accommodation yourself, using a flexible panel system. Ready-to-assemble panels are produced in standard sizes, and you can select the number of panels you require for your chosen design. Separate door units are also available. These panels are made of mesh fixed to a metal framework, which is more durable than timber or plastic. Although the finish is usually very good, you should check that there are no exposed sharp pieces of galvanized metal, which could be dangerous; parrots often climb around their quarters, and if one of these splinters penetrates a bird's fleshy tongue, it will not only be painful, but may also result in serious blood loss.

Easy access to the inside of the flight unit is important for cleaning and feeding purposes. Unfortunately, some designs do not incorporate a suitable tray to correspond to the dimensions of the flight. This means that to clean the floor properly you will need to lift the whole of the flight unit off the base. Apart from being quite heavy, a flight of this type will also be cumbersome in a confined space.

A mesh floor, made of the same panels as the side and roof of the flight, is the obvious solution, but you will have to use paper to cover the floor (rather than bird sand, for example) and the parrots are likely to shred this. You can place the paper beneath the cage, where it will be out of the parrot's reach, but the mesh will then become soiled and you will need to detach the mesh and scrub it frequently to remove the droppings, as well as changing the paper regularly.

The best solution may be to make a base to fit the dimensions of your flight. Allow a gap of at least 2.5cm (1in) between the bottom of the flight and the base unit to insert a separate sliding tray. If you decide to use metal sheeting, rather than timber with a plywood tray, you must ensure that there are no sharp edges on which the parrot could slice its toes. You should also check the corners carefully for any gaps in which the bird's claw could become caught.

If you come to the conclusion that the problem of cleaning a panel-system flight outweighs the advantages of its versatility and low cost, a ready-made indoor flight unit that comes complete with a base may be the answer. Several stylish designs are available; make sure that the model you choose is sufficiently robust for the species you want to keep. They can offer a particularly good way of housing cockatiels, which are particularly active.

Toys

It is important to provide some basic toys for a pet parrot living on its own, but do not be tempted to offer the plastic toys sold for budgerigars to larger species. A parrot will destroy these quite easily and there may also be sharp metal projections inside such toys that would be out of reach of a less destructive bird.

Cage toys suitable for parrots are often less readily available than those for budgerigars. though more are now being marketed, but resign yourself to the fact that any toys will ultimately be gnawed away by your pet. You can, of course, improvize. Suspend a clean wooden cotton reel (with its label removed) on a strand of wire coat-hanger and tie the ends of the wire out of the bird's reach outside the cage. The parrot will enjoy sliding this up and down. You will be able to replace the reel easily once the parrot has destroyed it. A mirror placed at perch level outside the cage can provide companionship for pet birds when you are out, as will a radio. For your room you may also want to provide one of the climbing playframes available for parrots ranging in size from budgerigars to macaws.

But most parrots appear to derive greatest pleasure from gnawing wood. You will probably notice that your bird's interest in attacking its wooden perches tends to vary through the year; parrots entering breeding condition will be especially destructive. But the parrot's beak will become overgrown if you provide nothing on which it can gnaw, and you may even need to have it cut back so your bird can continue eating. To distract it from the perches while encouraging it to exercise its beak, try supplying one of the special parrot chews now available, which often fit around a perch.

Positioning the cage in the room

To help your new pet feel secure in its new environment, position the cage unit alongside a wall, possibly in the corner of a room in which you regularly spend time. Once your bird is tame, it may not mind being moved to a more central location. Avoid draughty spots and never place the cage where it is exposed to direct sunlight – in front of a window, for example – as this could prove fatal.

It is a good idea to screen the back of the bird's quarters with a polythene shield to protect the wall from droppings or pieces of fruit, which it will scatter outside the cage. Allow a small gap between the cage and the screen so that the bird cannot

Left: Toys will prevent boredom and feather-plucking. A simple cotton-reel on a strand of wire is safe and robust.

damage it. You may also want to place a rug on the floor to protect the carpet; this should extend abut 30cm (1ft) around the edges of the cage or flight.

Ideally, you should position a cage so that the bird perches just below eye level. This will help the bird to become used to you, and will thus facilitate the taming process. It will also prevent you having to stoop to open the cage door and birds tend to feel more secure in a higher position that allows them a good overall view of the room.

Although you can buy special stands for smaller cage designs, many tend to be rather unstable and are easily toppled over, so they are clearly not recommended if you have young children. A piece of furniture will often make a better base. If the cage is equipped with castors, you will need to ensure that the floor is level, or lock the castors in place with a wedge to prevent the cage from sliding forward into the room.

Because of the amount of noise a parrot can make, it is best to avoid placing the flight unit directly against a shared wall, if possible. Amazon parrots and cockatoos, in particular, with their regular periods of screeching during the early morning and evening, are likely to disturb someone in an adjoining room; you may be able to minimize this problem by covering the parrot's cage or keeping the curtains closed until a reasonable hour.

Below: A variety of toys are available for pet budgies, but small plastic toys like these are not suitable, and may be dangerous, for larger species.

POSITIONING THE FLIGHT

HAZARDS IN THE HOME

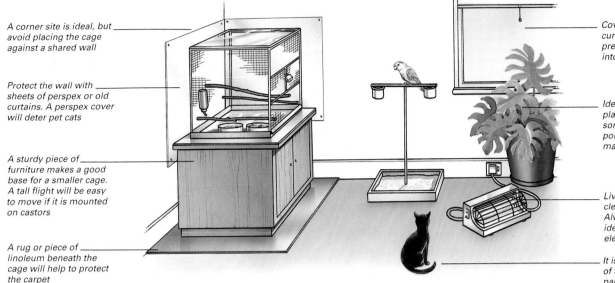

A corner site is ideal, but avoid placing the cage against a shared wall

Protect the wall with sheets of perspex or old curtains. A perspex cover will deter pet cats

A sturdy piece of furniture makes a good base for a smaller cage. A tall flight will be easy to move if it is mounted on castors

A rug or piece of linoleum beneath the cage will help to protect the carpet

Cover windows with a curtain or blind to prevent parrots flying into them

Ideally, remove house plants from the room; some may prove poisonous and others may be destroyed

Live or open-bar fires are clearly dangerous. Always unplug and, ideally, remove all electrical appliances

It is wise to shut a cat out of the room while your parrot is out of its cage

If you keep a cat, you will need to take particular care when introducing a pet bird to your household. (More active species, such as cockatiels, are likely to attract more attention from cats than larger parrots.) Choose a flight with mesh not more than 2.5cm (1in) square or the cat may be able to reach inside the flight with its paws. And it is not only the parrot that could be in danger; should the cat strike and miss, the cockatoo might retaliate and bite the cat's leg. A cat sitting on the roof of the bird's quarters presents the greatest danger, and you may want to add a false roof of plastic sheeting to deter any such confrontation.

Some cats prove more interested in pet parrots than others, and although you should never relax your guard entirely, a state of semi-harmony can be reached. Be careful, however, not to show too much overt affection to another pet in the presence of your parrot or it may become jealous and scream loudly for attention. This situation is more likely to occur if you obtain another pet once you have a parrot; the parrot will usually grow to tolerate established pets in time.

The early days

Place food and water close to a perch at first, because many birds are reluctant to feed on the floor in unfamiliar surroundings. If it is dark when you reach home with your new pet, leave a room light on for an hour or so to allow the parrot to settle down.

Some owners like to cover their parrots at night so that the bird is not exposed to abnormally long periods of light, which may interfere with the moulting cycle. If you decide to adopt this practice, you will need a thick cover, preferably of a non-woven fabric, so that the bird cannot catch its claws in it and injure itself. There is no need to tie this in place; simply drape it over the roof and allow it to trail down the sides, leaving a slight gap for ventilation at the bottom.

Avoid disturbing a newly acquired parrot more than necessary for the first few days, to allow it time to settle in its new surroundings. Keep a close watch on its food and water intake, as well as on its droppings; if you suspect anything is amiss, contact a veterinarian – early treatment can be vital in ensuring recovery.

Above: A site in the corner of a room should help your parrot to settle and feel secure. Tall flights such as this are easier to move to clean if they are mounted on castors, and it is a good idea to screen curtains and walls and protect carpets around cages housing larger parrots, which can be messy.

Left: Offer a piece of fruit or other foodstuff to your pet to encourage it to step onto your hand. Hand-feeding will reinforce the bond between you.

Teaching your parrot to talk

The length of time it takes to tame a parrot and teach it to talk varies considerably. Indeed, it may not even be possible to really tame an adult bird. Much depends, firstly, on how tame the parrot was when you acquired it, and, secondly, on how much time you can devote to the training process each day. Regular short spells of five to ten minutes during the day will be much more effective than a single lengthy session every weekend.

Most parrots, including budgerigars, find it easier to mimic the voices of women or children, although they often respond adequately to men as well, and some species prove more natural talkers than others. The Grey Parrot is universally accepted as the most talented member of the family in this respect, but budgerigars are also very able, and most amazons can also acquire a large vocabulary and have clear diction. Macaws and cockatoos are rather less talented in establishing an extensive repertoire, but can certainly be taught perhaps 30 or 40 words and Pionus parrots and *Poicephalus* species can also prove able mimics, though they are less often kept as pets. There is even a record of a parrotlet being taught a few words.

You will need to repeat a chosen word or phrase many times before the parrot will copy you. Start with something simple, such as ''Hello Joey'', when you go into the room; the bird will soon come to associate this phrase with your presence, and should eventually respond by repeating it. Build up the vocabulary carefully, so that the bird does not become confused. Although it may be amusing, a parrot whose repertoire includes swear words can be a source of embarrassment or problems later, in front of children, for example. It is also difficult to persuade a parrot to drop words from its vocabulary once it has mastered them. If your parrot does pick up an undesirable word or phrase, you could try covering the cage briefly when the bird uses it.

Taming your parrot

Within a few days, you can try offering pieces of millet spray by hand to a new budgerigar – or larger nuts to a young macaw – to win its confidence. If it initially refuses to feed in this way, try again later, perhaps in the late afternoon, as parrots normally feed then before retiring to roost for the night. A hand-raised bird will rarely refuse an offering, and may even beg for food, attracting your attention by head-bobbing and calling for food. Aviary-bred or imported youngsters may be more reticent, but you need not worry provided that the young parrot is clearly eating on its own. In the wild, the young of certain species, such as the large macaws, stay with their parents in family groups for a considerable period and may try to solicit food from an adult even when weaned.

Once the parrot is feeding readily from your hand, initially taking food pushed through the cage mesh and then inside the flight, you should find it quite easy to persuade a hand-raised chick to step from the perch onto your hand or arm. If the bird is reluctant, you can try to bribe it by holding a piece of fruit or other favourite food item, such as a groundnut (a peanut in its shell) just out of the parrot's reach while it remains on the perch. Place your arm in front of the perch to encourage the bird to step onto it to reach the food.

As with all stages in training, keep repeating the procedure until the bird is responding without hesitation. It should then allow you to stroke its head, indicating its request by tilting its head slightly to one side and ruffling its feathers. This is a clear sign of acceptance, which may not be extended to other members of your family. It is a good idea to encourage other people to be involved to some extent in the bird's care. It will help if the parrot will accept someone else's attention in your absence, though they should be cautious – your pet is unlikely to be as trusting with anyone else, and may bite unexpectedly.

Below: A tame parrot, such as the White-bellied Caique shown here, will allow its owner to stroke its neck. This clear sign of acceptance may not be extended to others in the family.

Left: Most parrots, including budgies, find it easier to mimic the voices of women or children. Special cassette tapes and records have limited success.

Studies of talking parrots have suggested that, in some cases, the bird is able to associate a particular word with a request, so that it can learn to ask for 'fruit please', for example. You can build up a parrot's vocabulary over many years. They are capable of learning over 500 words, and you can even teach them songs or nursery rhymes by training them to repeat a line at a time and then linking these together. In some countries – North America, especially – records and cassette tapes are available to help you train a parrot to talk, but these are usually less effective than may be imagined, largely because the bird cannot relate to the voice. Although there is really no substitute for spending time with your bird when you are teaching it to talk, it can be useful to play tapes of your own voice to reinforce the bird's talking lessons when you have to leave it alone.

Parrots will also pick up other sounds from their environment. Greys are especially talented whistlers, probably because their natural calls are comprised of a series of similar sounds, and they may also learn how to imitate a barking dog, or even the sound of a ringing telephone. This can be particularly disorientating, so try to keep your 'phone out of earshot of your bird, or you may have difficulty distinguishing between a genuine call and your parrot!

Letting your parrot out

Once your bird is perching readily on your arm and has settled well in the home, you will have to decide whether or not to let it venture out into the room. Generally this is to be recommended, especially if you can devote a particular time every day, perhaps during the evening, to playing with your pet. These times will undoubtedly strengthen the bond between you, and the parrot will soon settle into the routine of coming out, and then returning to its quarters. Indeed, after an initial investigation, it may perch happily on a special stand for much of the evening.

Suitable stands are sometimes incorporated as part of a flight cage, added above the roof, where parrots often feel most secure. Alternatively, many pet stores stock special stout wooden T-shaped stands with a food and water pot at either end and a tray beneath to catch seed husks and droppings. Do not be tempted to acquire a leg chain for a parrot, especially if your bird is not tame. If it is frightened for any reason, it will try

to fly off the perch, and is likely to be left dangling upside down from the chain.

Never leave a parrot loose in a room if you are not present. There are a number of potential dangers here (see page 23), including uncovered windows; parrots do not always appreciate the presence of glass, and may fly into a larger pane. Open or electric-bar fires are another hazard, as is live electrical flex. Macaws, especially, can bite through a flex with devastating speed and will receive a lethal shock from a live wire, so check that all appliances are switched off before you let the parrot out into the room. Some house plants may prove poisonous if the parrot eats them, and flaking paintwork that contains lead will also represent a hazard.

Adequate supervision is also important to protect your furnishings; many pet parrots can inflict serious damage to wooden furniture with their powerful beaks, and can also wreck curtains. Until used to being let out your bird may fly around wildly, knocking over ornaments and hurting itself, as well as damaging your home.

Below: A secure stand is useful for a tame parrot, such as this Grey, providing it with a place to perch and feed while out of its cage.

Wing clipping

With all the potential damage that a parrot could cause both itself and your home, you may decide to clip your parrot's wing to restrain its flight. Carried out properly, this procedure is quite painless, with no long-term effects; at the next moult (within a year), the cut feathers will be shed and replaced by a full set, enabling the parrot to fly again normally. (You may find, however, that your pet is rather withdrawn for a day or so afterwards, because of the indignity of being handled and restrained for this purpose.)

Try to find someone to help you clip your parrot's wings; with the larger species, especially, you really need one person to hold the bird, leaving the other free to concentrate on cutting the flight feathers. (If you are at all concerned, ask your veterinarian to carry out this task for you.) Open up one wing, and with a sharp pair of scissors (preferably with round rather than pointed ends), cut across the flight feathers in a straight line, leaving the outer two intact. Do not cut below the start of the individual feather shafts, but leave a small amount of feathering at the top; this part of the feather is dead so there will be no risk of bleeding. (When a new feather is growing, there is a blood supply within the shaft, and cutting the feather too short at this point will result in a haemorrhage.)

While parrots are not generally disturbed by having their feathers clipped in this way, some tend to pull at the remaining bare shafts. They may do this instinctively, as once the stub of damaged feather is removed, another full feather will grow to replace it. Try to divert their attention by supplying plenty of fresh branches for them to gnaw.

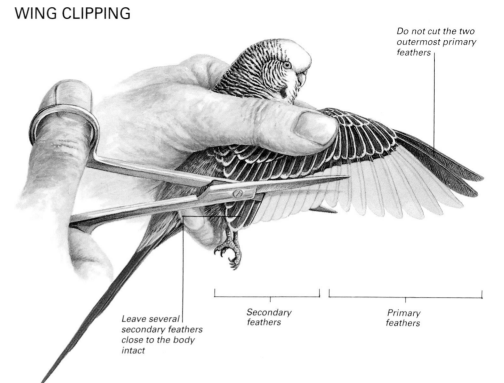

Do not cut the two outermost primary feathers

Leave several secondary feathers close to the body intact

Secondary feathers

Primary feathers

Above: You should be able to restrain a budgerigar yourself to clip its wing. Open up one wing, and with a sharp pair of scissors with rounded ends, cut across the flight feathers in a straight line, leaving the outer two intact.

Below: You will need someone to help you clip the wing of a large parrot, or ask your veterinarian to do it for you. Although your parrot may be withdrawn for a day or two after having its wing clipped, the procedure is painless.

Introducing another parrot

While cockatiels and budgerigars will usually accept a newcomer without any problems, other species – even the smaller birds, such as conures – are usually far less tolerant, and, in the early days, bloodshed may result unless you are very careful.

Start by keeping the newcomer in a room on its own for a fortnight or so, to ensure that it is healthy, before placing its cage in the same room as that of your established pet. Position the two cages so that the birds are within sight, but not within reach, of each other, or one bird may bite the feet of the other, inflicting a serious injury. Do not let one of the parrots out into the room while the other remains confined in its quarters; this is likely to lead to jealousy, especially if the established parrot is left confined while the newcomer is at liberty in the room, and if one lands on the other's cage, it is likely to have its feet bitten.

Once they have had time to adjust to each other's presence in the room, you can let both birds out together. Supervize them very carefully in these early stages and separate them at once if there is any overt sign of aggression. In most cases, however, the birds will be rather wary of each other at first and will avoid contact.

Over a period of weeks, they should come to accept each other and may even end up sharing their quarters. And, of course, should you have a true pair of parrots, you may even be able to breed them successfully in the home.

Dealing with feather dust

All birds produce feather dust, especially when they are moulting; as the new feathers emerge from the feather follicles in the skin, they are covered in a thin sheath and this covering is broken down by preening, enabling the feather to un-

wrap into its usual shape. This feather dust is distributed into the atmosphere and settles around the room, which is not only a nuisance, but can also provoke an allergic reaction in some people. Symptoms may include runny eyes and nose and, sometimes, a tight-chested feeling. Those who suffer from asthma are likely to be worst affected, but prolonged exposure to this dust can create an allergy in other people too. Cockatoos are particularly bad in this respect.

There are various ways in which you can help restrict the spread of dust in the environment; you may be able to buy a special clear hood to fit over the cage, or, alternatively, use a domestic ionizer, which will precipitate dust from the atmosphere and will help to make the room feel fresher.

You should also spray the parrot regularly with tepid water, which will damp down feather dust and keep the plumage sleek. Bathing will prevent the parrot's plumage from becoming excessively dry indoors. (In aviary birds, the preen gland, located near the base of the lower back, produces a weather-proofing agent, which the parrot transfers on to its feathers when it preens itself, helping it to stay sleek in appearance.) You can easily recognize a parrot that has not received a regular bath indoors by its rather ruffled feathering. Allowing the bird's plumage to become very dry could trigger feather-plucking; no longer able to arrange its

Left: Spraying parrots housed indoors with water helps prevent their plumage becoming too dry. Make a habit of doing this before you clean out their cage.

plumage properly, the parrot may resort to pulling out its feathers.

Fill a simple plant sprayer with tepid water and spray the bird while it is in its quarters. (Remove the food pots first to prevent their contents being soaked.) Be careful not to spray the water directly at your pet, especially if it is not used to the experience, but aim the jet so that the droplets fall on to it from above. Do not saturate the parrot or it will be vulnerable to a chill, especially if it has not received a bath for some months.

It is a good idea to give your pet a bath just before you clean out its quarters. Obviously, some of the spray will fall onto the floor of the bird's quarters, dampen-

Above: Introducing a new bird to the home needs to be done sensitively. Once they have adjusted to each other, the birds may even share their quarters.

ing down feather dust here and preventing it from being liberated into the room when you pull out the tray. A spray can also be useful to remove any faecal contamination or other dirt on the cage bars; use it in conjunction with one of the special wipes now marketed for cleaning cages. These have greatly facilitated the task of cleaning these difficult areas thoroughly and are also useful for wiping surrounding furniture on which dust has accumulated.

KEEPING PARROTS IN THE GARDEN

Before planning an aviary for parrots, you will need to consider whether their calls are likely to cause offence to close neighbours. Some of the smaller species, such as the parrotlets, lack the harsh screech of Amazon parrots and the large macaws, and an aviary for them will also prove far less costly. If you do want to keep large parrots in the garden, you may be able to design suitable birdroom accommodation for them. The parrots will breed without any problems in such surroundings; indeed, results can be better in a darkened environment, which offers greater seclusion.

The size of the aviary

The size of the aviary will obviously depend to an extent on the parrots you want to keep. Smaller species will thrive in an aviary with a flight 180cm (6ft) long attached to shelter 90cm (3ft) square. Medium-sized and larger parrots, such as the Senegal and *Pionus* species, will benefit from a flight that is at least 360cm (12ft) in length, and parakeets, which are particularly strong fliers, will show to best effect in an even longer flight.

The width of the flight is less significant, especially since most parrots are usually kept in pairs, rather than on a colony system. A width of 90cm (3ft) will suffice for the smaller short-tailed species, with 120cm (4ft) being adequate for most of the others, except the long-tailed macaws, for which a flight 180cm (6ft) wide is ideal.

Because most aviary mesh is approximately 90cm (3ft) wide, aviaries are usually constructed in 90cm (3ft) modular units. (You may be able to find mesh 120cm/4ft wide, which will save on timber costs if you are planning a flight 360cm/12ft long.) Mesh is also sometimes available in widths of 180cm (6ft), but this tends to sag on the frame without a central support.

Right: The size and thickness of the aviary mesh are important to exclude rodents and to prevent parrots from breaking the strands with their bills. The top two mesh samples shown here are 1.25cm (½in) square, the thinner one 19 gauge (19G) and the lower one 16 gauge (16G). The lower two are 2.5×1.25cm (1×½in), again 19G and 16G respectively. Sixteen-gauge wire is suitable for aviaries to house most parrot species.

HOUSING PARROTS IN THE GARDEN

PARROT GROUP	DESIGN POINTS	FLIGHT LENGTH
Budgerigars, cockatiels and hanging parrots	Can be kept in aviaries made from 19-gauge mesh.	1.8-3.6m (6-12ft)
Australian parakeets, fig parrots, parrotlets and lovebirds	16-gauge mesh is recommended for aviaries to house these birds.	1.8-5.4m (6-18ft)
Lories and lorikeets	Pay particular attention to the floor covering; it must be easy to clean.	2.7-3.6m (9-12ft)
Psittaculid parakeets and conures	These destructive species require flights built with 16-gauge mesh, and woodwork must be protected from their bills.	2.7-3.6m (9-12ft)
Amazon and *Pionus* parrots, caiques, Eclectus and *Tanygnathus* parrots	Strong aviaries are essential for these birds. Protect woodwork in the shelter, as well as in the flight.	3.6-5.4m (12-18ft)
Vasa parrots	Vasas will benefit from plenty of flying space.	4.6m (15ft)
Macaws and cockatoos	A steel-framed flight and blockwork will be needed for all but the smallest macaws.	2.7-5.4m (9-18ft)

* Note: Flight length will be influenced by the number of birds being kept together, their individual size and level of activity.

POSSIBLE AVIARY PLANS

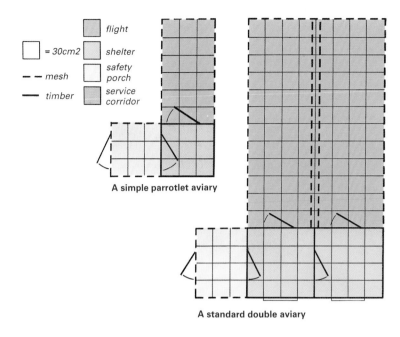

A key showing:
- □ = 30cm2
- - - - mesh
- —— timber
- flight
- shelter
- safety porch
- service corridor

A simple parrotlet aviary

A standard double aviary

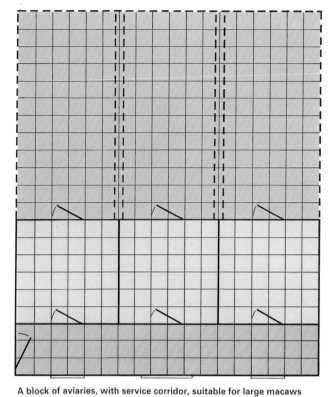

A block of aviaries, with service corridor, suitable for large macaws

Above: The size of aviary you decide on will depend to a large extent on the species you want to keep. Here are three possible aviary plans.

Siting the aviary

Where you site the aviary in your garden is an important consideration. The parrots will benefit from being kept in a sheltered and relatively secluded place, so try to avoid positioning the aviary where it will be exposed to the prevailing winds. During the winter months, the effects of the so-called wind-chill factor will expose the birds to much lower temperatures than if they were in a more sheltered spot. A site within view of the house would be agreeable and is especially advantageous if you want to have access to amenities such as water and electricity. A level site will make construction much easier.

Although they act as a windbreak, trees can be dangerous, especially if branches fall on the aviary. A more commonly encountered disadvantage, however, is that they provide cats with an easy means of reaching the aviary. (Although they may not be able to harm the parrots directly, cats can cause breeding birds to desert their nest, which often results in the death of young chicks, especially after dark.) You may, therefore, need to trim back trees in order to accommodate an aviary.

To avoid disturbing your garden more than necessary, try to plan the aviary to fit on a site near an existing path. (You will need to walk to the aviary every day and will want to avoid muddy patches on the lawn.) If you have children, it is a good idea to avoid their main play area, since noise close to the aviary is bound to disturb even committed breeding pairs.

Finally, it is always advisable to check with your local planning department before starting to build an aviary, even though, under most circumstances, official permission will not be required. You should also inform your neighbours.

A site next to a garden pond is also inappropriate. Apart from the possibility of flooding during periods of heavy rainfall, the birds may suffer from biting midges, which breed in the pond water.

SITING THE AVIARY

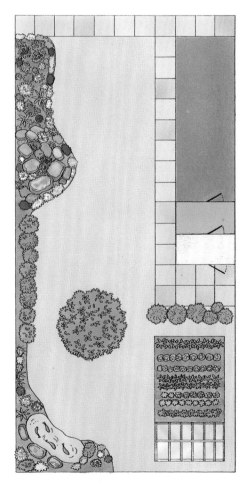

Parakeets are susceptible to the effects of the Laucocytozoon parasites, injected into the blood stream as the insect feeds on the bird's blood and giving rise to a form of avian malaria.

An aviary situated close to the house will enable you to observe the birds from indoors and keep a look out for troublesome cats at the same time. Bear in mind, though, that cockatoos can be quite noisy, and you may therefore prefer to site the aviary elsewhere in the garden, away from the house.

When you are designing an aviary, bear in mind that you may want to extend it at a later date. This flight measures 480cm (16ft) long by 120cm (4ft) wide and 180cm (6ft) tall – an ideal size for a pair of larger parrots, such as cockatoos.

In this basic aviary, a 180cm (6ft) square wooden shed has been subdivided to create a separate shelter and a storage area, which doubles as a safety porch. If you are building the shelter youself, 180cm (6ft) wood would be ideal. A basic safety porch need be only 120cm (4ft) square.

Conifers at the side of the aviary shield it from view. Avoid planting trees with overhanging branches that will cut out light in the summer months and drop leaves into the flight in the autumn.

With careful planning, the aviary can become the focal point of your garden.

The standard aviary

At its most basic, an aviary is comprised of an enclosed shelter and an attached flight area, which is constructed of wire mesh on a wooden framework. If you do not have the time or the skill to build an aviary yourself, a large number of firms now specialize in producing aviaries in kit form, which are easy to assemble on a ready-prepared base. The advantage of purchasing a sectional structure is that you can dismantle the aviary quite easily, and re-erect it elsewhere with the minimum of problems, if you move house.

Some firms will even erect the aviary for you. You may find it cheaper to purchase an aviary in sectional form than to build your own, particularly if you are interested in the grass parakeets, or other less destructive species, such as members of the *Bolborhynchus* genus. Ask at

A STANDARD AVIARY

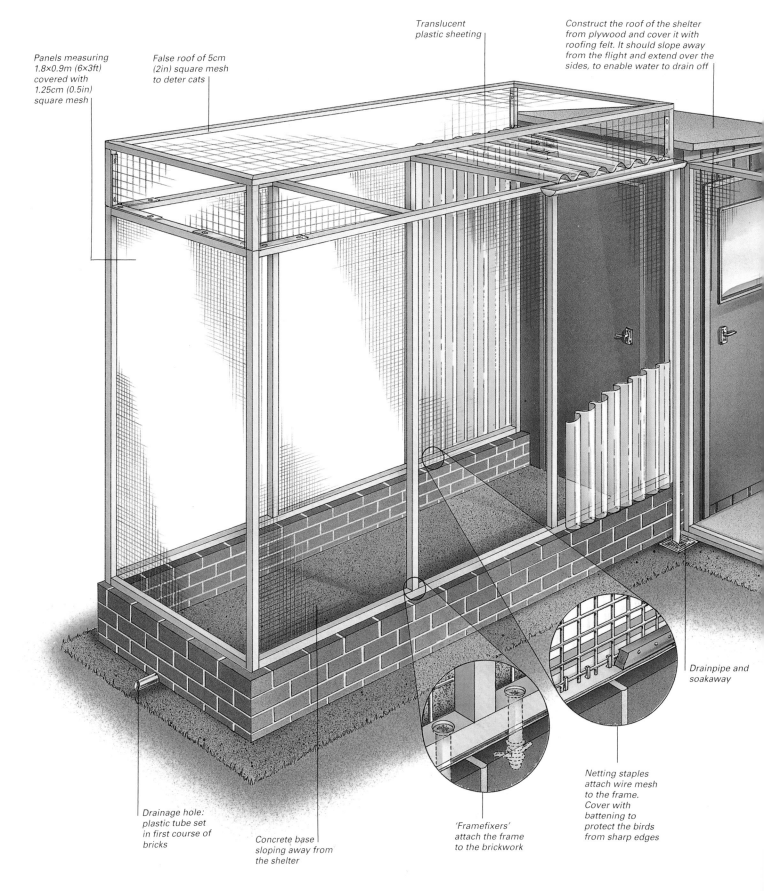

Panels measuring 1.8×0.9m (6×3ft) covered with 1.25cm (0.5in) square mesh

False roof of 5cm (2in) square mesh to deter cats

Translucent plastic sheeting

Construct the roof of the shelter from plywood and cover it with roofing felt. It should slope away from the flight and extend over the sides, to enable water to drain off

Drainpipe and soakaway

Drainage hole: plastic tube set in first course of bricks

Concrete base sloping away from the shelter

'Framefixers' attach the frame to the brickwork

Netting staples attach wire mesh to the frame. Cover with battening to protect the birds from sharp edges

your local pet store for the names of aviary suppliers near where you live, or trace them through their advertisements in a birdkeeping magazine.

Always try to visit a manufacturer's premises before making any choice, so that you can see the standard of workmanship

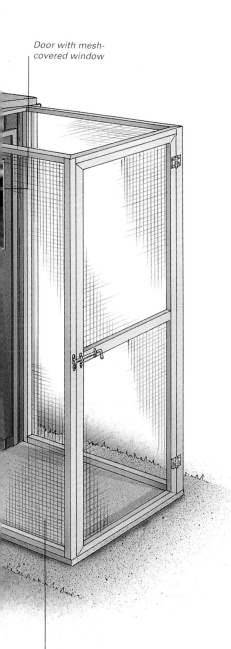

Door with mesh-covered window

Wire mesh safety porch with 5cm (2in) square timber frame

Above: Blocks of flights should be double-wired to prevent parrots inflicting injuries to the feet of birds in adjoining aviaries.

for yourself. A straightfoward comparison of prices can be misleading if you don't examine closely what is on offer. Look, for example, at the thickness of timber used, and the gauge and spacing of the mesh. The flight panel should be constructed from timber that is.at least 3.75cm (1½in) square. Check that the timber is safely weather-proofed (some companies charge extra for such treatment). Weather-proofing timber for outdoor use will greatly help to prolong its lifespan. Jointed panels should prove more durable than those made of lengths of timber that are simply nailed together.

Mesh should be fixed securely to the framework using special netting staples, rather than simply tacked in place with battening. You may be offered a choice of mesh. For smaller parrots, 19 gauge (19G) is adequate, and ideally the dimensions should be 1.25cm (½in) square, although 2.5 × 1.25cm (1 × ½in), which is cheaper, should exclude mice. The mesh should cover the inner face of the frame to prevent the birds reaching the woodwork.

If you are planning to build a block of flights, check that both sides of connecting panels are wired, so that birds in adjoining flights cannot injure each other's toes through the mesh. (It is, of course, possible to buy the timber, mesh and other materials separately and make your own flight, but, particularly if you want to build a block of aviaries, this is rarely economic.)

Where you position the entrance may depend on where you propose to site the aviary in the garden, but you can place a door into either the flight or the shelter. The latter arrangement will normally be most convenient as you will need to feed the birds here every day. You can enter the flight via the shelter as you will need to go into this part of the aviary only every week or two, to clean the floor. Try to arrange the doors so they are as unobtrusive as possible.

The shelter needs to be dry and well lit to encourage the birds to roost here at night, where they will be protected from predators and bad weather.

Tongued-and-grooved timber or heavy-duty marine plywood on a wooden frame are popular materials for the shelter. Set a window in one side, to provide natural light, and cover it with aviary mesh on its inner face, to prevent the birds injuring themselves on the glass. If you decide to construct a block of aviaries, then you will need to position windows at the back of each shelter unit.

It is a good idea to incorporate a safety porch into the design of the aviary. This is usually sited around the external door of the shelter, but you may also decide to place one at the end of the flight if you have an entrance point here. The porch, which you can construct of flight panels, will prevent any birds escaping when you enter the aviary. The arrangement of the doors is important here; hang the outer door of the porch so that it opens outwards and the one into the shelter to open inwards. This will give you enough room to enter the aviary with cleaning tools or perches when necessary. Fix a bolt on the inside of the safety porch door to ensure it remains firmly closed while you are inside.

Most shelters have a sloping roof, the highest aspect adjoining the flight. You will need to fix guttering along the lower edge to drain away rainwater and so prevent you being soaked by the run-off as you move in and out of the safety porch. To ensure that the interior of the shelter stays dry, cover the roof with a double layer of heavy-duty roofing felt. (You can check for, and fill, any gaps here once you have assembled the structure.) Ensure that the felt overlaps the edges of the roof and that it is firmly battened in place around the edges, or it may be torn off in a gale. You can help to prolong the lifespan of the felt by painting it white, which will reflect the sun's heat and so prevent the felt splitting prematurely. Replacing the felt, and carrying out any other repair work on the aviary, will cause considerable disturbance to the birds as you will need to remove them from the aviary; if the birds are breeding, they may well desert their nest. It therefore pays to buy the best available material, rather than a cheap grade with a limited lifespan.

Provide access to and from the shelter for the birds by cutting an entrance hole near the top of the shelter, next to (rather than as part of) the door. The size and height of the hole will depend on the species concerned, but 30cm (1ft) square is adequate even for macaws. Fix a landing platform, made from timber or thick plywood, beneath the entrance hole on either side. The depth of the platform will depend on the size of the bird, but, again, 30cm (1ft) on either side will be sufficient. Brackets provide the simplest means of supporting the platform. You may want to add vertical edges, creating an open box structure, to protect the interior of the shelter from direct winds. This is especially important with some species such as Grey Parrots, which, even when acclimatized, dislike cold weather.

REINFORCING THE FRAMES

1 *Choose timber at least 5cm (2in) thick to provide a greater surface area on which to attach the mesh using netting staples.*

2 *Cover the panel with 19G, 1.25cm (0.5in) square mesh to protect the woodwork from the onslaught of the parrots' powerful beaks.*

3 *Attach the sheet of mesh (size 2.5×1.25cm/1×0.5in or smaller) to the frame, tucking exposed ends underneath to prevent injury.*

Preparing the site

A secure base for the aviary is essential, not just to protect the structure in gales, but also to ensure that it does not start to rot prematurely. Start by removing any grass from the site, and from the immediate surroundings, as it is likely to be badly damaged during the building work. If you cut the grass carefully using a sharp spade, and fold the turf inwards so that the roots are uppermost, you should be able to replant it satisfactorily later on. Keep it in a shaded spot and do not allow it to dry out.

Mark out the site carefully and dig trenches around the perimeter to a depth of 45cm (1½ft). Set a course of blocks here, extending to a height of 30cm (1ft) above ground. This provides the base on which the framework will ultimately be positioned. Make sure that the trench is wide enough for you to stand in once the blocks are in place. Depending on local soil conditions, you may need to use shuttering to hold the sides of the trench in place.

Floor covering for the flight

Cleanliness in the parrots' quarters is very important, especially for those species, such as Australian parakeets, that will forage for food on the ground. A grass floor may seem attractive here, but is fairly impractical; the grass under the covered part of the flight soon dies back unless it is regularly watered, while elsewhere in the flight, water-logging will be a problem when it rains and mossy patches will start to develop. If you walk through the flight regularly, you are likely to create further areas of wear. Perhaps most importantly, a grass surface will be difficult for the parrots. It may be possible to have a compromise, with a central area of grass, gravel around the sides and undercover, and concrete beneath the perches.

If you use gravel, you will need to lay a fairly thick layer, or the flight may become flooded during wet weather, and you must include a hole in the base of the gravel at one end of the flight to facilitate drainage of rainwater from the flight. This is again hard to clean, however, and you may decide to lay concrete or paving slabs, which you can scrub down thoroughly, beneath the perches, and use a gravel covering elsewhere in the flight, where dirt is less likely to accumulate.

A concrete base is a rather more permanent option, but also likely to be the most hygienic. Start by preparing a 15cm (6in) layer of hardcore, and on top of this lay a mix of one part cement to three parts ballast. Finally, the floor will need a coating of sand and cement, in equal parts, to create a smooth finish. It is important to ensure that this mix is not too sandy, or the surface will crack and break up and, during the winter especially, unsightly algal growth will colonize the floor. You may decide to seek the help of a plasterer in order to ensure a smooth finish.

Make sure that the floor slopes slightly towards a drainage hole at one end of the flight. This will allow rainwater entering the flight to flow away, rather than forming puddles over the base. A solid concrete base to the aviary also has the advantage of preventing rodents burrowing beneath the foundations.

Aviaries for the larger parrots

Accommodation for larger species will need to be reinforced to withstand the onslaught of their more powerful beaks. Choose 5cm (2in) timber for the flight panels to provide a greater surface area on which to attach the mesh (again, using netting staples). The mesh size should not exceed 2.5 × 1.25cm (1 × ½in), not only to exclude rodents, but also to prevent the parrots reaching through it to the timber.

It is particularly important with the larger species that you fully cover the inner surfaces of the flight panels with mesh, so that they are not accessible to the parrots' beaks. As an additional precaution, tack a layer of 19G 1.5cm (½in) square mesh around the inner surface of the frame before applying the thicker mesh on top to cover the panel.

You will also need to protect the shelter by lining the interior with mesh so that none of the framework supports are exposed to the birds. Parrots will not be able to chew a flat surface, but if they find any unprotected edges, they will destroy the timber easily. A major area of weakness is likely to be the landing platform. You can protect the woodwork here by folding tin sheeting tightly over the exposed edges. Check that the metal is flat against the surface of the shelter and extend it about 10cm (4in) down the sides to minimize the risk of the parrots cutting their toes on the sharp edges of the metal. You may be able to bend the bottom cut edges up behind the sheeting so that they are completely out of the parrots' reach.

Several companies have now started to market all-metal structures, complete

A BRICK AVIARY FOR LARGE PARROTS

Attach mesh to the door making sure there are no sharp edges

The door leading from the shelter should be hinged to open into the flight. (A service corridor at the rear gives access to the shelters)

Attach the mesh securely to the brickwork

Right: This metal flight is made of units that clip together. These panels are ideal for constructing quarters for cockatoos and other large parrots within a wooden shed, as they avoid the need to cover all exposed timber.

with shelter, which solve the problems of how to construct a durable aviary for the larger parrots. A metal aviary may appear quite expensive, but it will save you the considerable time and trouble necessary to parrot-proof a more conventional timber-framed one.

As with timber-framed aviaries, sectional designs are preferable, as they will allow you to design the aviary to meet your own requirements. Such units are normally very easy to assemble on site, using nuts and bolts that fit through pre-drilled holes to hold the panels together. (It is usually easiest to assemble the sides and then slot in the roof section last.) You will have to devise a means of attaching the flight securely to the block or brick foundations once you are happy with its position. This can be achieved by bedding the frame in mortar, and also using frame fixers or bolts to ensure greater stability, as with a standard aviary.

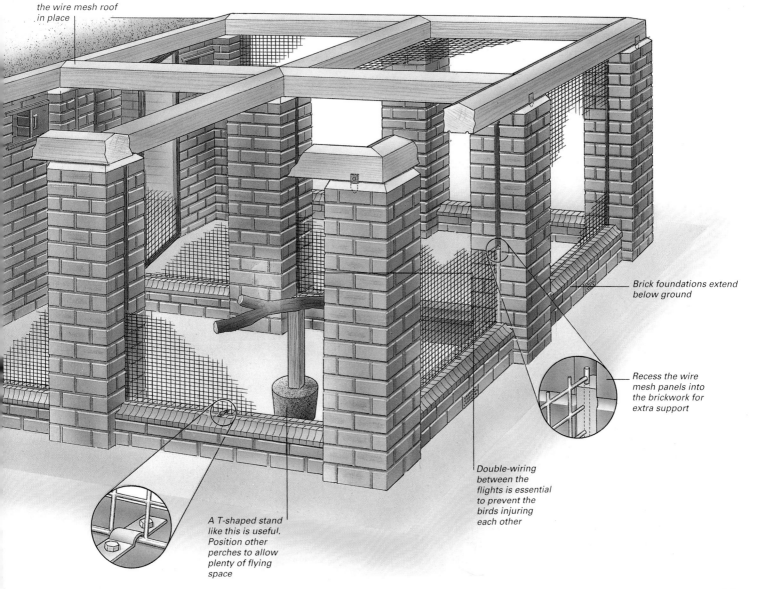

Timber beams anchor the wire mesh roof in place

Brick foundations extend below ground

Recess the wire mesh panels into the brickwork for extra support

Double-wiring between the flights is essential to prevent the birds injuring each other

A T-shaped stand like this is useful. Position other perches to allow plenty of flying space

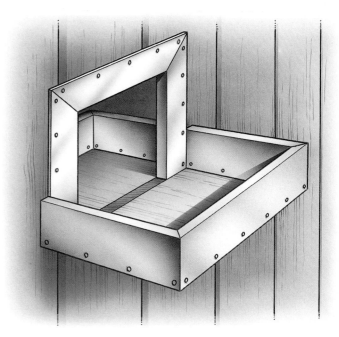

Above: A brick structure is ideal for the larger, more destructive parrot species. This one houses a pair of rare Red-fronted Macaws.

Below: Constructing suitable accommodation for cockatoos and other large parrots can be a problem; a stout all-metal aviary is one solution.

As an alternative to using one of these ready-to-assemble designs, you may be able to find a welder to make up metal panels for you, or you can buy wire mesh in sheets of the appropriate size. Suppliers of mesh panels often advertise in the birdkeeping magazines. Panels are available in various lengths, ranging from 180 to 360cm (6-12ft), and are easier to

Above: You will need to protect all exposed woodwork in an aviary for large, destructive species. One area that is often overlooked is the entrance hole. Use tin sheeting to protect woodwork here from the birds' strong beaks, remembering to fold back any sharp pieces of metal so that the birds cannot cut their feet.

work with than wire mesh on a roll. Check that no sharp spicules have formed on the mesh during the galvanizing process, as the sharp splinters could injure the tongues or feet of the cockatoos as they climb around their quarters.

Twelve-gauge mesh is suitable for the accommodation for most larger parrots, though for some species, such as Umbrella Cockatoos and the larger macaws, you may need to use thicker 10G mesh. The dimensions of the mesh are also important; in most cases 2.5cm (1in) square will be ideal; while more expensive than, say 2.5 × 7.5cm (1 × 3in) mesh, there are several advantages with its smaller size. Firstly, the parrots will be less able to gain leverage, so it will be harder for them to damage the mesh with their powerful beaks. It will also prevent sparrows and most other birds (though not mice and some small snakes) from gaining access to the aviary, where they could steal food and spread disease.

Unfortunately, snakes (where they are found) can prove a particular problem; although they are only casual visitors to aviaries, they will find their way into a nestbox and grab any chicks if they get an opportunity. Mice, which will be betrayed by their droppings, are most likely to eat seed. If you decide to opt for 2.5 × 7.5cm (1 × 3in) mesh, you may find that rats, too, are a problem. All rodents present a serious health hazard because they can introduce a variety of diseases, such as salmonellosis and yersiniosis, to a collection. You therefore need to make every effort to exclude them right from the outset. (For how to eliminate rodents if they do become a problem, see pages 38-39.)

A reinforced shelter

With considerable modification, a wooden shed can provide a suitable aviary shelter for larger parrots. You will need to construct an internal shell using sectional mesh panels to prevent the birds from gaining access to the interior woodwork. The face of the shelter that connects with the flight will also need to be protected, especially if the shed is made of overlapping boards, which will present an irresistible target to the parrots' beaks.

Don't forget to allow for the door and to provide a landing platform. You can build a ledge around the sides of the platform to minimize draughts in the shelter. Protect the platform with tin sheeting, as these parrots will gnaw and rapidly destroy any exposed wood.

Having made the landing platform, you will need to protect the remainder of the exposed woodwork on the side of the shelter that adjoins the flight. The simplest means of doing this is probably to screw a framework of 2.5cm (1in) square timber covered with 1.25cm (½in) square 16G mesh over the exposed woodwork. Although in time the timber on this frame may be destroyed, the covering should serve to protect the shelter itself from the parrots' strong beaks.

Metal flights sometimes come complete with a shelter, but these metal or fibreglass shelters tend to become very hot during the warmer months of the year and often lack windows. The thermal range within a brick or blockwork structure is less marked and you can easily include a window to provide light and adequate ventilation.

If you decide to construct a block or brick shelter for the parrots, you may decide to seek professional help from a builder. Don't forget to include a damp-proof course, as the birds will not thrive in wet or, indeed, poorly ventilated surroundings. Although a brick shelter will be expensive to construct, you will not have the problem of protecting the woodwork on the flight wall of the shelter, nor will you have the additional expense of including a flight within the shelter. As the parrots will have free access to the interior, you will need to cover windows with wire mesh to protect the birds from injury (they may not always appreciate the presence of glass).

Try to design a shelter of this type so that, should you move home and take the flight with you, the new residents will be able to use the building, for storing garden tools, for example. Otherwise unless the potential buyers share your enthusiasm, the structure may create problems when you try to sell your house.

USING A WOODEN SHED AS A BIRDROOM

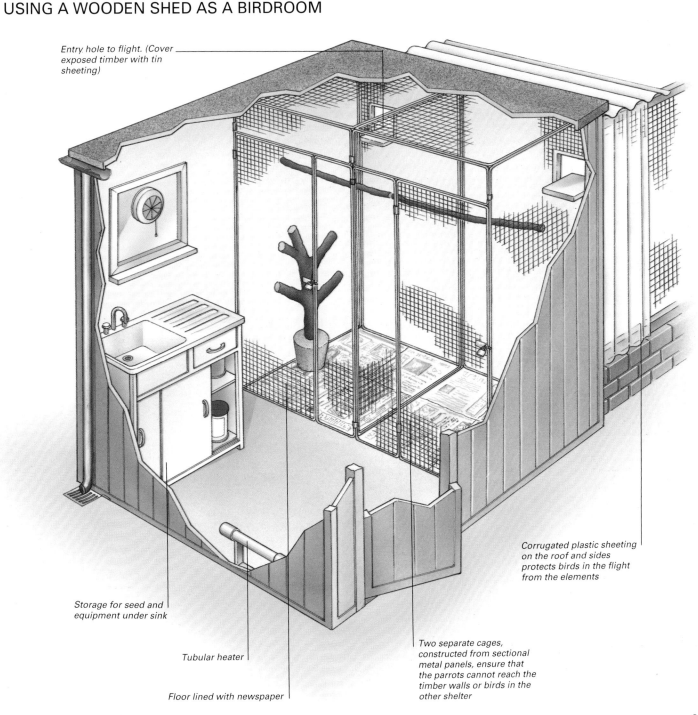

Entry hole to flight. (Cover exposed timber with tin sheeting)

Corrugated plastic sheeting on the roof and sides protects birds in the flight from the elements

Storage for seed and equipment under sink

Tubular heater

Floor lined with newspaper

Two separate cages, constructed from sectional metal panels, ensure that the parrots cannot reach the timber walls or birds in the other shelter

Above: Raised aviaries, such as this, are popular in North America, because they are cheaper to build than standard types, but they are not ideal, as access to the interior is limited.

Entrances to the aviary

The parrots should be fed in the shelter, so an entrance here will be essential and a connecting door will give you access to the flight. Apart from the need to inspect nestboxes (which, ideally, should be positioned under cover in the flight) during the breeding period, you will only need to enter the flight about once a week or so in order to clean the floor, so a separate door into the flight is really unnecessary and will increase the cost of the aviary.

Some aviary designs incorporate the single entry point into the flight rather than the shelter, but this will mean that you will need to pass the nestbox regularly, and some of the larger parrots are likely to become aggressive and may even attack you close to their nestbox when they are breeding. If you decide to incorporate an additional door into the flight, it should open inwards.

A safety porch is a vital part of a good aviary design, ensuring that there is no risk of parrots escaping when you enter their quarters. It needs to be about 90cm (3ft) square and 180cm (6ft) high to allow easy access and will be fairly easy to construct. Cover the inner surface of the wooden framework with wire mesh; thinner, 2.5 × 1.25cm (1 × ½in) 16G, rather than any more costly, heavy-duty mesh, will be adequate here. Use nuts and bolts to anchor the panels together; provided that you fit washers, you should be able to dismantle the entire structure at a later date if you move house.

There is no need to reinforce the timber of the safety porch, because if the parrots do slip out, they will be returned to the aviary before they can start to destroy the woodwork of the porch. Hinge the door of the safety porch so that it opens outwards to enable you to enter easily with perches and equipment.

The door of the aviary will need to be adequately protected, however, and you should fit bolts on its inner and outer faces

so that you can lock the door behind you when you enter the flight and be certain that the aviary is securely closed when you leave. It is a good idea to fix a secure hasp and padlock to the outer doors, as well, to deter thieves and vandals; combination locks are ideal as they avoid the need for keys.

Raised flights and shelters

As the cost of materials needed to build an aviary has risen, so birdkeepers have sought cheaper and more efficient aviary designs. Suspended flights – all-wire cages supported off the ground on block or brick pillars – have become popular, particularly in North America.

Although, in theory, suspended flights may appear an ideal option, in reality they are difficult to service. A simple task, such as replacing perches, becomes a problem, while the droppings are as likely to stick on the mesh as to accumulate on the floor. (The mesh needs to be at least 2.5cm (1in) square over the floor area for this reason.) Whereas a conventional flight can be anchored all around using frame fixers driven through to the framework, the suspended flight can be fixed only to the brick supports and is thus less secure.

Although suitable for nervous parrots, (as they prevent the need for you to enter their quarters), suspended aviaries are not suitable in all cases; there will be less space than in a conventional flight and a hen will therefore have less chance of escape if a cock in breeding condition turns aggressive.

A raised shelter may be a better option. Here, of course, you will need a safety porch not only around the shelter door, but also around any entrance to the flight, unless you have a block of aviaries, in which a service passage will alleviate the need for an additional safety porch at the rear.

Fitting perches and finishing off

You can help to divert the parrots' attention from woodwork in their aviary by ensuring that they have a good supply of perches. Cut lengths that will fit across the aviary, from non-poisonous trees (see page 19). You will find it easier to mount the perches on vertical uprights than to try to suspend them from the aviary framework, as the weight of the branches will place an unnecessary strain on the structure, and will also be difficult to replace.

Set a piece of 5cm (2in) square timber in a large cement-filled tub and screw the perch on to the top of the timber. When the perch needs replacing, you need only unscrew it, or lever it off and attach the new one. If you prepare a cement mould for the timber upright, rather than actually setting it in the concrete, you will be able to lift the post out of the supporting tub and replace both the perch and the length of timber when the parrots have destroyed it. You can simply attach the perch to one central upright, but for extra stability support the perch at either end.

If you have a fairly small aviary, you may prefer to attach perches to the aviary structure. Coil wire tightly around the

ends of the perches and loop it out through the aviary mesh, twisting it tightly around the framework. You may well find, however, that the parrots start to gnaw the branch from one end, in which case the perch will collapse.

Don't be tempted to clutter the aviary with perches, but allow the parrots adequate flying space. Two or three perches located at opposite ends of the flight will be adequate, but take care to avoid the doors; position two across the flight, for example, with a third angled across a corner. Fixing the perches in containers as described will give you flexibility to move them around, and if you adopt a similar system inside the shelter, the

AN AVIARY WITH A RAISED SHELTER

Safety porch for the shelter

Guttering

The safety porch door should open outwards

Set the safety porch on concrete paving slabs

Right: A rack system of perches is one option to consider in an aviary housing a colony of smaller species. You can construct this quite easily from dowelling and plywood, or buy it ready made from a specialist supplier.

perches will also serve to hold down the newspaper on the floor.

Finally you can face the blockwork on the outside of the aviary with mortar and then paint it if you wish. Replace the cut turves around the flight. It is a good idea to lay a path, or at least to set paving stones in the turves, so that you do not create bare patches on the lawn by constantly walking back and forth to feed the birds.

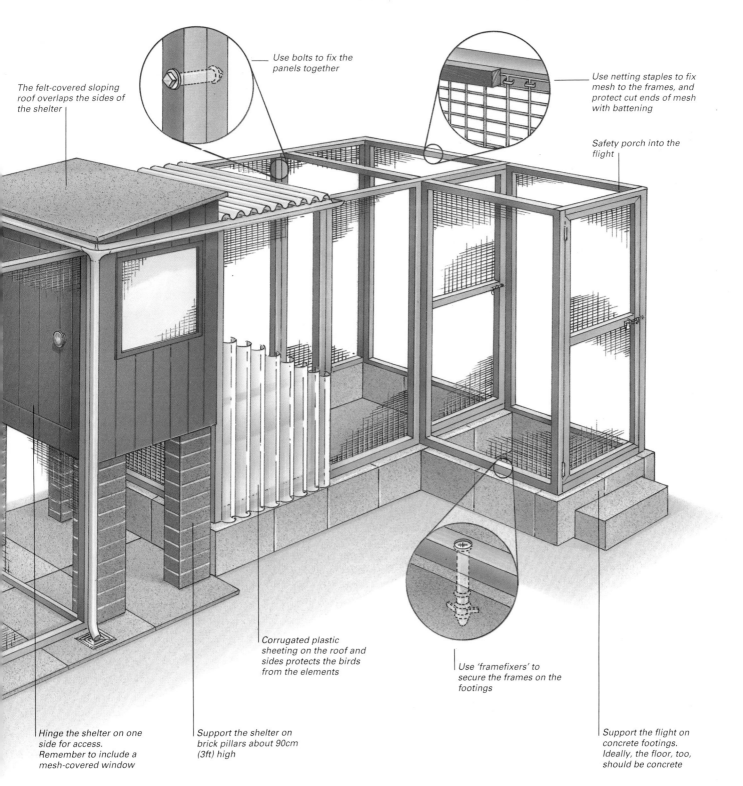

The felt-covered sloping roof overlaps the sides of the shelter

Use bolts to fix the panels together

Use netting staples to fix mesh to the frames, and protect cut ends of mesh with battening

Safety porch into the flight

Corrugated plastic sheeting on the roof and sides protects the birds from the elements

Use 'framefixers' to secure the frames on the footings

Hinge the shelter on one side for access. Remember to include a mesh-covered window

Support the shelter on brick pillars about 90cm (3ft) high

Support the flight on concrete footings. Ideally, the floor, too, should be concrete

PROTECTING THE AVIARY FROM CATS

Deter cats from climbing onto an aviary, particularly when chicks are in the nest.

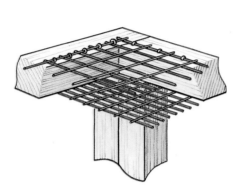

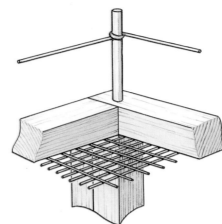

Introducing the birds

Before introducing birds to the aviary, make sure that you have fixed the food and water containers in place and that you have taped together sheets of clean newspapers on the floor of the shelter, so that they are not disturbed by the parrots as they fly around. Release the birds into the new aviary during the late morning, preferably at a time when you will be at home and can watch their progress. Release the parrots into the shelter at first and allow them to find their own way out; you may decide to confine them in the shelter for a day or two so that they become used to feeding here; they should then return inside to roost at night.

It is vital to supervise the parrots at this stage. Most birds, especially older stock, will settle in rapidly and soon find their way around their new surroundings, but young, recently fledged parrots can be more of a problem. If they have shown no sign of wanting to eat and drink by the start of the second day, close them in the shelter. This alone should be sufficient to rekindle the birds' appetite, provided they are otherwise healthy. If you are worried, contact your veterinarian without delay.

Once they have settled, you will need to check the parrots regularly each day to ensure that they are not ill or injured. They will need food and fresh water on a daily basis – twice a day (morning and afternoon) during the breeding season – especially if you are offering perishable greenfood. On each occasion, pause to look at the parrots for a few moments; when you have been doing this regularly for a few months, you will soon notice if any birds appear even slightly off-colour.

Aviaries and cats

Cats can be troublesome around an aviary, especially when the parrots are breeding. They may climb up the mesh on to the roof of the aviary and try to reach the birds from above and this will disturb the parrots and may lead to the loss of eggs and chicks.

Strangely enough, if you keep a cat yourself, you are less likely to have such problems. Although kittens may be troublesome, an older cat will soon realize that it will not be able to catch the birds,

and so will ignore them, and will probably deter other cats from entering its territory.

If you are plagued with cats, you can protect the aviary quite easily by stringing thin strands of wire on short poles around the top of the aviary. You can also add a false roof to the aviary by tacking another layer of 22G mesh, 5×2.5cm (2×1in) in size, onto the top wooden part of the roof frame. The wire around the sides of the aviary will make it difficult for the cats to climb onto the roof section and any that do overcome this barrier will find it hard to walk over the thin mesh. With both obstructions in place, the vast majority of cats will be deterred from disturbing the parrots. (If you need to modify an existing aviary in this way, remove the birds while you carry out the work.)

Eliminating vermin

If you have used the correct mesh for the aviary, and if you store seed in bins and keep the aviary clean (see pages 28 and 44), rodents should not, hopefully, be a problem you have to face. Rats are capable of killing parrots, and they will also scare them so much that they neglect their chicks. Small mountains of earth and longish, brown pelleted droppings are an indication of their presence. Eliminate rats without delay; if using poison around the outside of the aviary is not practical (perhaps because there are young children around), seek the help of a pest control officer.

Mice can also be serious pests, and can increase rapidly in numbers where food is freely available (calculations suggest that a single pair can produce over one hundred young mice during a year). Several mice can destroy an aviary quite rapidly, especially if they get behind the lining material on the walls of the shelter. At the very least, you will need to pull off the lining and clean behind it, which is an unpleasant task even once you have removed the mice. If you feed your parrots in the shelter, seed will be less accessible to the young of smaller rodents, which may be able to squeeze through the aviary wire. Once inside, the rodent may decide to nest in the aviary, and here you will not be able to use poison in case the parrots can reach it.

Below: Breeders with large numbers of parrots often arrange the flights in blocks, servicing them from a single corridor, as shown here.

You may be able to place a killer trap safely in the birds' quarters, provided you position it in the centre of a parrot cage and close the door securely. The mice will be able to move in and out between the bars of the cage, thus reaching the trap, whereas the parrots will be kept outside. Killer traps only take one mouse at a setting and the box traps that catch mice alive are more efficient at eliminating greater numbers; they can catch well over a dozen mice during the course of a night and have no dangerous components, so you can use them quite safely in an aviary.

It will take the mice several days to become used to a live trap, which consists of two parts, a base and a lid. Bait the trap with the lid off for the first few days, until the mice are feeding regularly here. Once the lid is in place, the mice can still enter easily, but cannot escape.

In a birdroom you may want to incorporate an ultrasonic rodent scarer as a deterrent. This device emits high-frequency sounds that are inaudible to the human ear and cause no adverse reactions in parrots, but that are highly disorientating to rodents.

Extending the aviary

You should make any additions to the aviary in the early autumn, after the breeding season. You may be able to place a second flight alongside the existing struc-ture, using one of the sides as part of the new unit. It is important to wire the outer face of the panel common to both structures so that there is a gap between flights, otherwise parrots in adjoining aviaries may bite the feet of their neighbours, which can result in serious injury. You must also check that the double-wiring remains intact. After a time, the lengths of mesh often sag slightly on the frame, so that the space between is reduced. Once the aviaries are assembled, it will obviously be difficult to rectify this problem, but the simplest way of dealing with it is to cut short lengths of battening and fit these through the mesh. You could even hold them in place with netting staples, although usually the pressure of the mesh alone holds them in place, while they serve to keep the strands apart. If the parrots nibble them away, you will need to replace these 'spacers' at regular intervals.

Breeders with large numbers of parrots often arrange a number of flights in blocks, servicing them from a single corridor that runs the length of the flights. With this design there is no need for a safety porch, as the outer door to the corridor

Below: This large block of cockatoo aviaries incorporates a service corridor at the rear. During cold weather, plastic-covered frames cover the openings at the front to provide additional shelter for the birds.

serves the purpose. Having closed this door, you can then safely enter the individual flights. Should a parrot fly out, it will simply remain trapped in the corridor and can be returned to its flight. The aviary shelters form part of the building in which the corridor is situated, so the indoor quarters are often made of a mesh framework, rather like the flight, instead of having solid walls. Internally, the shelters can be separated by blockwork partitions with a wire-mesh roof beneath that of the building. The wire mesh front of each shelter should incorporate an access door.

Birdrooms

Another option to consider is a series of wire-mesh flights accommodated within a larger building. Such a birdroom set-up is often favoured by commercial breeders. The sectional flights are similar in design to those used in the home, with a nest-box attached at one end, where it can be easily inspected from outside the flight.

If you decide to invest in a birdroom, various options are open to you: you can buy a birdroom, convert a suitable shed, or, if it is large enough, divide the existing shelter and use part of it as a birdroom. In the simplest design, the birdroom is attached to one end of the aviary flight. Part of the birdroom is partitioned off internally, using a wire mesh framework, and becomes the shelter. An outer safety

Lighting and heating

It will be useful to have an electricity supply running to the birdroom, but seek professional advice, as the regulations governing the external supply of electricity vary from one country to another. Electric lighting will enable you to feed the birds after dark when necessary, which may be unavoidable during short winter days. The birds will also benefit from increased lighting at this time of year, since they will have a longer period during which they can feed. Fluorescent strip lights, emitting a so-called 'natural' light, can also have positive health benefits for breeding parrots; the ultraviolet rays falling on the plumage of the birds may help to stimulate the synthesis of Vitamin D3, which plays a vital part in controlling the body's stores of calcium, essential in the formation of egg shell, for example.

You can connect an electronic time switch, which will turn the lights on and off automatically, along with a dimmer, which will reduce the light intensity gradually, so that the birds will not be plunged into sudden darkness, but will be able to return to their nests or roost before the lights go out. Various types of dimmer are available, the most sophisticated of which operate without being set to a time switch. When fixed close to a window, a photo-electric cell will trigger the lighting into operation once the level of illumination falls below a certain level. You should be able to obtain such equipment by mail order from one of the specialist suppliers, who often advertise in the various birdkeeping magazines.

The use of heating for parrots is a controversial subject. Artificial heating can be useful if you are breeding birds such as Madagascar Lovebirds during the winter months in temperate climates, especially during sudden chilly spells. This is the time of year that these small parrots often choose to nest, but cold conditions can lead to egg-binding in laying hens and, of course, young chicks will be more vulnerable in cold weather. A moderate degree of

Above: A garden shed, such as this one, can make an ideal birdroom, providing space for both indoor flights and storage. (Make sure it has windows.)

porch surrounds the entrance to the birdroom, thus ensuring that all the occupants are safe within, provided you close the outer door of the safety porch before entering the birdroom. There may be a window located in the door, or else at the front of the birdroom, alongside the flight.

Below: Birdrooms come in all shapes and sizes. This well-planned larger example incorporates a table and a sink with running water. Note the first-aid cabinet.

There should also be a window in the shelter area (see page 31).

This arrangement is favoured by budgerigar breeders; it allows several breeding cages to be stacked on the floor at the back of the birdroom, with a wooden or metal framework holding them securely in place. You may have space for an inside flight here, which can be useful for housing young stock prior to releasing them into the aviary, or as temporary holding quarters for birds that are to be sold. Other areas of space in the birdroom can be used for seed storage, and for training exhibition birds. You may also find it useful to have a table, ideally positioned directly in front of the window.

Below: Box cages offer a versatile means of housing breeding budgerigars, or other small species, and a number can be stacked up on the floor of the birdroom.

heat should help to ensure improved breeding results at this time of year.

Fan heaters are not suitable for use in birdrooms because the relatively high level of dust in the environment will interfere with their operation. Sealed electric tubular heaters, available in various sizes and wattages, are ideal; they are both durable and reliable and, unlike paraffin heaters, do not give off harmful fumes. Mount these heaters on the birdroom wall, rather than on the floor, to improve the circulation of heat through the building. You can obtain these heaters from specialist avicultural suppliers or from garden centres; they are also widely used in greenhouses. The wattages you will need for your birdroom will depend on the size of the structure, the degree of insulation and the external temperature; the supplier will be able to advise you.

A thermostat connected to the heater unit will reduce the costs of heating the birdroom and ensure that the temperature does not fall below a minimum level. The simplest type of thermostat plugs directly into the electrical socket, and the heater plug connects into the thermostat unit. Check the temperature range over which the thermostat will operate – this is usually between 0°C and 30°C (32-86°F) – and also that it is capable of operating all the heaters in the birdroom. As a general guide, you should set the thermostat to switch on the heating once the temperature falls to about 7°C (45°F) and to turn off the heaters when the temperature rises to 10°C (50°F).

Ventilation

Good air flow is an important, yet often forgotten, aspect to consider in planning a birdroom. A number of parrots kept together in a confined space will generate a considerable amount of feather dust, especially during the moulting period, and, although not harmful for the birds, this can lead to respiratory problems for their keepers. Typical symptoms of this allergic reaction – commonly known as 'bird-fancier's lung' – are a tight-chested feeling and difficulty in breathing soon after entering the birdroom.

Obviously, windows will help to improve ventilation, but it is not always possible to leave them open, especially during bad weather. An extractor fan (as used in the home) will actively draw the air and accompanying dust from the bird room, but may also cool the air, and some models can be rather noisy, though the parrots will soon get used to this. You can connect the fan to a time switch so that it will operate on a regular basis. Add a wire-mesh cover to the fan to prevent a bird that escapes into the birdroom from being sucked into it.

Another means of combating dust in the birdroom is to use an ionizer. This piece of equipment has become very popular since its introduction to the avicultural market several years ago. The needle-like tip at the end of the ionizer emits a stream of high-energy electrons, which generate negative ions that pass through the air and collide with dust particles and other microscopic debris, including bacteria. Dust particles bombarded with these ions take on a negative charge and are drawn towards an earthed surface, such as the floor. An ionizer also helps to prevent the spread of air-borne infections, by destroying bacteria and other disease-causing micro-organisms. The main drawback is that, although it reduces aerial pollution, an ionizer does not actually remove the dust particles from the environment; you will need to mop up the dust where it has settled with a damp cloth.

If you do not have electricity in your birdroom, you will probably be able to run an ionizer successfully at very low cost off a car battery. (Check that the model you purchase can be operated by this means.) Simply position it at a high point in the birdroom and leave it switched on; the difference in the atmosphere should become apparent within an hour or so. You will not need to screen the ionizer in any way, as it will not harm a parrot that escapes into the birdroom.

Probably the most effective means of dealing with feather dust is to use an electric air cleaner; various models are available to suit birdrooms of different sizes. They remove air-borne pollutants, including dust particles, fungal spores and bacteria, permanently from the environment, and, although they are more expensive than ionizers, their maintenance is simple and running costs low.

If you fit a false door in the birdroom, you will be able to leave the outer birdroom door open on hot days, secure in the knowledge that the parrots are safely confined within, out of reach of cats and other predators. This simple measure will help to improve the ventilation in birdroom, as well as reducing the temperature.

Below: Security devices are advisable, particularly to protect valuable birds. The invisible infrared beam from this device can cover a wide angle of about 120° and detects body heat. It is connected to an alarm and spotlights.

Security

As parrots have risen considerably in value during recent years, they have become an attractive target for bird thieves. It is sensible to take precautions to protect your aviary by installing one or more of the security devices now available, especially if you have valuable birds. Ask your local crime prevention officer for advice on systems to suit your needs.

Various companies are now marketing security systems specifically for bird-keepers. These include infrared devices, which are triggered when the invisible light beam is broken, and pressure pads, usually located near the entry point to the aviary or just inside the door. Alarms that ring in your home when an intruder is detected, dazzling lights that switch on automatically, and even camera systems, are also now available.

A sophisticated security package will require a fairly substantial investment so be certain that it meets your needs. Ensure, too, that the alarm will not be triggered by passing animals, such as rodents, other birds or even bats; your neighbours will not thank you for disturbing the peace with numerous false alarms, and if a genuine break-in does occur, you may be tempted not to take it seriously. Don't overlook simple precautions either, such as fitting windows and doors with locks.

In conjunction with these protective systems, you should also consider marking the birds themselves, so that if, in spite of your precautions, they are stolen, you will be able to identify them with certainty should they be recovered. A tiny microchip implant placed in the bird's breast muscle provides an invisible and indisputable means of identifying a bird. Each microchip contains a unique coding, which is read using a special scanner. A number of avian veterinarians can now provide such implants. There are also plans to establish a central registry, where code numbers are stored, and so deter bird thieves.

FEEDING PARROTS

Growth in the understanding of the dietary needs of parrots is one of the major factors that has led to the great improvement in breeding results with these birds over recent years. Seed and nuts form the basic diet of many parrots, but in order to keep these birds in good condition, you will need to provide a much wider range of foodstuffs, including fresh fruit and greenfood. Lories, lorikeets and hanging parrots are unusual in that they feed primarily on nectar and pollen gathered from flowers, and suitable substitutes – now readily obtainable – need to be offered to them.

Seeds for parrots

The seeds used for feeding parrots can be divided into two basic categories: oil seeds and cereal seeds. Oil seeds, which include sunflower, safflower, peanuts, hemp and pine nuts, are the main components of parrot seed mixtures. Cereal seeds, such as canary seed, millet and maize, are comprised mainly of carbohydrate. Canary seed and millet are the principal ingredients of seed mixtures for budgerigars, cockatiels, Australian parakeets and other smaller parrots.

Sunflower seed is likely to be the most prominent ingredient in a parrot seed mixture. The various strains available differ somewhat in size and coloration; the larger grades tend to be more wasteful because the kernel – the only part of the seed that is eaten – is usually no larger than in the smaller seeds. White sunflower seed has a higher protein level and

less fat than the striped or black forms but is more expensive because the yield per hectare is low. Black sunflower seed may be found in some seed mixes, but is not popular, especially for use as soaked seed; some birdkeepers believe that the dye it releases into the water is harmful. Safflower, valued for its protein content, at first glance resembles white sunflower, but it is smaller and plumper in appearance than the latter.

Peanuts, or groundnuts (so called because the seed pods develop underground), are another common ingredient of parrot food. Check the quality of peanuts carefully, and if they appear even slightly mouldy, discard them. *Aspergillus* moulds may develop on peanuts that have been stored in damp conditions, and these produce potent toxins, which will cause serious damage to the parrot's liver. Never use salted peanuts – they

could have a harmful effect on your parrot's health.

Hemp and pine nuts are two other oil seeds that are sometimes added to parrot foods. Hemp is a small, dark brownish circular seed. Pine nuts are not cultivated, but are collected in the coniferous forests of the Soviet Union and China. Parrots are quite capable of cracking the large grade nuts, and even parrotlets can crack the small Chinese variety without too much difficulty; providing a mixture of both sorts helps to provide variety, compensating for deficiencies that may result from local growing conditions. Check supplies carefully for any signs of green mould; you may discover this on damaged nuts where the kernel is exposed.

Some pet stores stock pine nuts, but you may need to go to a supermarket or health food store for other nuts. These are often appreciated by the larger parrots, in

OIL SEEDS FOR PARROTS

Striped sunflower
An ingredient of most parrot mixes. Larger grades tend to be more wasteful.

White sunflower
This sunflower has higher protein value and less fat than the striped form.

Peanuts
Another popular food. Check quality carefully and avoid salted nuts.

Hemp
This small, dark-brown circular seed is often popular with cockatoos.

Pine nuts
These nuts, found in the Soviet Union and China, provide valuable variety.

Parrot mix
A parrot mixture, such as this, provides the basis of a balanced diet.

CEREAL SEEDS FOR PARROTS

Canary seed
Provide this seed in a separate container. It is popular with Galahs.

Millet spray
Popular as a rearing food and for newly weaned birds, as it is easy to crack.

Millet
Like canary seed, this cereal is not routinely included in parrot seed mixes.

Flaked maize
You can also buy maize whole; larger parrots can easily crack the seeds.

Corn-on-the-cob
This is a useful food for larger species that you may be able to grow.

particular. Brazil nuts have a tough outer casing, but larger macaws can crack this quite easily. Walnuts are another favourite, and hazelnuts, too, are likely to be greedily consumed by parrots as an addition to their usual seed mixture. If you crack the nuts yourself, you can offer pieces to your bird and allow it to extract the kernel.

Maize is a common ingredient in parrot seed mixtures. You can buy this yellowish cereal seed crushed (kibbled), but the bigger parrots can crack the whole seed.

Parrot mixes
Branded parrot foods probably offer the best guarantee of quality and cleanliness, but are a rather expensive alternative to buying seed and mixing it yourself. Good mixes will include pumpkin seeds, which are broad, flat and whitish in colour, and red chilli peppers, often favoured by Amazons and macaws, in addition to the above-mentioned seeds and nuts. Some parrot food mixes also contain a variety of dried fruits and vegetables, such as carrot, apricot, pineapple, banana, and even alfalfa cubes (alfalfa is a form of grass), which are popular with many parrots. (It is worth noting that the nutritional value, in terms of carbohydrate, of dried fruit tends to be several times higher than that of fresh fruit.)

Budgerigar seed mixes
This type of seed mixture usually consists of two types of cereal seed: canary seed, which is brownish in colour and has pointed ends, and millet, which is rounded in appearance. Different types of millet may be apparent in such mixes, which, if supplemented with sunflower, may be used for other parrots with similar dietary requirements.

Canada and parts of North Africa, notably Morocco, are the major producers of canary seed, although crops from various other countries are occasionally available. It has been successfully grown in Europe (Spain used to be one of the main suppliers) and you should be able to cultivate this grass in the garden. Choose a sunny location, prepare the ground, and sow the seed in drills during the late summer. (If space is limited, you can sprinkle a little canary seed towards the back of a flower border, as it is not unattractive.)

Thin the resulting seedlings as necessary before the winter, and cut the grass when the seedheads have turned brown during the following summer. There is no need for the grass to be ripe unless you want to store the seed, since many parakeets, lovebirds and parrotlets will delight in feeding on fresh green seedheads. You should only cut larger quantities once they are dry, and then hang the seedheads upside down in a shed. Don't worry about threshing the crop – the birds will prize the seeds from the seedheads.

Millet can be grown in a similar way, although it may prove less hardy. The different varieties likely to be encountered in seed mixtures include pearly white, which is a relatively large seed, and the smaller

panicum and Japanese millets. You can also buy panicum sprays and these are very popular with many parrots.

Cheaper seed mixtures tend to contain a higher proportion of millet than canary seed. Both are cereal seeds, and thus low in oil (fat), but have a relatively high carbohydrate content. Canary seed generally contains slightly more protein than millet, but samples do vary, depending on the local growing conditions and other factors, such as the relative use of artificial

Above: This Blue and Gold Macaw is enjoying a brazil nut, which it has cracked with its powerful beak.

fertilizers. Some breeders prefer to feed a mixture of canary seed from various parts of the world in order to balance out nutritional shortcomings from any once source.

Below: A typical budgerigar seed mix includes two types of cereal seed: canary seed and millet.

Choosing and storing seed

Seed that has been properly cleaned should not be dusty. If it does appear dirty, there is a risk that debris, such as stones, or even sharp pieces of glass, could be present. Check that it smells fresh; a sickly sweet odour is usually indicative of fodder mites, which feed on the seed, rather than attacking the birds, but may spread disease through contamination. As it is not possible to eliminate fodder mites from seed effectively and safely, discard any affected seed.

Rodent droppings are another obvious menace to the parrots' health, and contaminated seed will almost certainly have been exposed to their urine as well. Obviously, you will have to dispose of it. To prevent rodents gaining access to seed, always store it in metal bins.

Good hygiene in the aviary is vital; without a reliable food source, rodents will not be attracted to the area. Feed the birds in the shelter and clean up thoroughly once or twice a week, so that spilt seed is not left to accumulate on the floor. If you suspect that mice could be entering the aviary, remove the seed pots just before dusk, sweep up any spilt seed, and only replace the pots the next morning. This should not cause the parrots any distress, but should dissuade mice, which normally feed after dark, from becoming established here.

Some seed and husks are bound to fall down between the mesh and the timber-clad wall of the shelter. Leave the netting staples protruding slightly near the floor

Below: Choose a bin with a lid in which to store seed; this will help to exclude rodents, damp and dust. A scoop will be useful for removing seed.

so that you can pull them out easily to sweep behind the mesh. If you line the floor of the shelter with clean newspaper, you will be able to tidy up spilt seed and other foods without difficulty, discarding the soiled sheets.

Parrot pellets

Pellets can help to compensate for the nutritional shortcomings of a regular seed diet but many birds show a marked and persistant reluctance to try them, especially if they have been used to an oil-rich diet comprised mainly of sunflower seeds and peanuts, which are the staple ingredients of many parrot seed mixes. Parrots that have been raised by hand are generally far less selective in their choice of food than adult imported birds, and you should find that a parrot that feeds readily on pellets will play a part in encouraging another bird to eat them.

If the birds do show an unwillingness to try pellets, it may be worth adding them to the usual seed mix. This method can be particularly successful with macaws, which, instead of taking single seeds, prefer to scoop up several at once, storing them under their prehensile tongue and cracking them and swallowing the kernels individually. Some of the African species, such as the Senegal, can prove especially difficult to wean across to a pelleted diet. Try gradually increasing the proportions of pellets to seed in the mix, so that the birds will be forced to eat at least some pellets as part of their daily food intake.

Several different brands of pellets are now being manufactured, and shape can play a part in attracting a parrot's interest. Fairly short, thick pellets, which more closely resemble seed, are preferable to

those that are long and thin. Check that you are purchasing the right size of pellet for the species concerned; there are usually small and large grades.

Some brands are available in two varieties: a maintenance diet, suitable for the pet bird and other parrots that are not breeding, and a breeding diet, containing a slightly higher level of protein. You should make the change between these diets over a period of a week or two, beginning before the likely start of the breeding period. The breeding pellets should have a stimulating effect on the parrots, as well as providing useful nutrients for the parent birds once they are rearing their chicks.

Fresh food

As well as a combination of dry seeds and pellets, parrots also require a regular supply of fresh fruit and greenstuffs. The choice available will obviously depend to some extent on where you live, and usually varies seasonally. In temperate regions, apples and grapes are traditionally popular foods for parrots, but there is no reason why you cannot feed other more exotic fruits, such as mango, to provide variety. Always wash perishable food items thoroughly before offering them to the parrots.

Macaws can hold a whole apple without difficulty and appear to enjoy gnawing chunks out of it, but you may need to cut fruit into pieces for smaller parrots. Cutting up the fruit also prevents wastage – parrots may throw a whole apple, or other fruit, on the floor, rather than eat it – and provides an ideal means of adding a food supplement to the parrot's diet – the dry supplement will stick to its wet surface,

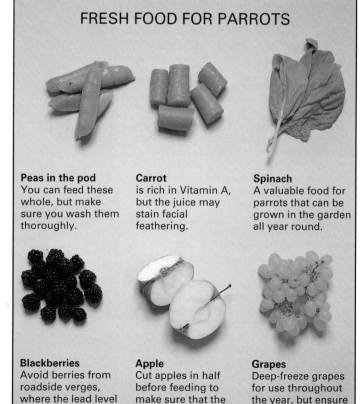

FRESH FOOD FOR PARROTS

Peas in the pod
You can feed these whole, but make sure you wash them thoroughly.

Carrot
is rich in Vitamin A, but the juice may stain facial feathering.

Spinach
A valuable food for parrots that can be grown in the garden all year round.

Blackberries
Avoid berries from roadside verges, where the lead level is likely to be high.

Apple
Cut apples in half before feeding to make sure that the core is not mouldy.

Grapes
Deep-freeze grapes for use throughout the year, but ensure they are defrosted.

Right: Carrot is a valuable source of Vitamin A. This Cobalt-winged Parakeet is enjoying eating a whole one, but you could grate it. In either case, you should wash and peel it first.

whereas it often just accumulates at the bottom of a seed pot. If you dice the apple you will be able to check that the core is not mouldy; red-skinned varieties that have been stored for a while are particularly prone to go bad.

You can deep-freeze some fresh foods for use during the winter; grapes, for example, will freeze well. Place them loose on trays in the freezer and, when they are frozen, tip them into clean, plastic boxes for storage. Corn-on-the-cob is also suitable for freezing, although you need to blanch it first. After defrosting, cook in the normal way and allow to cool before offering it to the parrots. South American and psittaculid species are particularly fond of this vegetable.

Various legumes, such as peas in their pods, tend to be quite readily accepted by parrots that may refuse other greenfoods, and are a valuable source of protein. One vegetable to avoid is avocado; although there is, as yet, no conclusive evidence, it appears that at least parts of this may be toxic for cockatoos and other members of the parrot family. Pomegranates can be stored successfully for several months and will be greedily taken by South American parakeets.

Some species, such as many Australian parakeets, prefer greenfood to seed and all species will benefit from a regular supply. Even if you do not have access to a garden, you can still provide fresh, uncontaminated greenfood; simply fill a clean empty margarine tub with soil and sprinkle some budgerigar seed on top, cover this with a thin layer of earth, place it in a warm spot, and keep it watered. The seeds will soon start to sprout and, once they have grown at least 8cm (3in) in height, you can cut off small amounts each day for your birds.

You should be able to find a variety of greenfoods out of doors, but avoid collecting from sites where potentially harmful chemicals may have been used, or from roadside verges, where vegetation is likely to be contaminated by lead from engine exhausts. The availability of greenfood varies seasonally; chickweed (*Stellaria media*) is widely used by budgerigar keepers and tends to be most prolific in the late spring and early autumn. It is quite easy to grow, too; plant it in a shaded spot and keep it well watered in dry weather. Towards the end of summer you may be able to collect seeding grasses, such as Meadow Grass.

You can also offer cultivated greenfoods to parrots. Spinach beet is easy to grow from seed and you can harvest it for the birds even during the winter. (Allow it to warm up if the temperature is below freezing.) Various strains of spinach beet (*Beta vulgaris*) are available; choose one that contains low levels of oxalic acid, as this chemical can interfere with the absorption of calcium – an important mineral, particularly for breeding stock.

Although parrots will often gnaw at the thicker stalks of spinach, chop up large leaves to prevent them becoming soiled with droppings. Lettuce is not a popular choice with most breeders, since it is said to lead to scouring (loose droppings), and although freshly cut lettuce, fed in moderation, will do no harm, it has little nutritional value compared with other vegetables. Wash all greenstuff before feeding.

As winter proceeds, and greenfood is in shorter supply, you can offer your parrots carrots, washed, scraped, and either cut into pieces or grated. Carrot is a valuable source of Vitamin A, so although not all birds take it readily, you may want to persevere to encourage a parrot to sample it. (Avoid feeding carrot to exhibition stock before a show, as the juice is likely to stain the facial feathering.)

Below: Try to offer the birds some greenfood two or three times a week all year round, and daily during the breeding period. You may be able to grow your own regular supply.

Grit and minerals

Parrots use their beaks to crack seeds and, if necessary, to gnaw their food into pieces sufficiently small for them to swallow easily. Under normal circumstances, food passes into the crop before continuing through to the proventriculus and then the gizzard, where the digestive process begins in earnest.

Grit fulfills several functions. Firstly, it helps to prevent the seed from forming lumpy aggregates by breaking it down into smaller pieces on which the digestive enzymes can work effectively. The walls of the gizzard in a seed-eating bird are very muscular, assisting this grinding process. As the grit itself breaks down, it releases valuable minerals, which are absorbed into the bird's body.

It is useful to mix oystershell grit and mineralized grit to improve the bird's intake of minerals and vital trace elements, such as iodine, which are needed in smaller amounts. Packets of both sorts of grit are available from pet shops. Provide grit in a separate container from seed, and fill up the pot each week, so the parrots have a regular supply and can forage for particles of their choice.

Smaller species will take budgerigar grit; pigeon grit (as sold for racing pigeons) is recommended for larger parrots. However, larger species often seem reluctant to consume grit of any size, and whether or not to supply grit for larger parrots has long been a source of dispute among birdkeepers. Nectar-feeding parrots will also sample grit on occasions, and should always have a supply available to them. In some cases, parrots will swallow wood chips, gnawed from perches, and these perform a similar function to grit when they reach the gizzard.

You should also offer the parrots calcium, in the form of cuttlefish bone or a block. This mineral is very important for healthy bone structure, and a lack of it, particularly when the birds are young, can result in permanent skeletal weaknesses. Calcium is vital for breeding hens; a deficiency can result in soft-shelled eggs (especially in the more free-breeding species, such as the Eclectus Parrot), and may cause further complications, notably egg-binding. Gnawing on a cuttlefish bone will also help to keep the parrots' beaks from becoming overgrown.

If you live near the sea, you may be able to find cuttlefish bones washed up on a beach, especially after a storm. Provided that they are not contaminated with oil, you can clean them for offering to your parrots. Soak them thoroughly in a bucket of clean water, changing it once or twice daily for a week or so. Then scrub the bones with a clean brush and leave them to dry off thoroughly, either outside, or on top of a radiator. You can store them in a clean plastic bag until needed. Attaching the bone to the mesh with one of the special metal clips available from pet stores will usually hold it fast.

Studies have shown that budgerigars require a relatively high amount of iodine. This is used by the thyroid glands, located in the neck region on either side of the windpipe, to produce hormones that in-

Above: Cuttlefish bone is a valuable source of calcium and minerals. Hold it in place with a special clip.

fluence various body processes, including moulting. A shortage of dietary iodine is likely to lead to the condition known as goitre, which results in an enlargement of the thyroid glands, possibly to as much as ten times their normal length of about 2mm (0.1in). This in turn causes pressure on the windpipe, causing an affected bird to breathe noisily. Most supplements now contain iodine, but it is also worth giving budgerigars, in particular, an iodine nibble, which you can fit into the bars of a cage or the aviary mesh.

Treats

Various treats for pet birds are widely available. These include seed rings, which fit round the perch, and feeding sticks, which attach to the side of a cage. Sometimes the seed is dyed, or other ingredients, such as honey, have been added. Some of these products contain colouring that may alter the colour of the parrot's droppings, but this need not cause concern. Use these treats sparingly, however, especially if they contain sugar in the form of honey; although they are safe in limited quantities, it has been suggested that excessive use could be a factor in the apparent growing incidence of *diabetes mellitus* in pet budgerigars.

FOOD FOR PARROTS

SPECIES	SEEDS	FRUIT AND GREENSTUFF
Budgerigar	Plain canary seed, millets and millet sprays.	Chickweed, seeding grasses and sweet apple.
Cockatiels, grass parakeets, parrotlets, and lovebirds	Plain canary seed, millets and millet sprays, plus some groats and sunflower. A little hemp in the winter.	Chickweed, seeding grasses, sweet apple and carrot.
Lories, lorikeets and hanging parrots	Nectar, with a little canary seed or millet sprays. Restrict sunflower.	A good variety of fruit, plus greenfood.
Psittaculid parakeets, amazons, *Pionus* and vasa parrots and caiques	Sunflower seed, groats, pine nuts, safflower, millet sprays and peanuts.	Fruit and vegetables. Do not feed these or other parrots avocados, which can be poisonous.
Poicephalid parrots, Grey Parrot and cockatoos	A good-quality parrot mix with limited amounts of peanuts.	Prefer fruit to greenfood. Often reluctant to sample unfamiliar items.
Eclectus and *Tanygnathus* parrots	Parrot seed mix	Plenty of greenfood (limit cabbage as this has a depressive effect on the thyroid glands). Also corn on-the-cob, carrot and fruit.
Macaws	Parrot seed. Dwarf macaws may take millets and canary seed; larger species enjoy brazils and whole maize.	Prefer fruit, but also eat carrot and some greenfood.

Above: Soaked seed is popular with breeding parrots. To sprout seeds – canary seed and millet are most suitable – rinse them and drain them twice a day for about four to five days.

Above right: Millet sprays can be fed dry or soaked, which makes them an easily digested and valuable food for young chicks. Remember, though, that soaked seed is a perishable foodstuff.

Nectar foods

Lories and lorikeets and hanging parrots require a supply of fresh nectar every day. In the past, such mixes were made from a variety of ingredients, but proprietary nectar foods are now widely available. You can buy these either as a paste or as powder, which needs to be dissolved in warm water and then topped up to the correct volume with cold water. Try not to prepare more food than will be required for a day, as it will not keep.

Offer nectar mixes in a sealed drinker, which you should wash out after each feed, to prevent the food being soiled with droppings. If you supply nectar in an open container, the birds may attempt to bathe in it, which could have catastrophic consequences if their plumage becomes saturated with the sticky solution.

Dry (powder) diets, which can be mixed with the bird's daily ration of fruit, have now been developed for this group of parrots. Such foods more closely replicate the kind of diet that they receive in the wild and reduce the fluid content of their droppings. (Whether you use powder or a paste the birds will, of course, also need fresh drinking water.) Dietary changes should be made gradually, over the course of several weeks; sudden changes can upset the digestive tract of these, and may result in a fatal toxaemia. While nectar-feeding parrots, especially hanging parrots, may eat some seed, this should not form the major part of their diet.

Soaked seed

Soaked seed makes a welcome addition to the parrots' diet, especially during the breeding season. You can prepare canary seed, millets (including sprays) and even sunflower in this way by covering a small amount of seed with hot water, leaving it to stand for a day, and then rinsing the seed very thoroughly under a running tap. After draining off the surplus water, transfer the seed to a clean container.

The advantages of soaked seed are, firstly, that it is more digestible, and therefore of particular value as a rearing food and, secondly, that the protein level of the seed is increased. Once seed has been soaked, it becomes a perishable foodstuff and you will need to remove any that is not eaten before it starts to turn mouldy. Most birds will take soaked seed very readily, so you only need to leave it in the feeders for a few hours. Wash containers immediately after use.

When there are chicks in the nest, some parrot breeders offer their birds wholemeal bread soaked in an equal mix of milk and water. Again, it is absolutely essential that such a mixture is fresh and so it is generally an unsatisfactory option in warm climates. The parrot's ability to break down the milk sugar has also been queried, and it is thought that it may give rise to digestive upsets in some cases.

Softbill food is a better option; this may already be available to hanging parrots housed in a mixed aviary. (Softbills do not eat seed but rely on 'soft' foods; species suitable for keeping with non-aggressive parrots include zosterops and fruit doves.) There are various brands of softbill food on the market, some of which can be offered straight from the packet, others of which need mixing with water. A number of parrot species will eat softbill food quite readily, especially during the breeding period, and it provides a valuable source of essential amino-acids. Offer a small quantity regularly before the start of the breeding season so that the birds have an opportunity to sample it. Canary rearing foods are also suitable, but, again, make sure that they do not turn sour.

Food containers

There are a variety of bird feeding containers on the market, and many are suitable for use with parrots. Cages usually come equipped with two food pots, one at each end. You can fill these with seed and grit respectively, but take care to arrange the perches so that they do not directly overhang the containers, or droppings will contaminate the food. If the pot has a covered hood, as is often the case in those supplied with budgerigar cages, start by sprinkling a little seed on the floor of the cage around the base of the feeding container. This should encourage a young (and probably reluctant) bird to place its head under the hood to feed. A millet spray fixed on the side of the cage close to a perch will also encourage a youngster to start feeding in new surroundings. Hold millet sprays in place with a metal clip (or clothes peg, for smaller species).

Seed pots sold for budgerigars will be suitably robust for other small parrots and parakeets. Avoid filling them right to the top, to prevent seed being scattered around the floor. Special plastic bases that fit around the neck of upturned jam jars are frequently used in box-type cages, but are not suitable for most ordinary cages, the doors of which are too small to allow the seed reservoir to be placed inside. Plastic tubular containers, some of which can be refilled from outside the cage, provide a more versatile means of feeding budgerigars in cages, but it is important, especially with narrow-spouted feeders of this type, to ensure that the flow of seed is not impeded, and these designs are not suitable for dispensing larger seeds. Tubular containers are also useful for water.

Metal seed hoppers are frequently used in aviaries as they are indestructible and keep the contents free from the birds' droppings. An enclosed tray, included in most designs, collects the seed husks and prevents them littering the floor of the shelter. Not all models are suitable for dispensing sunflower seed so check on this before choosing one. Hoppers of this type are often sold on the basis of their seed capacity and the number of feeding holes for the birds. A large-capacity hopper will save time, and should hold enough seed to last the parrots several days, which will be particularly useful at holiday times, when someone else will have to look after them. (Never just leave birds over a week, even if they have plenty of seed and water; they need to be checked once, and preferably twice a day in case one falls sick or is injured.)

Position open, hook-on food pots alongside perches; if the birds need to fly on and off the rim of the container to feed,

Supplements

Parrots that are receiving a nutritionally balanced diet, made up primarily of pellets and seed or nectar, with greenstuff and fruit offered on a daily basis, should not generally require food supplements. There are times, however, when such items can be useful. For example, recently imported birds may be suffering from nutritional deficiencies, especially of Vitamin A, and supplementation at this stage can prove very valuable. Fig parrots are known to have a specific requirement for Vitamin K, a deficiency of which can cause haemorrhages.

The various food supplements are produced in powdered form, which will adhere easily to the cut surfaces of fruit, or to damp greenstuff. In addition to vitamins and minerals, a general supplement will contain essential amino-acid residues, which form the chains of protein. One such, lysine, is needed for feather growth.

Less comprehensive supplements tend to be administered in the drinking water. Position the drinker in a shaded part of the aviary, as exposure to sunlight may affect the potency of the vitamins in solution. Exposure to bright sunlight also encourages the growth of algae in the drinker, creating a green slime over the sides, especially when there are dissolved nutrients present. Wash all drinkers at least once a week, using a bottle brush of the appropriate size to clean difficult corners and spouts.

Right: Solid, heavyweight feeding bowls are ideal for parrots. Make sure that you wash thoroughly every day any that have been used for fresh food.

they are more likely to spill the seed. If you cannot conveniently fix the seed container to the aviary mesh, mark the position of the hooks and drive two netting staples half way into the woodwork to provide ready-made supports to accommodate the hooks of the food pot.

For larger parrots, you may be able to purchase stainless-steel feeding containers, which bolt onto the mesh. The bowl section will detach from the arm for ease of cleaning. Loose stainless steel bowls are less satisfactory as they are light and easily overturned. The best option for large macaws is to use heavy ceramic bowls, as sold in pet stores for dogs. Fill these with seed or fresh items, and simply place them on top of the newspaper lining the shelter. The parrots will be unable to overturn them and they will be easy to clean.

If you find that the parrots are spilling large amounts of seed, you may want to invest in a winnower to reclaim the seed. This machine separates seeds from husks and other debris, although not all designs can cope with sunflower seed. Try to position the food pots so that dry seed is confined in one area and fresh, perishable foods to another elsewhere in the shelter. This will make it easier to collect good seed and discard any that is damp or contaminated with droppings.

Do not provide water in an open container, as it will soon be fouled by seed husks and droppings, especially if it is next to food pots. A separate drinking bottle, which attaches on to the outside of the cage with hooks, is the best option for larger parrots; they will soon learn how to obtain water from it by pushing on the ball within the spout.

Unfortunately some macaws and cockatoos may decide that the drinker is a toy; larger species, such as the Green-winged Macaw, are capable of crushing the stainless steel spout, and if this happens you will have to resort to an open drinker. Others like to unhook the drinker and, while it may simply fall to the floor, there is the risk that it may split, especially if it is full. If you cannot reinforce the hooks so that the bottle remains firmly in place, you may be forced to offer drinking water in an open container.

Never fill drinkers containing either nectar or water to the top during cold weather, or the container may split as the water freezes, and for the same reason, avoid pouring boiling water over the plastic to melt ice. Instead, float the drinker in warm water and within a fews moments the ice plug will be dislodged from the interior of the drinker, which you can then refill. If you are keeping a large number of parrots in cages, in a birdroom during the breeding period for example, you may consider an automatic drinking system.

A plastic seed tray is ideal to prevent greenstuff being pulled onto the floor. Greenfood racks, which are sold for use in both cages and aviaries, are ineffective –

Above: A tubular drinker should ensure that the birds have a supply of clean water available, but may not be suitable for more destructive species.

Right: A clever device for feeding parrots from the service corridor, this 'serving hatch' would be very useful in an aviary housing breeding pairs.

the parrots simply pull the leaves out of the rack. Offer other perishable foods separately from dried seed, in open pots. Wash these containers thoroughly after each feed, taking care to rinse them properly after using a detergent.

You may also need to wash the feeding area itself, especially if you are providing fluid nectar. (Ideally, use tiles, or a similar impermeable surface that you can simply wipe over regularly.) This will prevent build-up of bacteria in the vicinity of the parrots' food.

HEALTH CARE

Parrots are normally very healthy and long-lived, once established in their quarters. Try to minimize changes to your new parrot's environment by asking the seller about its diet and the temperature in which it has been kept. Even if the weather is mild, do not transfer a new bird straight into a flight with another parrot. The newcomer may be persecuted by the established bird (whether or not the two are of the same sex). Keep it in isolation for at least two weeks, or it could spread an infection to other birds. Take particular care with newly imported birds, which will need time to acclimatize.

General care of sick parrots

Signs of illness in parrots are often non-specific, and accurate diagnosis is very difficult without tests. Unfortunately, such tests are generally impractical because, especially with bacterial and viral diseases, the bird's condition deteriorates rapidly and, if you wait for a diagnosis, it may be too late to start treatment. As a result, broad-spectrum antibiotics, which are effective against a range of bacteria, are often prescribed in the early stages of an illness.

A sick bird will appear slightly dull and less active than usual. Its droppings may also have altered in appearance; instead of being well formed, they may be watery, with a higher proportion of white uric acid (the urinary component). A parrot whose plumage appears ruffled, sitting with both feet gripping the perch, its eyes closed, and showing little interest in its surroundings, is in need of urgent attention.

Parakeets, especially, will often attempt to carry on feeding, and may even spend more time than usual picking at the seed when they are ill, but closer examination usually reveals that the bird has simply been dehusking the kernels. (Canary seeds are darker when dehusked.) In these circumstances, you should catch the parrot and feel for signs of weight loss around the breastbone.

For treating sick birds at home, invest in a dull-emitter infra-red system, consisting of a bulb that gives off heat rather than light, (so that the parrot will be kept warm and will not be dazzled or disturbed by bright light), with a holder and a surrounding reflector shield, which helps to concentrate the infra-red rays. Some systems also incorporate a control unit, enabling you to adjust the heat. Suspend the lamp over the wire top of the bird's cage to create a thermal gradient here. The warmest position will be directly beneath the infra-red bulb, while the tem-

Right: This Jardine's Parrot is clearly poorly; note its ruffled plumage, half-closed eyes and the way it grips the perch with both feet. Veterinarians will often prescribe antibiotics at the first sign of ill health.

Right: An infra-red lamp – use one that emits heat rather than light – is ideal for keeping a sick parrot warm. Secure it to the cage with clips, as here, or suspend it above an all-wire cage.

perature will fall slightly on either side, so that the bird can adjust its position according to its need for warmth. You may be able to obtain a purpose-built hospital cage, but these are less flexible than using an infra-red lamp. Such cages are generally too small for parrots, although some designs may be suitable for budgerigars and other smaller species.

Parrots usually recover quite rapidly, provided that appropriate treatment is begun early enough. Once the bird begins to become more alert, lower the heat supply gradually to reacclimatize the bird. Avoid reducing the temperature too rapidly, and be guided by the parrot's response; if it starts to appear uncomfortable, ruffling its plumage, then increase the temperature again.

Tempt the parrot's appetite by placing a favoured food item, such as a millet spray, within easy reach of the bird; water, too, should be readily available. If you are using a soluble powder treatment, such as an antibiotic, provide just one drinker containing the medication. Given a choice of medicated and non-medicated drinkers, the parrot is more likely to drink the untreated water than the antibiotic solution, which tends to taste bitter.

It is best not to hurry a sick bird's return to the aviary, and you certainly should not return it to an outside flight when the weather is bad. You may have to keep it in a stock cage until weather improves.

First aid kit

It is worth keeping a few basic items available for routine health care or emergencies. You will need a styptic pencil to control minor bleeding, which may occur following a torn claw, for example. Alternatively, keep a supply of powdered alum (potassium aluminium sulphate), which you can make into a solution to curb blood loss. A tube of ophthalmic ointment is useful to deal with any minor eye inflammation. You will need to apply the ointment directly to the affected eye, several times a day, and hold the bird for a few minutes afterwards, so that it does not wipe the medication off on the perch. For exhibition birds, eye drops may be preferable, as ointment tends to matt the plumage. However, you may find drops harder to administer – if the bird blinks, it will scatter the fluid. Hold the bird still to allow the drops to settle.

An eye dropper is useful for dispensing medicine directly into the mouth. A pair of bone clippers, stocked by larger pet stores and grooming parlours (where they are used to trim dogs' claws), will be needed to cut back overgrown claws or beaks.

Right: Eye drops are generally preferable to ointment, though they may be difficult to administer. After applying the eye drops, hold the bird for a few minutes to allow the medication to mix with its eye fluid.

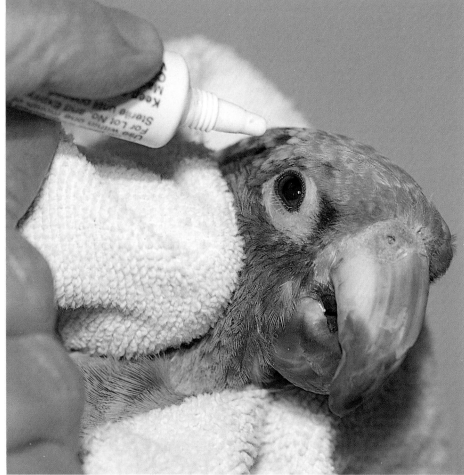

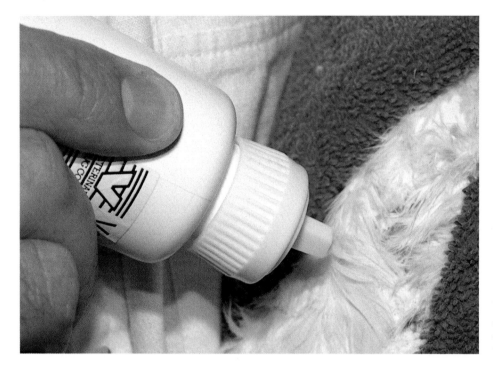

Left: This cockatoo is having a wound dressed with a powder treatment. Injuries should be rare, but conflicts may arise between breeding birds.

Fractures of the wing and leg occur occasionally, although they are not common. There may be an obvious swelling at the site of the fracture, and the parrot will be clearly lame. Seek the advice of an experienced avian veterinarian about splinting. Avian fractures heal within a few weeks if they are properly supported, although the bird may suffer some loss of movement in the affected limb. Parrots usually adjust well under these circumstances, and their breeding capacity is usually unaffected.

Claw and beak trimming

Aviary birds rarely need to have their claws clipped, but you will probably need to clip a pet budgerigar's claws from time to time to enable it to perch comfortably. Trimmed beaks tend to grow back faster, so avoid clipping them, if possible.

Do not use scissors for trimming claws or beaks, as they tend to tear the tissue. Use bone clippers, and carry out this task in good light, so that you can see the blood vessel, which, in light-coloured claws, appears as a narrow red line extending down each claw from the base of the toe. Clip a short distance beyond the end of this to avoid bleeding. It is harder to

Below: To trim the beak of a smaller parrot, hold the bird's head between your index and middle fingers, taking care not to press on its neck.

Physical injuries

Parrots are normally very healthy birds, and you will probably encounter more injuries than illness in your stock. Parakeets are particularly prone to injury, especially if they are disturbed after dark, causing them to fly wildly around the aviary, sustaining superficial cuts, or even a brain haemorrhage, which is rapidly fatal. Australian parakeets are the most vulnerable, partly because they are more nervous by nature, but also because they have thinner skulls. If you find a parrot on the floor of the aviary looking dazed, examine its head closely to try to find the point of impact. There is really nothing that you can do, however, apart from moving the bird to a quiet, darkened environment in the hope that it will recover. A box lined with paper towelling is ideal, but leave it in a secure place, away from cats and other possible disturbances. Hopefully, the bird will be showing signs of recovery within a few hours.

There is usually no need to worry about minor bleeding, as clotting will occur rapidly. But if bleeding is more severe, perhaps from a torn claw, you may need a styptic pencil, or a solution of cold potash alum, to stem the blood loss. Apply the alum on cotton wool, pressing it tightly on the cut end of the claw; the bleeding should stop within minutes. Try to discover the cause of any injury by inspecting the bird and the aviary. If a parrot's claws become too long, and start to curl round at an abnormal angle, the bird may get caught up in the mesh and break a claw while freeing itself.

Frostbite is another, less obvious, cause of bleeding, and may occur if parrots have roosted in the open part of the aviary. The first signs you are likely to find are traces of blood on the perches, and the parrots will be reluctant to use their injured toes, which will appear red and swollen. Unfortunately, there is little effective treatment, although massaging the damaged toes or holding them in warm water may help. If the injury is severe, the blood, and

thus the oxygen, supply to the extremities will be lost, and the affected toe will shrivel up over the course of ten days or so and drop off. The parrot may have difficulty in perching, depending on the number of toes that are affected.

Some species, notably the Long-tailed Parakeet, appear especially susceptible to frostbite, and should be protected during periods of cold weather, even if otherwise they are properly acclimatized. They may use a nestbox for roosting, but if not, you will need to shut them in the shelter each evening before dusk during cold weather.

locate the blood supply in the beak; look for a dark, triangular area on the inner surface of the upper beak, and clip below the lower point. The lower beak is easier to trim; simply cut back the surplus growth in line with the upper beak. If in any doubt, however, seek your veterinarian's advice.

Tumours

Budgerigars are particularly prone to tumours of various kinds; watch for any swellings on your bird's body, particularly as it gets older. Lipomas, which consist of fatty tissue, are common benign (non-cancerous) tumours in these birds, often close to the breastbone, restricting the bird's ability to fly. The development of lipomas may be linked to lack of exercise, since they are far less common in budgerigars housed in aviary surroundings; caged budgies do not have to expend much metabolic energy on maintaining their body heat, and so are more susceptible to obesity.

Abnormal growths of this type are not common in other parrots, although the Galah Cockatoo can also be prone to lipomas, perhaps due to an excessively rich, fatty diet. It has been suggested that a standard parrot mix contains ten times more fat than is actually needed for the health of these cockatoos. Galahs, like budgerigars, occur in arid areas of Australia, where food is scarce, and they are probably ill-adapted to storing surplus food in the form of fatty tissue. Birds that have been fed a relatively low-fat diet in the first few months of life are less likely to become obese at a later stage, and you can avoid the risk of obesity and lipomas by providing your birds with a food choice of cereals, along with plenty of greenfood right from the start.

If your bird does develop a lipoma, you can try improving its diet, and your veterinarian may recommend the use of thyroid hormones. Alternatively, it may be possible to remove the tumour surgically but, unfortunately, they often recur. If left untreated, it becomes harder to remove the lipoma surgically, and the bird may lose its ability to fly. The situation worsens as the bird takes less exercise, and further tumours may develop on the body.

Internal tumours are hard to detect, and usually prove fatal. The reproductive organs are a common site; a tumour here will ultimately affect the cere coloration of budgerigars, turning it brownish in a cock bird, and pale, almost whitish, in hens. The kidneys may also be affected, and the bird will lose weight. Again, you should be able to detect such weight loss over the breastbone, and the bird will become progressively weaker, although it may appear to maintain its appetite. Eventually, the budgerigar will be unable to perch, as the tumour affects the spinal cord close to the kidneys. Obviously, by this stage, it would not be fair to allow your bird to suffer, and it should be taken to your veterinarian, who will painlessly euthanase it, usually by injection. Some tumours may be caused by viruses, so always disinfect and rinse the cage thoroughly before you buy another bird.

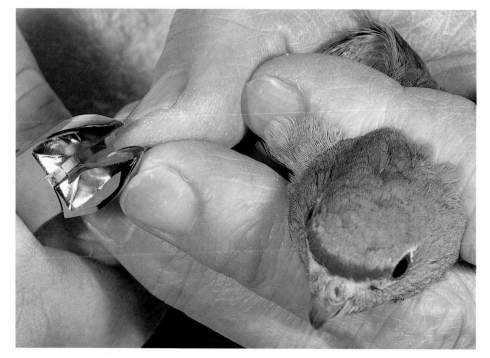

Parasitic infections

Parrots are potentially at risk from a variety of parasitic infestations, but by careful monitoring of new stock you should be able to avoid any problems. Parasites can be divided into two categories, those living on the feathers and skin, and those found internally.

Scaly face, caused by *Cnemidocoptes* mites, results in growths resembling coral and is thought to spread from adults to nestlings by direct contact. However, the mites appear to survive away from living organisms; kakarikis, transferred to

Above: A bird's claws sometimes become overgrown and will need to be trimmed with a stout pair of clippers. Locate the blood supply before cutting.

accommodation where infected budgerigars were previously housed, subsequently developed scaly face. The mites can also infest the feet, leading to scaly feet, and may spread over the rest of the body. Use a proprietary remedy at the first sign of the disease – snail-like tracks across the upper beak; if you delay treatment, the beak may become distorted.

LIFE CYCLES OF PARASITES

■ Other factors that play a part in the life cycle

Direct life cycles

Disease can be introduced by new infected birds, by earthworms via worm casts, and on contaminated shoes

Infection spreads quickly in a flight difficult to clean. Birds that feed on the ground ingest many worm eggs

Food pots soiled by droppings, and the grass under perches are common routes of infection. Worm eggs can survive for months and are hard to eliminate

Indirect life cycles

The parrot can only become infected by eating an invertebrate containing an immature tapeworm

Here, parasites are spread indirectly via tapeworm eggs passed out from the gut in segments, called proglottids

Beetles and woodlice eat the eggs. Only then will the tapeworm start to develop from the egg – a vital stage

Once outside the bird, the proglottids containing the eggs will rupture. The eggs then spread through the aviary

PREVENTING DISEASE IN THE AVIARY

A number of potential dangers to your parrot's health lurk in and around the aviary. By taking precautions, you can prevent disease and ensure healthy stock.

New birds
Disease can be introduced to established stock by new arrivals. Keep them in quarantine for at least two weeks.

Perches
Avoid using dead wood for perches, as it may be contaminated with fungal spores. Parrots are susceptible to fungal disease, including aspergillosis.

Rusty mesh
Parrots use their beaks for climbing around their quarters, and rusty or badly galvanized mesh is therefore very dangerous. Sharp metal splinters may penetrate a bird's fleshy tongue or even embed in the wall of its crop.

Food pots
Dirty food containers provide a focus for bacterial and fungal growth. In particular, pots used for perishable foodstuffs, such as soaked seed and fresh fruit, will need to be washed daily.

Plants
Certain plants and their seeds may be poisonous to birds. (In any case, most parrots are likely to destroy any vegetation in their aviary.)

The aviary floor
A solid floor – concrete is ideal – will prevent rodents gaining access to the aviary and will be easy to keep clean.

Wild birds
Spilt seed will attract wild birds, which, if they can gain access to the flight, will not only steal the parrots' food, but may also spread disease and parasites. Ensure that the mesh is undamaged and that the dimensions of the strands are sufficiently small to exclude sparrows and other small birds (see page 28).

Rodents
Rats and mice may enter the aviary via holes in the mesh, or by burrowing in through the floor. They will contaminate food, and may even harm the birds directly. Store seed in bins and keep the aviary clean, and, if rodents are still a problem, eliminate them without delay using suitable live traps.

Wash the birds' quarters thoroughly with an effective disinfectant once treatment is completed, and replace the perches, where the mites may be hidden.

Red mite is a particular hazard during the breeding period. Heavy infestation in a nestbox can result in anaemic chicks, and may trigger feather-plucking because of the irritation caused by the mites. There is also evidence to show that red mites are responsible for transmitting some microscopic blood parasites, which may cause avian malaria. It is possible that wild birds, such as sparrows, may spread the mites to aviary occupants. Take regular precautions against red mites by spraying all newly acquired birds with a specially formulated avian aerosol, and wash nestboxes thoroughly at the end of each breeding season, using one of the preparations marketed for this purpose. It is a wise precaution to give the parrots' quarters a good clean at the same time. A population of red mites can grow very quickly under favourable conditions, and they are capable of surviving from one year to the next without feeding.

The *Leucocytozoon* parasite is a blood parasite, spread by flies that breed in stagnant water, rather than by mites. Infestations most commonly arise in aviary stock housed close to standing water, such as ponds. There are few signs prior to death, which results from heart failure, when a post-mortem examination reveals the parasites encysted in the heart muscle. If you live in an area where this disease is known to occur, probably the only satisfactory solution will be to cover the aviary with mosquito netting to prevent flies gaining access to the birds. If you cannot drain the water where the flies are breeding, ask your veterinarian for preventive medication for your birds.

Other blood parasites, which are often found at routine screenings, can be divided into two groups. The first consists of malarial-like micro-organisms (of no danger to people), which appear to have few, if any, adverse effects on the bird. The second, *Microfilariae,* are more serious. These immature parasitic worms spend part of their life cycle in the circulatory system, and kidney damage may occur as a result. Imported cockatoos, as well as Long-tailed Parakeets, are known to be vulnerable, but, unfortunately, there are often no visible signs of infection, and the affected bird simply dies suddenly.

Giardiasis is one of the most frequent causes of diarrhoea in cockatiels, more often in North America than in Europe, for reasons which are not understood at present. The resulting diarrhoea tends to be rather mucoid, forming strands as it is voided from the body, and usually has a highly unpleasant odour. Diagnosis depends on examining faecal samples, and treatment with a drug called dimetridazole is possible. The droppings are infectious, so strict hygiene is essential to prevent the disease spreading.

Other parasites can be found in the parrot's gut; roundworms are the most common form, and can pose a dangerous threat to the birds. The symptoms of a roundworm infection are surprisingly varied. Some parrots show little adverse reaction, while others lose weight and appear generally sickly and dull. Death can be quite common, especially among young birds, so no breeder can afford to ignore this potential problem.

Roundworm eggs are voided in the parrot's droppings and millions can rapidly accumulate in the environment — they thrive in dark moist surroundings and may remain viable for years. If a parrot eats a piece of greenfood contaminated with droppings containing mature roundworm eggs, further roundworms will develop in the bird's gut. On a soil floor, earthworms may also ingest the parasitic eggs, and introduce them to a neighbouring flight as part of a worm cast. Thorough cleaning of the parrot's quarters is absolutely essential to prevent reinfection occuring, and obviously, once you have a parasitic problem of this type, it is very difficult to resolve without considerable effort. As well as taking sensible precautions to keep roundworm out of the aviary, you should always deworm all new parrots properly before releasing them into your collection. Do not assume that they have already been dewormed — there is no guarantee that they have received an adequate dose of treatment and they could still be infected. Regular preventive deworming is standard practice with most birdkeepers; ideally, you should treat the birds twice a year, giving the first dose just before the onset of the breeding season. A pet parrot, kept in isolation, is less in need of regular treatment.

Your veterinarian can test for the presence of parasitic worm eggs in the parrot's droppings and prescribe a dewormer. The medication will be more effective if you treat each parrot individually, rather than simply adding the drug to the drinking water. Dewormers are generally bitter, and the parrots will be able to detect this, in spite of their rather limited sense of taste. When administering fluids of any kind to a parrot, be careful to avoid the windpipe, which is evident as an opening at the back of the mouth — if fluid enters here accidentally, the parrot may choke. For this reason, experienced parrot-keepers often medicate their birds using a tube, which they pass down the throat into the crop. Do not undertake this without seeking proper advice and assistance however, or you may cause serious or fatal injury to the parrot. It is best to keep the parrots caged for a short time after treatment, until the effects of the drug have worn off. You will be able to see the worms on the floor of the cage.

If you suspect that a parrot is suffering from a particularly bad infestation, offer a little olive oil at the same time as dosing with the vermifuge. The parrot's gut narrows as it progresses through to the cloaca, and dislodging a knot of worms high up in the gut could lead to a fatal blockage lower down. The olive oil will act as a laxative to lessen this risk.

Australian parakeets and cockatiels are commonly infested with parasitic worms, probably because they spend more time on the ground, where there is the greatest concentration of worm eggs, but an increasing incidence is now being recorded in lovebirds kept in flights previously occupied by such birds.

Tapeworms, in contrast to roundworms, rarely pose a serious threat because of their indirect life cycle. These flat worms are attached to the gut, and segments containing their eggs are voided in the droppings. The eggs are not a direct hazard to the parrot, and the bird will only become infected if it eats an invertebrate, such as a snail, that has itself consumed the tapeworm eggs. Occasionally birds may eat an infected insect, on a piece of fruit, for example. A recent study has suggested that up to 20% of all imported cockatoos could be infected with tapeworms, which suggests that they must at some stage, either deliberately or inadvertently, consume invertebrates as part of their diet.

Symptoms of a tapeworm infection in-

Below: In some cases, you may need to administer medicine directly into a bird's crop. Be careful to avoid the windpipe, evident as an opening at the back of the mouth, or the bird may choke.

clude loss of condition, and weight loss, which is particularly apparent across the breastbone. Diagnosis is possible either by analysis of the droppings, or by microscopic examination of the white blood cells, although this will only show the presence of a parasitic problem rather than identifying it precisely. Treatment with a suitable deworming medication should lead to a full recovery, and the likelihood of reinfection in aviary surroundings is slight. It is probably worthwhile screening and treating cockatoos for this group of parasites, particularly if the birds have been imported recently.

Liver flukes are another group of parasites that can be encountered in cockatoos, although they are generally very rare in other parrots. They can impair liver function, and cause general poor condition. Up to a hundred flukes have been detected in the liver of a Sulphur-crested Cockatoo; enough to prove fatal. Your veterinarian may be able to diagnose the infection by examining a faecal sample under a microscope and will give advice on treatment. The medication used to treat tapeworm is effective in some cases.

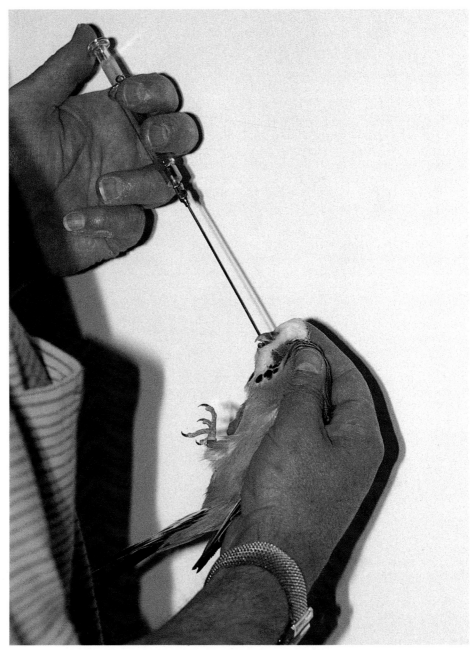

Sour crop

This is a relatively common budgerigar ailment, especially in hens that are in breeding condition but have not bred, indicating that the disease may be influenced by hormonal changes in the body. The most obvious sign is retching – you may see evidence of this in a mucus discharge on the head of an affected bird. Closer examination usually reveals that the crop at the base of the neck is distended with air and contains little food. Empty the crop by massaging it gently towards the neck while holding the bird upside down. Add potassium permanganate crystals to the bird's drinking water, sufficient to create a pale purple (10%) solution. This should resolve the problem within a couple of days, enabling the bird to start eating normally again. If the problem recurs, you should obtain suitable medication from your veterinarian, as the cause may be a protozoal infection.

Bacterial diseases

A wide variety of bacteria can be linked with disease in parrots, and a general course of antibiotic treatment will usually be prescribed by your veterinarian for such conditions. In its simplest form, antibiotic is available as a powder, to be mixed with the bird's drinking water, and the solution should be made up twice daily to retain its potency. It is important to offer the antibiotic solution in a glass or plastic container, which will not react with treatment. The main problem with administering antibiotics in solution is that recovery is entirely dependent on the volume of fluid that the bird will drink; it may not consume enough for the drug to be effective. (Never exceed the recommended dose, however, as this can lead to adverse side-effects.)

Your veterinarian may decide to administer the drug by injection or tablets. It is relatively easy and safe to inject larger parrots, and tablets may also be useful in certain circumstances, although they have to be placed directly inside the parrot's mouth – a hazardous undertaking with a large macaw. You will need another person to restrain the bird, while you place the tablet at the back of the bird's mouth on the tongue. Hold the beak closed for a few moments afterwards to ensure that the parrot swallows the tablet rather than spitting it out. Another method of administering an antibiotic is to pass a tube down into the crop, and flush antibiotic solution directly into the digestive tract.

In all cases, it is important to seek proper veterinary advice and follow the recommended treatment regime carefully. Birds usually recover quickly once appropriate treatment has begun, and you should notice a distinct improvement within a day or so. With any course of antibiotics, complete the treatment, even if the bird appears to have recovered, or the bacteria may multiply again.

Unfortunately, the beneficial bacteria normally present in the parrot's digestive tract are also likely to be adversely affected by a course of antibiotic treatment. This may interfere with the manufacture of certain B vitamins, for example, or even allow another harmful infection to gain easy access to the parrot's system. Some veterinarians recommend natural live yoghourt, given on fruit, to help a parrot through the convalescent stage – live yoghourt contains *Lactobacillus* bacteria, which will help to colonize and protect the gut. You may also be able to obtain *Lactobacillus* in a powdered form direct from your veterinarian. Probiotic products have been formulated to encourage the development of helpful bacteria after an illness. Such products may be obtainable from more specialist pet shops and bird farms, and they can be administered on food or in drinking water.

If, in spite of treatment, the parrot dies, it is worth arranging an autopsy, especially if the bird has been in contact with others in your collection. A post-mortem examination will identify the bacterium responsible for death, and it should then be possible to find a specific antibiotic for any other parrots that fall sick, and prevent further losses.

Try to establish how the infection gained access to the aviary. Two serious diseases, salmonellosis and yersiniosis, may be introduced by rodents and can result in heavy losses of birds. *Salmonella* bacteria often cause bloodstained droppings, while yersiniosis can result in either sudden death, or a more prolonged illness, during which the parrot loses condition and becomes progressively more depressed. Treatment is rarely successful, largely because of the damage caused to the liver by these bacteria. Yersiniosis can be diagnosed quite easily at a post-mortem examination, because it produces white spots on the liver that are reminiscent of avian tuberculosis – for this reason it is also known as pseudo-tuberculosis. Humans can catch both these diseases from rodents or infected birds, so take sensible precautions when handling a sick parrot. Wash your hands after touching the bird or its surroundings, keep it isolated, and clean its quarters thoroughly with a disinfectant solution. Disinfectants are less effective in dirty surroundings, so scrub the flight with water before washing it out with disinfectant. Don't forget to clean perches and foodpots, too, and rinse them thoroughly if they are to be re-used.

A number of bacteria, such as *Escherichia coli*, can give rise to digestive problems in parrots, notably enteritis, before spreading into the blood stream and affecting the body organs. Good hygiene is vital to prevent the spread of enteric diseases; *E. coli* is often present in the environment, and can be spread by dirty hands, when you are cutting up fruit, for example. An infected parrot's droppings will alter in consistency, and, in the later stages of infection, the bird's appetite will decline. Your veterinarian can arrange for a sample of droppings to be cultured, in order to confirm the diagnosis.

Chlamydiosis, sometimes known as ornithosis or psittacosis, is potentially the most serious disease affecting parrots. Some groups are more susceptible to this disease than others – amazons, for example, are more likely to be affected than cockatoos, which appear quite resistant to the bacteria, *Chlamydia psittaci*. It is now known to occur in a wide range of mammals, including sheep, cats, and even amphibians, as well as birds. It can also be transmitted to people, often producing severe influenza-like symptoms. The disease is spread by inhalation of infective particles present in the droppings,

PARROT DISEASES

Budgerigars	Watch for fatty lumps (lipomas). Also susceptible to parasitic mites and protozoal ailments.
Cockatiels, Australian parakeets and lovebirds	Intestinal parasitic worms are common in these birds.
Conures	May represent a hazard to other parrots as symptomless carriers of Pacheco's Disease.
Psittaculid parakeets	Vulnerable to egg-binding if nesting during a cold spell.
***Pionus* parrots**	Susceptible to aspergillosis.
Amazon parrots	Prone to eye and nasal ailments.
Grey parrot	Feather-plucking can be a particular problem in these birds.
Vasa parrots	Feather discoloration, leading to areas of white plumage, may be linked with Psittacine Beak and Feather Disease (PBFD).
Fig parrots	Suffer spontaneous haemorrhages if the Vitamin K level of their diet is low.
Macaws	Vulnerable to proventricular disease.
Cockatoos	Susceptible to Psittacine Beak and Feather Disease.
Lories and lorikeets, Eclectus and *Tanygnathus* parrots	At risk from candidiasis, especially if the Vitamin A content of their diet is low.

or in secretions from the nose and eyes. Antibiotic treatment is usually effective, but on a very few occasions, the disease can be fatal. However, there is really no great likelihood of you or your family contracting chlamydiosis from keeping parrots, particularly if you buy your stock from reputable dealers or breeders. There are only about 10 cases of people contracting the disease each year in the UK, and a high percentage of those affected have not even been in contact with birds.

In most countries, parrots entering quarantine are routinely medicated against chlamydiosis, but reliable diagnosis of the infection can only be made in the laboratory. Unfortunately, some parrots are imported illegally, notably across the Mexican border into the United States, and these birds will not have been quarantined or innoculated.

Swelling round the eyes is sometimes linked with chlamydiosis, but may equally be a symptom of other more common diseases, or inflammation from a scratch. A local infection can arise, blocking the nostril on the same side of the head, and requiring antibiotic treatment. Swelling of the eyelids can also be caused by a deficiency of Vitamin A in the diet. If you feed plenty of greenfood and other fresh items, such as carrot (which is rich in Vitamin A), along with a vitamin supplment, the bird should soon return to normal. If the parrots have been receiving a balanced diet, the swelling is more likely to have an infective than a nutritional cause.

Fungal diseases

Fungal ailments are more common in recently imported birds, especially if they have received a poor diet. Antibiotics are not generally very effective against fungal disease, and a prolonged course of treatment can trigger a secondary fungal infection in some cases.

Candidiasis is a problem associated particularly with Indonesian parrots, such as the Great-billed, which appear to need relatively high amounts of Vitamin A in their diet. Recently imported lories and lorikeets may also suffer from this disease. Vitamin A is notably deficient in dry seed, and birds receiving a seed-based diet are particularly vulnerable. Offering foods that are naturally rich in Vitamin A, such as carrots, should assist their recovery.

Signs of candidiasis are most likely to be apparent in the mouth. The affected parrot will play with its food, rather than eating it, and you may notice a sticky whitish discharge from the beak. If you look inside the mouth, you will see whitish patches of the *Candida* fungus. You can obtain specific medication from your veterinarian, but you will also need to improve the bird's diet, to assist recovery and prevent any recurrence.

Symptoms of candidiasis are rare in adult cockatiels, so that you may not realize a problem exists until the infection is passed to the chicks during feeding. Since chicks lack effective immunity, *Candida* spreads rapidly through their system and can cause quite heavy mortality in newly

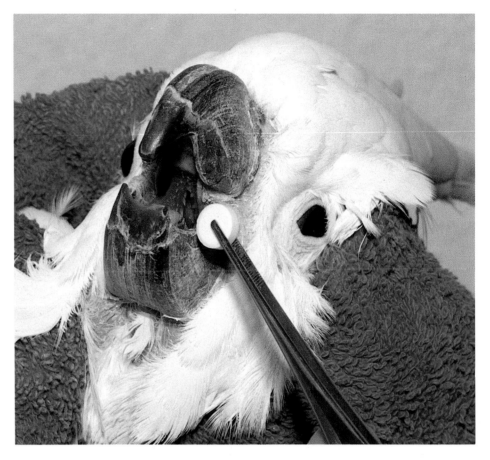

hatched birds. Visual diagnosis is difficult under these circumstances, but if you find that young cockatiel chicks are dying in large numbers, ask your veterinarian for advice on testing for candidiasis. Hand-reared chicks can also become infected, especially if they are being fed by a tube that damages the lining of their throat, enabling *Candida* to colonize the damaged tissue. Growths appear in the mouth and throat, and may well spread further down the digestive tract.

The other major fungal problem encountered in parrots is aspergillosis. Research is continuing into drugs to treat this disease and some promising remedies have been developed. The disease usually spreads through the bird's airways, from inhaled fungal spores. The bird has difficulty breathing, and the condition worsens as the fungus develops, especially if the bird is stressed. Aspergillosis develops slowly, and an affected bird's health will decline over several months. Diagnosis can be confirmed by an endoscopic examination (see page 60), when the strands of the fungus will be clearly visible. Treatment may be possible, provided that the condition is not too far advanced.

Viral diseases

The most common viral disease affecting parrots is Psittacine Beak and Feather Disease (see page 12), which gives rise to poor, scanty plumage over the parrot's body, and may cause the beak to become a brownish colour. In its early stages, PBFD can be confused with chronic feather-plucking, but the characteristic changes to the beak and claws are not seen in feather-plucking cases.

Above: Use a pair of tweezers or forceps to adminster a tablet to a sick parrot, placing the tablet well back in the mouth, then holding the bird's beak closed to encourage it to swallow.

It is now possible to diagnose PBFD from small feathers containing traces of blood, rather than skin biopsies. The disease affects the bird's immune system and fatalities are often caused by a secondary infection rather than the virus itself. In a few cases, however, the immune system appears to overcome the virus, and affected birds recover, but it is possible that such birds remain carriers of the virus, and so represent a threat to other parrots. Recent research has shown that parvovirus can also be implicated in some cases of PBFD.

The most serious viral disease affecting parrots is Newcastle disease, which can be spread to poultry, and causes a sharp fall in egg production, as well as high mortality, depending on the strain of virus. The possible effect of this disease is one of the major reasons that quarantine regulations are enforced for the movement of psittacines from one country to another. Provided that the parrots have been properly quarantined, there is little risk of them contracting this infection.

Pacheco's disease, which is caused by a psittacine herpes virus, has caused increasing concern during recent years. It is most commonly linked with parrots from Central and South America, although similar symptoms have been seen in African species. The disease usually becomes apparent during the quarantine period, although the susceptibility of individual genera varies. In severe outbreaks, there can be very high mortality,

Right: An advanced case of PBFD in a Lesser Sulphur-crested Cockatoo. There is currently no cure for this progressive viral disease, which affects the bird's immune system.

especially among amazon parrots and Grey Parrots. In many cases, there are few obvious signs, and birds that have been eating and drinking normally, die within hours. Larger macaws may suffer a more protracted illness, often with the characteristic symptom of orange-coloured diarrhoea. Parrots suffering from Pacheco's disease will suffer increased thirst as a result of fluid loss, and you will need to guard against dehydration. Affected birds rarely recover.

A vaccine against Pacheco's disease is now available in some countries, but it is not entirely effective. As an extra precaution, you should take particular care when adding recently imported conures, which are known to be symptomless carriers of the virus, to an existing collection of parrots. Some species, such as the Patagonian Conure and the Maroon-bellied conures, may appear quite healthy themselves, but introduce the virus to other parrots with potentially catastrophic consequences. Some breeders keep such birds in the company of cockatiels initially, so that illness in these birds will be apparent, before it can spread to more valuable members of their collection.

Parrots can also be susceptible to the herpes virus, which is the cause of cold sores in people, and treatment using human medication has proved effective. The virus affects the feet, causing small, wartlike swellings. It seems likely that owners could infect their birds; you might spread the virus to your pet by kissing it, or offering it food from your mouth.

Parrot pox is a viral disease that occurs in warm climates. The virus is spread by biting insects, and has been a particular problem in some lovebird collections. The skin around the eyes typically swells up, with scabs soon starting to form here. There is really no treatment for the disease, but affected birds that recover will be immune to this disease for the rest of their lives. Discharges or scabs may contain the virus, which can then infect other birds directly, so thorough disinfection is essential after an outbreak.

Behavioural problems

Some cocks can become murderous towards intended mates, often with little previous warning of their intentions. This is most likely to occur at the start of the breeding season, possibly because the cock is more advanced, and ready to nest, while his mate fails to respond. This behaviour may also sometimes be seen in bonded pairs that have bred previously without any signs of aggression. You may be alerted to an attack by the desperate screeching of the hen; separate the birds at once and remove the cock to separate quarters. Left to his own devices, the cock could kill his mate in minutes, or seriously mutilate her beak. When you reunite the pair later, watch the birds closely in case

the cock decides to renew his assault. There is little that can be done under these circumstances, apart from trying to find other partners that are more compatible. The problem is most likely to arise in cockatoos and some Australian parakeets.

The abnormal screeching of some pet parrots has already been mentioned, and such birds are also likely to pluck their feathers. This may be a sign of sexual frustration in an adult bird, especially if feather loss is confined to the lower chest. There are various sprays available that deter birds from plucking their feathers, but they are often ineffectual, since they do not address the underlying behavioural causes of this problem. A number of other factors may be responsible for triggering feather-plucking; inadequate bathing facilities, an alteration in daily routine or even a change of environment or owner. A specialist avian veterinarian may be able to help you unravel the cause, but treatment is difficult. A parrot may develop into an habitual feather-plucker, removing the new feathers each time they begin to emerge, so that a rapid, experienced assessment of a particular case will be vital.

Adult cockatiels, unlike cockatoos, rarely pluck their own feathers. An interesting observation from the United States suggests that birds that pluck themselves are infected with the *Giardia* parasite, which appears to trigger a severe skin irritation. In these cases, successful treatment of giardiasis can resolve the problem of feather-plucking.

Loss of feathers is also a relatively common problem in young lutino cockatiels, and usually occurs just as the birds are beginning to feather up. One or both

Below: Feather-plucking, as seen in this Citron-crested Cockatoo, can quickly become an habitual vice. Causes include a frustrated desire to breed, dietary deficiencies and boredom.

parent birds may be responsible for the feather-plucking, directing their attention first to the back of the youngster's neck, and often progressing to a much wider area of the body. This situation can also arise in budgerigars. It may be that the adult birds are keen to breed again, and attempt to drive their first round youngsters from the nestbox by removing their feathers. The youngsters are mutilated very quickly – often within a few hours – so that it is difficult to take effective action. To some extent the condition may be inherited, and there is little that can be done to correct it. However, if you have a pair that are known feather-pluckers, you can take steps to prevent a recurrence of the problem. Try sprinkling powdered aloes around the necks of the chicks every day as they begin to feather up – the bitter taste of the aloes may deter the adult birds. Another possibility is to provide a second nestbox in the cage or flight, in the hope that the breeding pair will use it for their second round of eggs, rather than persecute their existing offspring. Once they leave the nestbox, the plucked chicks will grow new feathers in the course of a few weeks, and become identical in appearance to their fellows. There is rarely any recurrence of feather-plucking once the birds have finally left the nest.

Below: Some cocks turn very aggressive at the start of the breeding period, and may suddenly attack the hen. Keep a careful watch on pairs at this time and separate the birds if necessary.

Breeding problems

The most common reproductive problem in parrots is egg-binding, when an egg forms a blockage in the lower part of a hen's reproductive tract, and she cannot expel it from her body. The underlying cause is usually in the surrounding muscles, which are responsible for forcing the egg out. Factors involved may include lack of muscle tone, cold weather (which decreases muscular activity) and low levels of calcium, (which is required for muscular contractions). If keeping the affected hen in the warm for an hour or so proves fruitless, seek veterinary help immediately. The most effective treatment is often an intramuscular injection of calcium gluconate, with a dose of 0.5mg per 100g of body weight. Although it may be possible to manipulate the egg out of the body (this should be left to a veterinarian), using a suitable lubricant, there is a risk that the egg could break, especially if it has a soft shell, leading to peritonitis (a severe infection of the body cavity).

In order to prevent egg-binding, parrots should have an adequate supply of cuttlefish bone, or a calcium block, throughout the year. The more prolific species, such as the parrotlets, should only be encouraged to breed during the warmer months of the year, and restricted to a maximum of three clutches of eggs during this time.

Always keep a close watch on laying hens, so that you can spot the signs of egg-binding early, as this is a serious disorder that requires rapid treatment. An affected hen will usually emerge from the nestbox appearing unsteady on her feet. Before long, she will not be able to perch, and her legs may seem to be paralyzed. Once the egg is removed, the parrot should soon be able to perch normally, but you should not allow her to breed again for a further year.

Cloacal prolapse is a complication of egg-binding that is relatively common in both budgerigars and cockatoos. The pink fleshy mass, which protrudes through the vent, must be cleaned and replaced. Ask your veterinarian for advice; in some cases prolapses recur, and it may be necessary to insert a purse-string suture around the vent for a few days to retain the tissue in the body.

Prolapses not associated with egg-binding can occur in cockatoos of either sex. They are triggered by a sudden increase in pressure within the abdomen, which causes tissue to emerge through the vent. Viral infection, and a deficiency of Vitamin A, have both been suggested as possible causes, but further research is required. It is also important to distinguish a prolapse of this type from cloacal papillomatosis, which is a sexually transmitted disease. Nodules, called papillomas, develop in the cloaca, and may ultimately protrude through the vent. Anaesthetizing the parrot and then carefully cauterizing the papillomas with silver nitrate can affect a cure, but it is likely to be at least a year before the parrot is free from infection, and it should be kept in isolation through this period.

BREEDING AND REARING PARROTS

Increasing numbers of parrots are bred each year by breeders around the world, and a considerable amount of new information has been gleaned about their reproductive needs. While budgerigars, cockatiels and Australian parakeets have long been considered the most prolific species in aviary surroundings, similar results are now starting to be obtained with other species, including the bigger parrots. Here we look at sexing, suitable diets and nestboxes for the breeding birds, as well as how to hand feed and rear the chicks, if necessary, until they are independent.

Breeding patterns

Provided that you have a compatible pair of parrots, there is no reason why they should not nest satisfactorily, even in indoor surroundings. Larger parrots will normally lay only one clutch of chicks when housed in an outdoor aviary in most temperate areas because of their long incubation and rearing periods. Eclectus Parrots tend to be an exception, however, and will lay repeatedly, and parrotlets are also prolific, sometimes nesting several times during a breeding season.

In some years, you may find that an established pair do not attempt to breed. A change in their environment may be responsible, but it could simply be that they are resting. It is unlikely that every adult pair breeds every year in the wild. The long lifespan of parrots means that once you have established a compatible pair, you may well be rewarded with chicks over a period of decades. One pair of Citron-crested Cockatoos, successfully reared chicks for 20 consecutive years.

Some parrots mature more quickly than others. Cockatiels may be ready to mate at only six months old, but they should be prevented from breeding until their second year, when there is less risk of young hens becoming egg-bound as a result of immaturity, and the overall fertility rate is likely to be improved.

Budgerigars are not usually difficult birds to breed, but to ensure that breeding stock is fully mature, do not use birds under about 10 months old. Cocks tend to have a longer reproductive life than hens, and will sire chicks successfully when eight or nine years old. Most exhibition breeders concentrate on breeding from budgerigars during their second and third years, so you may be able to obtain older quality stock at a relatively low price.

Parakeets vary in their breeding requirements and habits. Some species, such as the grass parakeets, are happy to breed in an aviary of fairly modest dimensions, whereas others, such as Crimsonwings, do better in more spacious surroundings. Most parakeets need to be kept in separate pairs, especially during the breeding season, but you should buy a small group of *Brotogeris* parakeets, as these birds appear to need the company of others of their kind to stimulate breeding. Similarly, other South American species, such as the Quaker Parakeet and *Bolborhynchus* species, often breed more successfully when kept in groups.

Certain parakeet species will prove quite prolific – many Australian parakeets nest twice during the warmer part of the year. In contrast, New World parakeets rarely hatch more than one round of chicks each year in outside aviaries. You will find the latter more challenging, as they are also less keen to reproduce than their Australian counterparts.

Although their aviary requirements and breeding habits differ, the care needed by parrots and their chicks remains fairly constant for all species. If birds are moved it could take them time to settle down in new surroundings, and a change of nestbox may also dampen their enthusiasm to nest. If you need to replace a nestbox, do so at the end of a breeding season.

SURGICALLY SEXING A PARROT

Stage One
Having anaesthetized the parrot (with an injection or a gaseous agent), the veterinarian will prepare the site for incision – on the left-hand side behind the last rib – by removing a few feathers and cleaning the area.

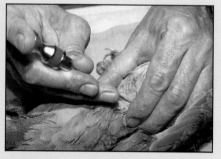

Stage Two
The small hole into which the delicate endoscope will be inserted is being made here by an instrument known as a trocar. (This hole will not be sutured. By the time the bird has regained consciousness it will be barely visible.)

Stage Three
With the trocar in position, the veterinarian can carefully insert the delicate endoscope, with its black eyepiece, into the parrot's body cavity. The inspection to determine the bird's gender will take only a minute or two.

Stage Four
The endoscopic examination will not only enable the veterinarian to determine the sex of the parrot, but will also reveal any diseases, such as aspergillosis, which may be difficult to confirm by any other, non-surgical means.

Sexing methods

In the past it was impossible to identify the sex of individual birds reliably by visual means. This often meant that supposed pairs were simply birds of the same sex housed together. Mutual preening and feeding are not clear indicators of breeding pairs, since two birds kept together for any length of time may behave in this way, irrespective of their sex. In some cases, it is possible to detect slight variances in physical appearance; hen macaws, for example, have a narrower head and are slightly smaller overall than their male counterparts. But such differences could equally be due to regional variations, as many of these species have a very wide distribution.

In recent years, there have been a number of advances in methods of sexing parrots that are not sexually dimorphic; by surgical sexing, chromosomal karyotyping, and faecal steroid analysis.

The advent of surgical or endoscopic sexing allowed birds to be sexed accurately, and can also provide valuable insight into the overall health and reproductive state of the individual parrot. The technique entails looking directly into the bird's body cavity, using a thin probe called an endoscope. A veterinarian will carry out this procedure for you, and will be able to advise on the treatment of any problems, such as infection of the air-sacs, which may be detected at the same time.

You will probably need to withhold food from parrots on the night before they are to be sexed, but check this with your veterinarian in advance. If you suspect that the bird may be at all poorly, particularly if it has a respiratory problem, you should inform the veterinarian, as this may affect the choice of anaesthetic. Obese parrots can also present complications, and if you have recently acquired a bird that has been kept as a pet for a long period, it may be wise to get it fit, in avian surroundings, before taking it to your veterinarian to be sexed. The veterinarian might give the bird a gaseous anaesthetic or use an injection. Recovery is surprisingly quick after the former, but in either case, you should keep the parrots quiet post-operatively. The site of the tiny incision, on the left flank, heals rapidly and does not usually require stitching.

A number of dealers now offer surgically sexed pairs of parrots for sale. (The initials 'S.S.' alongside the pair in question will indicate that they have been sexed in this way.) They may also offer a veterinary certificate to this effect, but this provides no absolute guarantee of sex, unless the parrots have been ringed or marked with a microchip implant. Such details should be shown on the certificate. Although surgical sexing is reliable, there remains the slight possibility that a pair could have become mixed up after being sexed.

Surgical sexing is a very safe procedure and its only real drawback is that it is impossible to sex young birds with any degree of certainty. This can place an intolerable burden on aviary space, should you want to keep chicks to establish a captive-bred strain. You will have to keep them for several months before they are old enough for surgical sexing to be reliable.

Chromosomal karyotyping avoids this problem, as parrots can be sexed by this means before they leave the nest, (although it is more usual to wait until the birds have fledged). This laboratory method isolates the bird's sex by a study of its chromosomes, present within the nucleus of all living cells. One pair – the sex chromosomes – are responsible for determining the bird's gender. In cock birds, the sex chromosomes are of equal length – referred to as a ZZ pairing – whereas in hens, one chromosome is shorter than the other. Hens are described as having a ZY conformation, with Y indicating the shorter chromosome.

Various laboratories provide the service, requiring only a small sample of body feathers with blood in their tips. The dividing cells in the growing feathers are cultured and collected, and a chromosomal map, or karyotype, is prepared, where the pair of sex chromosomes will be located. The cost of this service is higher than surgical sexing, and you will have to wait longer for the results, but it can be carried out easily, efficiently and safely, and, as it is a non-invasive method, it is worth considering with rare or valuable birds, such as Palm Cockatoos.

Faecal steroid analysis is a less common laboratory method of sexing, using a comparison of the levels of male and female sex hormones in the droppings to determine a bird's gender. Unfortunately, unlike chromosomal karyotyping, it is a ratio method, and is less reliable because it needs a proven baseline against which results can be interpreted.

BREEDING PARROTS

Budgerigars	Easy to sex, and breed readily, although pairs housed entirely on their own may be reluctant to nest.
Cockatiels	Prolific, but colony breeding may result in losses of eggs and chicks through chilling, if more than one pair decide to share a nestbox.
Lovebirds	Some species, such as the Peach-faced, are much more ready to nest than others. Pairs are best housed on their own to prevent fighting. Supply them with nesting material, such as leaves and branches.
Parrotlets	Breed readily, sometimes nesting several times during a breeding season. Remove chicks as soon as possible as they may be attacked by adult birds, especially the cock.
Hanging parrots	Require nesting material, in the form of leaves and branches, like lovebirds.
Lories and lorikeets	Some pairs may display a tendency to pluck their chicks.
Australian parakeets	Generally reproduce well, often rearing two rounds of chicks in a breeding season, but watch for signs of aggression from the cock, and remove youngsters as soon as they are feeding independently.
Fig parrots	Hens may prove rather susceptible to egg-binding, and rearing of chicks can be problematic. Hand-raising may often be necessary if a pair fail repeatedly.
Psittaculid parakeets, Eclectus and *Tanygnathus* parrots	Hens tend to be dominant for most of the year, when not breeding, so try to pair an experienced cock with a young hen for greatest likelihood of compatibility.
***Poicephalus* parrots**	Frequently prefer to nest during the winter in northern temperate areas. Their accommodation must be planned accordingly.
Amazon parrots	Nest rather late in the year in the northern hemisphere, rarely laying before May.
Grey parrot	Compatibility is very important in these parrots. Swopping partners, where there are problems, may result in almost immediate breeding success.
Vasa parrots	Swelling of the vent area and feather loss on the head appear to be normal features of the breeding pattern of these birds.
Macaws	Young pairs may prove poor parents, but generally improve with experience.
Cockatoos	*Cacatua* species, in particular, will tend to favour one chick, and any others in the nest may need to be removed for hand-raising if they are to survive.

Feeding breeding birds

Unless parrots are properly fed, as well as suitably housed, they will be unwilling to start nesting. Before the onset of the breeding period, you may want to increase the protein level of the diet, to stimulate breeding condition.

Mineral intake is particularly important for hens during the breeding season, and you will find that you need to replace cuttlefish bone frequently as the time for laying approaches. This is one of the first signs that the birds are ready to start nesting in earnest. Some breeders, especially in Europe, also offer rock salt, to Australian parakeets in particular. Rock salt, which is available from many large supermarkets, contains various trace elements, such as iodine, that may stimulate breeding behaviour.

Nestboxes

The basic design of the nestbox does not vary greatly, but the size will differ depending on the species. Some parrots, especially larger Australian parakeets and the psittaculids, feel more secure in a fairly deep nest box. You can buy nestboxes either complete, or in kit form for home assembly. The timber or plywood used for their construction needs to be at least 2.5cm (1in) thick in nestboxes intended for larger parrots, and ideally double this thickness for macaws, which are the most destructive species.

The dimensions of the nestbox will obviously vary, depending on the species – parrotlets can be bred quite satisfactorily in budgerigar nestboxes; macaws will need a much larger structure. An internal

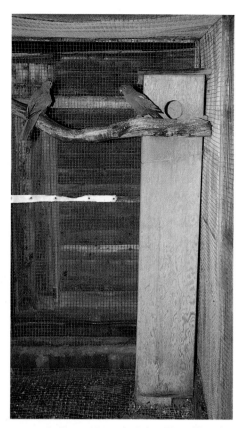

Left: Some species, especially Crimson-winged and king parakeets (shown here), prefer a deep 'grandfather clock' nestbox, which appears to offer greater security to the breeding pair.

area of about 25cm (10in) will suffice for the *Poicephalus* species, while a slightly larger box should be adequate for *Pionus*, Grey and amazon parrots. Allow a floor area of about 30cm (12in) square for the medium-sized macaws, and 45cm (18in) for the larger species.

The roof of the nestbox should be hinged, so that you can remove it for cleaning, and an inspection flap is also an advantage, positioned on one of the sides, out of the parrots' reach when they are on the floor of the box, but located so that you can reach down inside if neces-

sary. This will enable you to remove either eggs or chicks in an emergency, with the minimum of disturbance, and will also be useful if you intend to take the eggs away for artificial incubation. Attach a small bolt to the flap to ensure it remains securely closed when not in use.

The size of the entrance hole, which should be positioned near the roof of the box, will depend on the parrots – if it is too small, the birds will attempt to enlarge it. To calculate the approximate size of the hole, measure across the broadest part of the parrot's back, at the top of its wings. The more destructive species will persist in attacking this hole, so it is worth reinforcing it with tin sheeting (see page 34). Make sure there are no exposed edges, on which the parrots could cut their toes, by folding the cut edges.

It is also usual to incorporate a simple ladder inside the nestbox. By helping the parrots climb in and out of the box, this will minimize the risk of the birds accidentally harming their eggs or chicks. Aviary mesh, fixed in place with netting staples, makes an ideal ladder, but again, ensure that there are no sharp projections. Cutting a section from the side of a roll will give you one smooth edge, and you can then trim the opposite side, the top and the bottom, to the nearest strand and file down the stubs until they are smooth. You can simply tack this mesh onto the inside of the box, from the en-

Below: These Umbrella Cockatoos are using a conventional nestbox. Once they have taken to a nesting site, the birds are likely to breed here for many years.

Below: A stout nestbox is essential for breeding cockatoos because of their destructive natures. A hollow tree trunk, with an added lid, is one option.

Right: Note the metal sheeting that has been used to reinforce the entrance to this nestbox, and the inspection flap, which must be kept securely closed. Incorporate an internal ladder.

A STANDARD PARROT NESTBOX

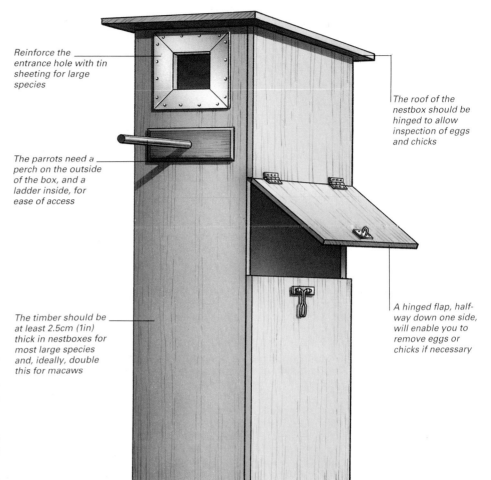

Reinforce the entrance hole with tin sheeting for large species

The parrots need a perch on the outside of the box, and a ladder inside, for ease of access

The timber should be at least 2.5cm (1in) thick in nestboxes for most large species and, ideally, double this for macaws

The roof of the nestbox should be hinged to allow inspection of eggs and chicks

A hinged flap, half-way down one side, will enable you to remove eggs or chicks if necessary

trance hole to the base, or fix it first onto two lengths of thin battening, about 0.635cm (¼in) thick, to create a small ladder. You can then attach this firmly in place in the nestbox, using panel pins driven through the battening onto the inner face below the entrance hole. Make sure it is securely fixed – if the parrots manage to dislodge the ladder, they will be unable to reach the eggs or chicks.

Although hollow logs often provide suitable nesting sites, they are not available to many birdkeepers. It can also be difficult to see inside the nesting chamber, and the parrots may eventually gnaw through the log, particularly if the wood is decaying. The interior may become contaminated with fungal spores, and will be harder to clean than a conventional nestbox.

Beer casks, usually made of oak, which is a fairly durable wood, and reinforced with metal supports, can be used as a nesting site for large macaws and cockatoos, instead of a more conventional box. Cut the entry point in the side, or at one end, and mount the cask on a sturdy base in the aviary. Because of its weight, you may need to provide support in the form of a blockwork base. You should be able to attach smaller boxes securely to the aviary framework using brackets.

Position a conventional nestbox at a relatively high spot under cover in the aviary flight. Here there will be no risk of it being flooded during heavy rain, chilling any eggs or chicks inside, and the parrots are less likely to be disturbed by cats or other animals. You may decide to offer a choice of nestboxes, positioning one in a fairly secluded spot outside in the flights, and the other in the shelter; some parrots prefer dark surroundings, and may ignore a nestbox in the flight. This is especially true of *Poicephalus* parrots, which often nest more readily in the shelter.

Most nestboxes have an exterior perch located just below the entrance hole, but as the parrots often destroy this at the start of the breeding period, it is worth positioning an aviary perch close to the entrance, so that the parrots can land here before darting into the nest.

The birds will require some time to prepare the nest before starting to lay and a satisfactory floor covering in the nestbox is essential. Most species prefer to make their own nest lining by gnawing up short lengths of softwood battening placed inside the nestbox. As an alternative, you can use coarse wood shavings, sold by pet shops for small animal bedding. Avoid sawdust, however, which tends to create too much dust. Although peat is sometimes used as a nest lining, once it is dry, it becomes very dusty, and many parrots appear to dislike this material and will scratch it out of the nestbox.

Wood is a good insulator and the birds will be reasonably warm inside the box, even in cold weather. (Warmth is particu-

larly important for the youngsters of the Plum-headed Parakeet, as the adults cease to brood the chicks at night before they are fully feathered.) Some parrots will use their nestbox site at night, and this is obviously to be encouraged in winter. If possible, transfer the box into the shelter during the winter period and move it outside again (after washing it thoroughly) in early spring. If you do not return it soon enough, the parrots may lay their eggs in a seed pot or even directly onto the floor. Most Australian parakeets will only use their nestbox during their breeding season and, since its presence may encourage them to lay during the winter, you should remove it in autumn.

Below: Converted beer casks, although difficult to inspect, are popular for larger species, while adapted hollow logs may encourage reluctant pairs to nest.

OTHER SUITABLE NESTBOXES FOR LARGE PARROTS

A BUDGERIGAR NESTBOX

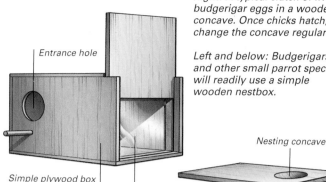

Right: A typical clutch of five budgerigar eggs in a wooden concave. Once chicks hatch, change the concave regularly.

Left and below: Budgerigars and other small parrot species will readily use a simple wooden nestbox.

Entrance hole

Simple plywood box

Viewing panel

Nesting concave

Budgerigar nestboxes

You can buy budgerigar nestboxes from many pet stores or from specialist suppliers advertising in birdkeeping magazines. Choose a design that enables you to check the interior easily, and that you can clean without difficulty. Nestboxes with hinged lids are not really suitable; breeders commonly use a box that opens at one end, usually with an outer sliding plywood door with a piece of glass behind it. This will prevent eggs or chicks falling out when you slide the outer door upwards in the runners.

The interior of the nestbox is lined with a 'concave'. This is a flat piece of wood, with a depression hollowed out, usually at one end. The hen will lay her eggs here, and the concave will help to prevent them being scattered when she leaves the nestbox. Place this away from the entrance hole, so the birds are less likely to damage the eggs as they come and go. Some breeders place the concave in a wooden box, the sides of which extend up to just below the level of the entrance hole, enabling them to remove the chicks easily from the box, while ensuring that they cannot fall out. You will need a supply of concaves for each nestbox, as these will have to be changed regularly once the chicks have hatched. Nestboxes and concaves are traditionally wooden but plastic versions are also available. Although these are easy to clean with a damp cloth, adult budgerigars are deprived of an opportunity to gnaw inside the box and so may resort to feather-plucking. Condensation can also be a problem in the interior of plastic nestboxes, and wooden concaves are still generally preferred.

It is possible to buy breeding cages with or without nestboxes attached. Alternatively, you can purchase the wire fronts and construct your own cage. Build the box with 6mm (¼in) plywood. Some breeders prefer to use hardboard instead of plywood as it is cheaper and easier to cut, leaving cleaner edges, but it is less durable, and warps more easily, especially when washed. The component pieces can also be bought already cut to size, so that you can simply assemble them to form the box unit. You may not need to build a wooden framework; you should be able to tack the individual pieces together with small screws or panel pins. (Avoid glue, as it may prove

toxic if consumed by the budgerigars.) Ensure that the various components fit together well, and that there are no loose edges which the budgerigars can gnaw. Before assembling the panels, paint the interior of the cage with a light-coloured emulsion. You may need two or three coats to give an adequate covering, depending upon the material.

So-called double-breeding cages are especially popular. These are made by incorporating two separate fronts into one relatively large cage. A removable partition is then placed between them and nestboxes can be attached to either end. Later in the year, you can convert this to a stock cage for young birds by pulling out the partition, and closing off nestboxes.

Cage breeding

If you are interested in breeding exhibition birds, or in producing a specific colour, then cage breeding is usually recommended to ensure the parentage of the chicks. Budgerigars are fickle in their choice of mates and, in a colony system, a hen may mate with several partners in succession. It is possible to keep individual breeding pairs in small flights, and the fertility of birds housed in flights is often better than that of budgerigars housed in cages, but the cost and space

Below: A suspended breeding cage in use in a birdroom. Some pairs may prove nervous, especially when breeding for the first time.

required generally precludes this system of management.

You can fix nestboxes onto the side or front of a breeding cage; it is easier to inspect a nestbox positioned at the side, but you will need to cut a hole through part of the breeding cage to correspond to the entrance hole of the nestbox and make a smaller hole for the perch. Secure the box firmly in position with a bracket. Where space in a birdroom is at a premium, you may prefer to fix the nestboxes to the front of the breeding cage, usually in the top righthand corner. This will mean cutting away part of the mesh, and you should ensure that there are no sharp projections; use battening to sandwich the cut ends out of reach. It is not practical to fix the nestboxes within the cage itself, as they take up a large amount of space and can also be difficult to clean thoroughly.

When you first introduce a pair of budgerigars to the breeding cage, close off the entrance to the nestbox for a few days to prevent the hen from retreating inside, and not emerging long enough for mating to take place. This is unlikely to be a problem in aviary surroundings, since the hens have to fly further afield in order to obtain food, and mating often occurs at this time. You should also spray the adult birds with a preparation to kill red mites (*Dermanyssus gallinae*), which can become a major problem within the confines of a breeding cage.

Provided that the hen is in good condition, she should lay within about a fortnight of being given access to the nestbox. If you are concerned about the humidity in the birdroom, you can obtain a humidity gauge, (often described as a hygrometer), which will measure the relative humidity on a percentage scale. A relative humidity of about 50%, is ideal. Low humidity is most likely to be a problem in a heated environment, such as in the home, or if you are breeding birds during the colder part of the year, in the birdroom, and supplying artificial heat. You can correct dry atmosphere with a humidifier, which is basically a tray of water that evaporates by gentle heat, raising the humidity of the atmosphere, or by spraying around the nestbox with a plant mister, wetting the wood.

Once the hen is settled in the nestbox, check inside each day to ensure that all is progressing well — it is a good idea to accustom the hen to this procedure before she actually lays. Gently tap on the outside of the nestbox, and give her a few moments to emerge before opening it.

Colony breeding

This is the simplest breeding system, and is often used for budgerigars and cockatiels. The nestboxes are fixed in place in the aviary, under cover, and the birds choose their own mates. If colony breeding is to be successful, they must have an adequate choice of nesting sites available, which means that you should provide about double the number of nestboxes to the number of pairs. Within a group of budgerigars, a distinct order of dominance will develop, so try not to have

any unpaired individuals in the aviary, especially hens, which may prove very disruptive. Don't introduce any new birds to an existing colony during the breeding period; in the resulting disturbance, eggs and chicks may be lost.

Fix all the nestboxes at the same height; this will reduce the risk of fighting, since hen budgerigars, in particular, are likely to dispute ownership of higher boxes. You may find it easiest to secure all the nestboxes onto one long piece of wood using brackets, and then position the complete row in the aviary. Allow sufficient space between the nestboxes so that you can inspect the interiors and clean them out easily. Avoid the temptation to provide the birds with nesting facilities before spring; breeding results are invariably better during warmer weather, and there is less risk of complications, such as egg-binding (see page 59).

When hen budgerigars are in top breeding condition, their ceres turn deep brown, and they become more destruc-

Above: The nestboxes have been placed at the back of these breeding cages to give the birds a sense of security.

tive, shredding paper on the floor of their quarters, for example, and gnawing intently at the perches in their aviary. Cocks become more vocal, and their musical prowess is often accompanied by vertical movements of the head, which can be a prelude to mating. At this stage, the pupils contract, so that the eyes appear whitish. Cocks pursue the hen of their choice around the aviary, occasionally pausing to tap their beaks repeatedly on the perch, and singing forcefully. Both budgerigars and cockatiels are often fickle in their breeding habits, however, and several cocks may mate with one hen, although one particular cock usually remains in close attendance. It is also not unknown for hens to share a nestbox.

Below: Cockatiels are often bred in a colony. Provide plenty of nestboxes.

(Only in the case of the Cockatiel, some black cockatoos and *Charmosyna* lorikeets does the male play an active part in the incubation process.) The hen will usually emerge for a brief rest each day, often just after feeding time, or to take a bath in a rain shower. Never be tempted to drive her out of the nestbox, or she may scatter, and possibly damage, her eggs.

Hatching problems
When calculating the incubation time, remember that this will be longer for the first, (and possibly second), eggs, which will not have been incubated initially. If the eggs fail to hatch, it may be because they were not fertilized, or the embryo may have died at a very early stage, before it could develop. In either case, the eggs will appear translucent when held in front of a bright light. Conversely, if a chick has formed, but failed to hatch, the eggs will be opaque – such losses are often described as being 'dead in the shell'. There are many potential causes; the egg may have been damaged, or nutritional deficiency and chilling may play a part. The parrots may lay again, even if they normally have only one clutch each breeding season.

Contamination of the egg shell by droppings allows bacteria and other harmful micro-organisms to enter the egg, and this, too, can kill the embryo. Second rounds of eggs are particularly at risk when the first round chicks are still using the nestbox. In the case of budgerigars, continue changing the concave to minimize contamination, and always wash your hands thoroughly before handling the eggs to ensure that you do not transfer bacteria to the eggs.

Incorrect humidity is often cited as a reason for deaths of chicks before hatching. In the normal process of incubation, the egg loses water, but if the volume lost is inadequate, the chick may 'drown' inside the egg before it can free itself. Conversely, excessive water loss may cause the shell membranes to become very tough, making it harder for the chick to cut its way out of the shell.

In some instances, an egg may 'pip', (the chick makes a small hole in the shell), but hatching does not progress normally. Under these circumstances, you may decide to assist the chick out of the shell – leave it for at least a day, however, before taking any action, especially if blood vessels are apparent in the shell membrane, in the hope that it will free itself. There is no risk of the chick starving while it remains in the shell; the yolk-sac reserves that nourish it through the incubation period will sustain it even a day or so after hatching. If you do need to help the chick out of the shell, position the egg on a flat surface at a convenient height and, using a pair of tweezers, cautiously lift the shell away from the opening already made by the chick. If the membrane stuck to the shell is very tough, you may need to snip it carefully with a small pair of clean scissors. Enlarging the opening in this way, and chipping the shell with the tweezers, may be sufficient to allow the chick to free

The breeding period
In the wild, where they usually nest in tree holes, parrots and macaws will lay their eggs on a bed of wood chips. As the breeding period approaches, you will notice that your birds become far more destructive, attacking the perches and any exposed woodwork in their quarters with their beaks. Both members of the pair will spend time in the nestbox, whittling down the wood here to form a nest lining. This may be one of the earliest signs of breeding activity.

Check the interior of the nestbox at regular intervals and add extra wood as it is whittled away – the wood chips will provide a clean and absorbent bed for the chicks when they hatch. You may see the parrots mating; they need to mate successfully only once in order to produce a fertile clutch of eggs. The hen will consume noticeably more cuttlefish bone during this period, and both members of the pair are likely to be more noisy than usual. As the laying time approaches, the hen will spend increasing periods of time in the nestbox, although she may appear rather nervous at this stage.

Just prior to laying, the hen's droppings will have a very pungent odour and become noticeably larger in size; this is not a cause for concern and they will return to normal after she has laid. Amazon parrots and cockatoos often become very territorial at this stage, so take care when

Above: Try to avoid disturbing a pair of birds during the breeding period, but keep a regular eye on them to make sure that all is going well.

approaching their nestbox. Some species are worse than others in this respect; Bare-eyed Cockatoos can be particularly pugnacious. Even tame birds can lose their rapport with their keeper and may bite if they feel threatened.

Most hens do not start incubating in earnest until they have laid a second or third egg. This helps to ensure that the chicks hatch closer together, so they will be of a more equal size, which favours their survival. All parrots lay white eggs, and those covered in this book usually lay on alternate days. The clutch size depends to some extent on the species; budgerigars, for example, lay a clutch of between four and six eggs, on alternate days.

Try to avoid any disturbance, leaving the parrots alone as much as possible – keep an eye on them from a distance to check that all is going well. Food pots will provide an early indication of any problems, (if she is ailing for any reason, the hen, in particular, will consume less food than usual).

Apart from an occasional case of egg-binding, problems are rare during this stage, and incubation usually proceeds uneventfully. The hen sits alone, but may be joined for short periods by her mate.

itself, provided that it is not too weak; if it has not broken out several hours later, remove more of the shell. During this process, dab the chick's navel with an iodine solution, which acts as a disinfectant and dries up exposed tissue. Chicks that have been helped out of the egg are not necessarily weaklings, and their subsequent development often proceeds normally.

The rearing period

The parent birds should not be disturbed at the end of the incubation period. You will probably hear the young chicks begging for food before long, and only if they call persistently throughout the day is this a sign that something is amiss. Parrots usually prove reliable parents, and once they have started breeding they will nest repeatedly over many years. But young, inexperienced pairs of macaws, for example, may lose their first chicks. It is difficult to know what to do for the best in such a situation; on the one hand, you will want to save the chicks, but on the other, the parent birds need to gain expertise. You can take the chicks away and raise them by hand if you feel that everything is not going well, but the problem may then simply recur the next time the birds breed.

Avoid unnecessary interference to nervous birds. It may be possible to tempt the adult birds out at a regular time each day with supplies of fruit and greenstuff, which will give you an opportunity to check the chicks quickly without causing a major disturbance to the nest. Healthy chicks appear pinkish in colour, neither pale nor noticeably red. More significantly, a strong chick will normally raise its head to beg for food, especially if there is little remaining in its crop, which should be clearly visible at the base of the neck, its food contents appearing whitish through the skin. A chick should be reasonably capable of supporting itself, even at a young age, and one that lies on

Right: A group of newly hatched lutino cockatiel chicks. Their eyes are still closed at this stage, but their pinkish colour indicates that they are healthy.

Above left: Avoid interfering with the chicks if all appears well. Some pairs will be intolerant of nest inspection.

Above right: Note the crop of these young Ring-necked Parakeets, visible as a swelling at the base of the neck.

its side is definitely weak and sickly.

You can offer a variety of food supplements to the adult birds throughout the rearing phase (see pages 47-48). Soaked seed, particularly in the form of millet sprays, is a popular rearing food with many parrots. The food and water intake of the adult birds will rise as their chicks grow, and they may require larger or additional containers.

There is no need to clean out the nestbox on a regular basis, except perhaps in the case of budgerigars, and occasionally nectar-feeding parrots, if the floor of the nestbox has become very damp. Simply change the concaves in a budgerigar nestbox, once the chicks are about eight days old. (While you are doing this, transfer the chicks to a spare nesting box.) Open the nestbox, change the concave and brush

out the interior before replacing the chicks on a clean base. Clean the soiled concaves by immersing them in a bucket of water for several hours, and then scrubbing them thoroughly. After a good final rinse in clean water, leave them to dry in the sun, or in a warm spot.

Keep a watch on the chicks as they develop to ensure that their toes do not become encased in droppings. Some pairs of budgerigars, called 'wet-feeders', have chicks that produce fairly fluid droppings, so that the interior of the nestbox soon becomes wet, and their feet can easily become caked with excrement. Never attempt to pull off this dirt; you are very likely to remove a claw at the same time and ruin the exhibition prospects of the bird before it has even feathered up. Instead, fill a clean empty yoghurt pot with tepid water and soak the foot to soften the droppings, and then remove these carefully with your fingernail. You should also check inside the bird's mouth for accumulations of droppings and food residue, which can distort the beak. Gently prize away the obstructions using the blunt end of a matchstick.

Above: Applying a closed ring to a young cockatiel chick. First, bunch the three longest toes carefully together.

Above: With the toes held in place, slide a closed ring of the correct diameter to the centre of the foot.

Above: Pass the ring over the little toe. Be sure to carry out ringing before the foot is too large.

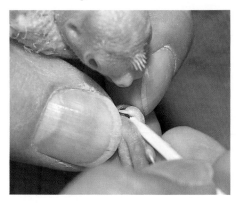

Above: Use a blunt matchstick to free the little toe. Finally, check that the ring slides easily up and down.

Ringing

Healthy parrot chicks grow rapidly, and can be fitted with closed rings by the time they are five days old. This is especially important in the case of exhibition stock. You will not be able to fit closed rings later in the bird's life, simply because the toes will be far too big for the ring to slide over. Ringing is not a difficult task, but you may find it useful to have experienced help available for your first attempt. Gently hold the bird's three longest toes together, and slide the ring over the ball of the foot. Then fold the fourth, smallest, toe up the leg towards the knee and gently move the ring over it – use a matchstick to ease the toe through the band. Once this toe is released, the ring should slide freely, directly above the foot.

It is particularly important to keep careful records when you have a stud of exhibition birds, and it is a good idea to set up a card index, or a computerized record, of the ring numbers, to enable you to identify all your birds and their ancestry. As well as closed aluminium bands, you can also use split celluloid rings of various colours to distinguish between individuals in an aviary. These are more versatile, as they can be fitted at any age, and their contrasting coloration means that you will be able to recognize birds of the same plumage colour easily without having to catch them.

Some budgerigars react badly to closed rings as they get older, and swelling around the ring can occur. If this is the case, you should cut the ring off to prevent the blood supply to the foot being impaired, which can result in gangrene and loss of the toes. A special tool is required to remove the ring, to avoid damage to the bird's leg, and you should seek veterinary help. In most cases the swelling subsides without further problems once the band has been removed.

Infertility

Recent research into the viability of budgerigar eggs has revealed poor levels of fertility. Only about half the eggs in the study hatched (a figure well below that of poultry) and over three quarters of those that failed to hatch were unfertilized, rather than containing chicks which had died in their shells. There are several possible explanations.

The proportion of infertile eggs tends to be higher in birds bred in cages; often, this can be attributed to the incompatibility of individual pairs. Many parrots do form significant pair bonds, and if a pair from an aviary are split up they may be reluctant to accept new partners. Many exhibition breeders house cocks and hens in separate aviaries outside the breeding period, to prevent the formation of strong pair bonds.

The physical changes that have occurred in exhibition budgerigars may also be a cause of infertility. As with canaries, there are two recognizably distinct feather types: 'yellow' and buff. The 'yellow' plumage is relatively soft, whereas the buff-feathered individuals have fairly coarse plumage, which may obscure the vent opening of both cock and hen birds and significantly reduce the likelihood of successful mating. You may have to trim the plumage around the vent carefully before placing buff budgerigars in a breeding cage.

Egg eating

Some pairs of birds acquire the bad habit of destroying their eggs as they are laid. Either the cock or hen can be responsible; you may be able to identify the culprit by yolk stains on the feathers around the beak. If you suspect that the cock is destroying the eggs, remove him from the breeding cage, allowing the hen to continue laying on her own. You may also decide to transfer the eggs to another pair that have laid at around the same time, rather than leaving the hen to rear the chicks on her own. In an emergency, however, she may be able to cope successfully with a few chicks.

If you identify the hen as the culprit, you will need to remove the eggs for fostering, unless you can break this habit. Place one or two dummy eggs, as used by canary breeders, in the nestbox of the egg-eating pair when they have destroyed an egg – the offender will often cease this destructive behaviour, when it is unable to break the dummy egg. In order to safeguard any eggs laid in the meantime, you will need to adapt the nestbox by including a false floor. Cut a hole large enough for the egg to roll through, and support the false floor on a block of wood at each corner, so that it is raised off the floor of the nestbox. Place a thick layer of wood shavings or paper bedding (as used for hamsters) under the false floor, especially directly beneath the hole. When the hen lays her egg, it will roll safely through the hole onto the soft bedding beneath, out of reach. Mark the egg with a small dot using a felt-tip pen, and transfer it to another pair, or an incubator. Since budgerigars will readily accept the eggs, and even the chicks, of other pairs, it is best to use foster parents. Having marked the eggs in this fashion, you will be able to see whether they hatch successfully. Choose a nest with relatively few eggs, at a similar stage of development so that the chicks will hatch almost simultaneously and have an increased chance of survival.

Occasionally, you may find that an egg has been damaged slightly in the nest, for example, if the shell is punctured by the overgrown claws of the parent birds. Repair minor damage by applying nail varnish, or similar, over the area of the crack. Be sure to cover the punctured area fully, but avoid spreading the varnish too widely over the remainder of the shell's surface, as this will block the pores and reduce the chances of successful hatching.

Rearing problems

It is not unusual to encounter problems during the rearing period – not all pairs of parrots make good parents and some will neglect their offspring, often the youngest chicks. If a chick is left, its decline will be irreversible and it will soon die. There are

A CONCAVE ADAPTED TO PREVENT EGG EATING

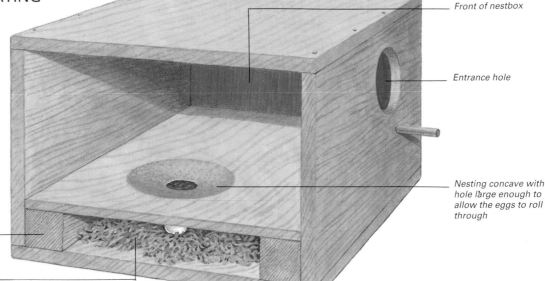

Front of nestbox

Entrance hole

Nesting concave with hole large enough to allow the eggs to roll through

Wood blocks to raise the concave

Thick bedding of sawdust or paper to protect the eggs

several reasons why adult pairs may fail to care for their chicks properly. It may be that the cock is not playing his part and is trying to interfere with the hen instead, or the diet may be inadequate, either because of insufficient variety or because the birds refuse food.

Some cockatoos, notably the Red-tailed and some of the other black species, become insectivorous when they are rearing chicks. You can offer the parent birds mealworms, kept in plain chicken meal, but bear in mind that these larvae of the Meal Beetle (*Tenebrio molitor*) have a rather wide ratio of calcium to phosphorus, which means that they could contribute towards skeletal weakness in the chicks, and are not a nutritionally balanced form of livefood. Tebos, where available, are a suitable alternative. For variety, provide other commercially available livefoods, such as small crickets and locusts – place these in a container in a refrigerator for a few minutes to slow their activity, so that it will be easier for the parrots to catch them.

Young parrots begin to feather up properly by the time they are about three weeks old. The cock bird in some pairs may start to pluck the chicks as they feather up, often starting around the back of the neck. The resulting devastation is often rapid; the chicks can be almost denuded in the space of a morning, so you will need to act quickly. Keep a supply of powdered aloes available for emergencies of this type, and sprinkle the powder over the chick's plumage at the back of the neck and over the wing feathers. The bitter taste of the aloes should deter the cock.

Such behaviour in cocks may be caused by a desire to nest again, feather-plucking being an attempt to drive the first round of chicks from the nest. Only occasionally will hens resort to feather-plucking their chicks. Even if the chicks have been badly plucked, their appearance should improve once they fledge, and the plumage will regrow as normal.

Below: The body plumage of cockatiel chicks is well developed at about 16 days. At this stage, they are vulnerable to feather plucking by the adults.

Hand-rearing chicks

Hand-raising parrot chicks is a demanding occupation, especially as it will be several months before the offspring of the larger species can feed themselves. At first you will need to feed them about every two hours, virtually around the clock, (although a longer gap from about 2 to 6 a.m. is acceptable), to ensure that they always have food in the crop. Although some birdkeepers allow a longer feeding interval, there is a risk that this will adversely affect the growth rate of the chicks over a period of time.

If you are not in a position to hand-raise chicks yourself, seek the assistance of a professional to undertake this for you, either for a fee or a percentage of the chicks. You should be able to find someone offering such a service by personal recommendation, or from advertisements in birdkeeping magazines. It is a good idea to make the necessary enquiries in advance, in case you find yourself in such a situation; for example, if a hen dies suddenly, leaving a clutch of young chicks that the cock will not feed.

Some breeders use a service of this kind on a regular basis, removing the first clutch of eggs from their parrots for artificial incubation, and having the chicks raised by hand. With their eggs taken away shortly after they were laid, the adult pair will be encouraged to nest again quite rapidly, often within a few weeks, and the reproductive potential of a pair is effectively doubled.

If you decide, or need, to incubate and hand-raise chicks yourself, you should start by obtaining a reliable incubator. A number of designs now have a proven track record in hatching parrot eggs, and details can be found in birdkeeping magazines. Forced-air incubators, which rely on a fan to drive warm air through the unit, are more commonly used than still-air types.

The eggs will need to be turned perhaps six times a day to prevent the embryo becoming stuck to its surrounding shell membranes. Choose an incubator that incorporates an automatic turning system, so this can be done without opening the incubator and losing vital heat from the unit. The temperature needs to be maintained in the range 36.9-37.5°C (98.5-99.5°F), and you will need a thermometer that can register changes of 0.5°C (1°F). The relative humidity in the incubator should be kept at 40-50%, and this is usually measured using a wet and dry bulb thermometer, which may be supplied with the incubator.

Once the chicks hatch, maintain them at incubation temperature for the first couple of days or so, before gradually reducing the temperature. You will need a separate brooder, in which to rear the chicks, with an adjustable heat supply, under accurate thermostatic control, and ventilation holes. Transfer the chicks to

Right: Suitable brooders are not widely marketed at present, and you may need to make one if you need to hand-raise chicks. These Grey Parrot chicks are being reared in a wooden brooder.

Above: Hand-feeding a young parakeet chick using a spoon with its edges bent to form a funnel. Special hand-rearing diets are now produced.

the brooder, in clean margarine containers lined with tissues, in small groups to help them maintain their body warmth.

Hand-rearing is much more straightforward than it used to be, as there are now specially-formulated diets available. Previously, breeders were forced to rely on human infant foods, which needed to be diluted with water for feeding chicks. Mix only enough rearing food for one feed, and offer it at a temperature not exceeding about 40°C (105°F). Feed the chick in a warm environment, (so that it does not become chilled while out of the brooder), using a teaspoon with its sides bent to form a funnel. Allow the chick to feed slowly at its own pace; if you rush this procedure the bird may choke. Always wipe the chick's soft beak tissue after a

feed to remove any food deposits before they can harden and cause any malformation. Keep a close watch on the crop and fill it at each feed; by the time the crop has emptied, the chick will be ready for another meal. It is a good idea to weigh the chicks at the same time each day, so that you can monitor their growth.

As the chicks start to feather up, you can add ground sunflower seed kernels to the feeding mixture. As the time for weaning approaches, offer the chicks seeds, which they may play with and start to crack. They will also begin to take less interest in the hand-feeding mixture, and will be difficult to feed with a spoon.

Do not rush to place the chicks in an outside aviary as soon as they are eating independently – they will be used to a warm environment, and will need careful acclimatization. If you intend to breed these young birds, you should keep them together, to prevent them relating more closely to people than to other parrots.

Leaving the nest

Young parrots will start to leave the nest from five weeks old, and the cock bird is largely responsible for feeding them until they are independent. In the meantime, the hen may be incubating her second clutch of eggs. Restrict the birds to a maximum of two or three rounds in a breeding season, so as not to overburden them. This can be harder when breeding is taking place on a colony system, and it may be necessary to transfer hens that have already raised their chicks to separate accommodation for a short period until all breeding activity has ceased. Do not merely close off nestboxes in the aviary, since there is likely to be squabbling over the remaining nesting sites.

Once the chicks are feeding themselves, move them to a flight cage. If you wish, you can then dispose of surplus stock as pets. However, it is very difficult to assess the likely exhibition potential of young parrots until after their first moult. Time spent with the young birds at this stage will be helpful in taming them, so that they will be easier to train for exhibition purposes later in life. Remove chicks reared in the aviary on a colony system as soon as they are independent, so that they do not interfere with their parent's subsequent nesting activities. You can then return them to the aviary, along with any new stock, after all the nestboxes have been removed.

The immediate post-fledging period is the time when signs of French moult are likely to become apparent (see page 12). Watch for any chicks that drop their tail and flight feathers at this stage. Although no treatment is available to cure this viral disease, you should thoroughly disinfect the nestbox, concave and surroundings to avoid spreading the infection, as the virus can be transferred from one nestbox to

Right: Here, at 10 weeks old, the same cockatoo chick is almost weaned. This can be a protracted process with some youngsters; it may help initially if you offer seeds by hand.

Above: This young, three-day-old Leadbeater's Cockatoo is clearly ready to be fed. A chick will not survive long once its crop is empty.

Above: Here the crop of the chick and its food contents are clearly visible. Normally, food is stored in the crop before passing into the digestive tract.

another both by the chicks themselves and also by their droppings. Affected birds are acceptable as pets, but you should house them separately and, obviously, you should not use them as future breeding stock.

Remove affected chicks from the nest to another aviary, or inside flight, as soon as possible after fledging, even though this will create a disturbance if the hen has laid a second clutch. Leave the hen in the flight, and try to catch the chicks in the shelter – this will cause less upset, and avoid the risk of the chicks flying into the mesh, and injuring themselves, a problem particularly prevalent in young Australian parakeets. Alternatively, if you have screened the far end of the flight with conifers or climbing plants, the fledglings will recognize this as a barrier.

GENETICS AT THE CELLULAR LEVEL
– HOW SEX CELLS ARE FORMED

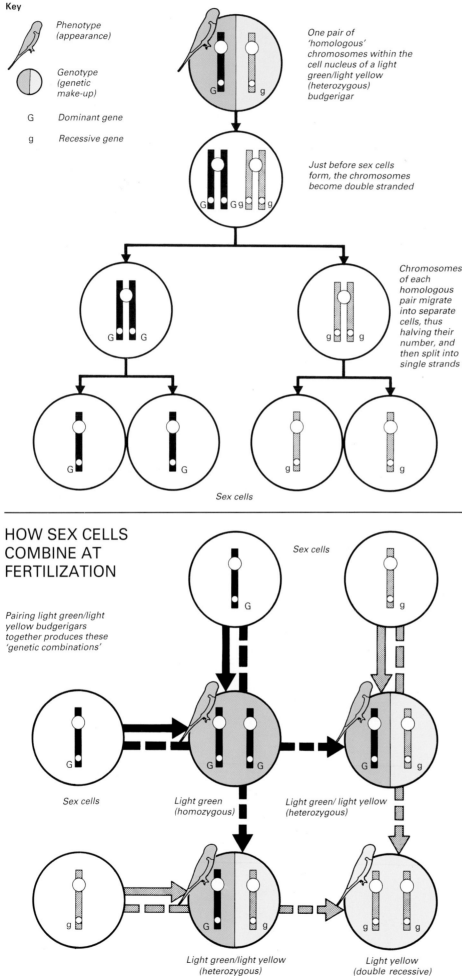

Key

Phenotype (appearance)

Genotype (genetic make-up)

G   Dominant gene

g   Recessive gene

One pair of 'homologous' chromosomes within the cell nucleus of a light green/light yellow (heterozygous) budgerigar

Just before sex cells form, the chromosomes become double stranded

Chromosomes of each homologous pair migrate into separate cells, thus halving their number, and then split into single strands

Sex cells

HOW SEX CELLS COMBINE AT FERTILIZATION

Pairing light green/light yellow budgerigars together produces these 'genetic combinations'

Sex cells

Sex cells

Light green (homozygous)

Light green/light yellow (heterozygous)

Light green/light yellow (heterozygous)

Light yellow (double recessive)

Genetics: heredity and mutations

One of the fascinations of the budgerigar has been the large numbers of colour varieties that have been developed through the years. Now such colours are becoming available in other birds, including lovebirds, cockatiels, ring-necked parakeets and many Australian species in particular. If you want to breed birds with specific colours and markings, it is essential to understand how these characteristics are passed on from one generation to another. Certain colours will start to predominate over a period of time, depending on the original stock. When birds are able to mate in a haphazard fashion, it is impossible to guarantee the parentage of the resulting chicks, and breeding specific colours can be difficult.

This section considers the basic rules of genetics – the 'science of inheritance' – and explains some of the terms commonly used to describe the biological processes, structures and results involved, followed by a number of case studies that are examples of 'genetics in action'.

Basic rules and terms

The basic rules of genetics were first laid down by Gregor Mendel, an Austrian monk who brought the analytical eye of a mathematician to the results of the exhaustive experiments he carried out, initially with pea plants. Working in the mid-1800s, Mendel recorded the inheritance of simple characteristics from one generation to another and developed a series of statistical 'rules' on the basis of the outcome. It was not until the early 1900s that Mendel's pioneering work and the emerging science of cell biology were harnessed into a better understanding of the mechanism of inheritance. Today, when electron microscopes can probe the inner secrets of the cell, Mendel's basic 'laws' of genetics still hold true.

What Mendel knew simply as 'inherited characters' we now recognize as genes on the threadlike chromosomes within the cell nucleus. Chromosomes occur in pairs, and these become separated in the sex cells of the parents (sperm and eggs) and are recombined at conception. This splitting up and recombination process lies at the heart of genetic variation; it allows the genetic 'cards' to be 're-shuffled' in each succeeding generation. As a result, offspring receive genes from both their parents. This does not mean that offspring display a 'mixture' of their parents' characteristics. Quite the opposite, for some genes (and hence characteristics) are dominant over others and these alone may be evident in the physical appearance of the offspring. The two types of genes are 'dominant' and 'recessive'.

There is an important distinction between the genetic make-up – the so-called genotype – of an individual and the outward expression of those genetic characteristics in the physical appearance – the phenotype – of the individual. Thus, two individuals can have the same phenotype (appearance) but different genotypes (combinations of genes).

Where two identical genes for a certain

Above: Genetically, appearances can be deceptive; this light green budgie may carry the recessive gene for yellow.

characteristic occur opposite one another on the paired chromosomes, such as two dominant or two recessive genes, the individual is called homozygous for that characteristic. If the genes are different, the individual is heterozygous, or 'split', for that characteristic.

Just a few more words of explanation will help you to follow the case studies below. There are two kinds of chromosomes in most animal cells: one pair that determine the sex of the individual, the 'sex chromosomes', and the remaining ones, called 'autosomes'. In parrots, there may be 16 pairs of chromosomes in each cell, of which 15 pairs are autosomes, and one pair are sex chromosomes. The parrot's sex chromosomes are designated ZZ for male and ZY for female, the 'Y' chromosome being shorter than the 'Z' chromosome. (This is quite different in humans, where males have the shorter 'Y' chromosome and are designated XY, while females are XX.)

In the accepted notation of genetics, the first generation from a particular pairing is called the F1 generation. If those offspring are paired, the next generation is F2, and so on.

Now let us see how these genetic processes work out in a representative selection of examples.

An autosomal recessive case study

This is the commonest type of mutation, where mutant genes arise on the autosomal chromosomes, rather than on the single pair of sex chromosomes. These genes are considered recessive if pairing the mutant with a light green budgerigar (dominant to all other colours) produces no mutant offspring in the first generation (F1). This supposes that both the recessive and the light green budgerigar are homozygous, i.e. with identical genes on opposing chromosomes. (In effect, 'double dominant' and 'double recessive'.

Alternatively, as we have seen, it is possible for the dominant colour to mask a

gene for the recessive colour on the opposing chromosome, so that although the budgerigar in question appears light green, it is also carrying the recessive characteristic in its genetic make-up, or genotype, and its appearance (phenotype) is not the same as its genotype. Such 'split' birds cannot be distinguished from homozygous individuals, except by breeding results.

In this example, the mutant colour is light yellow. Starting with a light green ('double dominant') paired with a light

yellow ('double recessive'), all the possible pairings are shown. As you can see, if any light yellow offspring arise from mating an apparently normal (i.e. apparently 'double dominant') light green budgerigar with a light yellow budgerigar, then this confirms that the normal is 'split' for light yellow (i.e. carrying one dominant gene and one recessive gene). Furthermore, if two light green budgerigars paired together produce any light yellow offspring, they must both be 'split' for light yellow.

AN AUTOSOMAL RECESSIVE CASE STUDY

These drawings show all the possible pairings, starting with a light green and light yellow budgerigar. The letters A-E refer to the panels, in which the tint reflects the bird's phenotype (appearance)

A	Light green	×	light yellow	→	100% light green/light yellow	
B	Light green/ light yellow	×	light green/ light yellow	→	50% light green/ light yellow	25% light green	25% light yellow
C	Light green/ light yellow	×	light yellow	→	50% light green/ light yellow	50% light yellow	
D	Light green	×	light green/ light yellow	→	50% light green	50% light green/ light yellow	
E	Light yellow	×	light yellow	→	100% light yellow		

A SEX-LINKED RECESSIVE CASE STUDY

Cinnamon cock	× normal hen	→	50% normal/cinnamon cocks		50% cinnamon hens	
Normal cock	× cinnamon hen	→	50% normal/cinnamon cocks		50% normal hens	
Cinnamon cock	× cinnamon hen	→	100% cinnamon			
Normal/ cinnamon cock	× normal hen	→	25% normal cocks	25% normal/ cinnamon cocks	25% normal hens	25% cinnamon hens
Normal/ cinnamon cock	× cinnamon hen	→	25% normal/ cinnamon cocks	25% cinnamon cocks	25% normal hens	25% cinnamon hens

A DOMINANT CASE STUDY

Spangle light green (df)	× light green	→	100% spangle light green (sf)		
Spangle light green (sf)	× light green	→	50% spangle light green (sf)	50% light green	
Spangle light green (df)	× spangle light green (df)	→	100% spangle light green (df)		
Spangle light green (sf)	× spangle light green (sf)	→	50% spangle light green (sf)	25% spangle light green (df)	25% light green
Spangle light green (df)	× spangle light green (sf)	→	50% spangle light green (df)	50% spangle light green (sf)	

A sex-linked recessive case study
Here, the recessive mutation affects genes located on the pair of sex chromosomes. Because the hen has sex chromosomes of different length (ZY), there will only be one gene to consider rather than two, and she cannot be split for a mutation of this type, since there is no corresponding gene on the opposite short Y chromosome. Therefore her phenotype must correspond with her genotype. In order to maximize the number of sex-linked mutant offspring, it is vital to concentrate on keeping cocks of the required colour, since, in pairings with normals, a relatively higher number of mutant chicks can be produced. The possible pairings and the results are shown below.

A dominant case study
In a few instances, mutations have arisen that are dominant to light green. Thus the dominant feature can arise in the first generation, following pairing to a homozygous light green. Dominance may be either single factor (sf), (if just one of the chromosomes in the pair is affected), or double factor (df), (when both members of the pair carry dominant genes). It is only possible to distinguish between single and double factor individuals if normal chicks result in the first generation of a pairing to a homozygous light green; if they do, the budgerigar in question is a single factor bird. The most recent dominant mutation is the spangle, which affects the markings. Budgerigars with normal markings cannot be 'split' for this characteristic, as the normal light green characteristic is recessive to the spangle.

Crested mutations
There are three different mutations of crested budgerigars, all of which are dominant in their mode of inheritance, but there is also a lethal factor associated with them which precludes the survival of double factor birds of this form. As a result, all crested budgerigars are single factor, and the standard pairing in this particular case is:
Crest (sf) × normal → 50% crest (sf) + 50% normal.

Crested budgerigars are never mated together, because this automatically means that the anticipated 25% of double factor birds are not viable, reducing the overall hatchability. In other respects, crested budgerigars present no difficulties in terms of their care and breeding.

Incomplete dominance
Where there is no clear dominance, it is possible to distinguish visually between single and double factor birds. This applies to the so-called 'dark factor', which exerts a darkening influence on the budgerigar's coloration. The presence of a single dark factor in the green series birds produces the dark green, while the double factor counterpart is described as olive green. Their respective equivalents in blue series birds are cobalt and mauve. Apart from this difference in coloration, their projected pairings are identical to those set out under the dominant case study above.

Right: A cinnamon Cockatiel (hen). Like the cinnamon form of the Budgerigar, this is a sex-linked recessive mutation.

How the colours are formed

It is now virtually impossible to calculate how many different varieties of budgerigars can be produced – it could well be over a million – and it is this variety which is one of the reasons for their popularity. Mutations and colour combinations are also now well-established in both the Cockatiel and the Peach-faced Lovebird, with a growing number also recorded in the commonly kept grass parakeets. The way in which these mutations affect the plumage is similar in all cases.

The change in coloration results from genetic alterations to the distribution of colour pigments within the feathers. As is apparent from the diagram opposite, yellow pigment is normally present within the outer part of the feather. Beneath this is a reflective layer that creates the impression of blue coloration, although in reality there is no blue pigment as such. Cockatiels lack this 'blue' pigment (and there is a similar lack of the blue pigment layer in cockatoos, which explains the rather limited range of colours in this group of parrots, and the fact that they have no green or blue plumage).

Under normal circumstances, the combination of yellow and blue produces green feathering. When visible yellow pigment is absent, the body coloration appears blue and the face becomes white. Since the Cockatiel lacks the blue layer, its coloration is restricted to shades of yellow or grey (see above).

Dark coloration results from the pigment known as melanin, which is located in the centre of the feathering. When melanin is diluted, the black markings become brown and the black eyes lighten to a plum colour. Absence of melanin produces the bright yellow appearance of the lutino. This is more muted in the Cockatiel than in other species; in lutino budgerigars even the dark mask is missing (in contrast to the light yellow, where sufficient melanin pigment is retained, so the eyes are black rather than red). When both yellow and melanin pigment are absent, the so-called albino results. Albino budgerigars may have a bluish tinge in certain lights, and this is due to of the presence of the blue layer.

In pied birds, there is a variable and sporadic absence of dark pigment over the body, so that individual birds can vary quite widely in appearance. Some will be much more yellow, whereas others will closely resemble normals, having just a trace of yellow in among green plumage. It is impossible to predict the distribution and extent of pied markings.

Primary mutations can be divided into three basic categories. There are those that affect the bird's coloration, such as the sky blue mutation in the case of the Budgerigar. Then there are those that are confined to the wing markings and body patterning, such as the cinnamon or pearl mutations, and the yellow-faced characteristic in budgies. The final category of mutations create feather variants. These are least known in psittacines; only in the crested and long-flighted budgerigar mutations has there been any noticable change to the bird's physical appearance

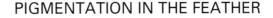

PIGMENTATION IN THE FEATHER

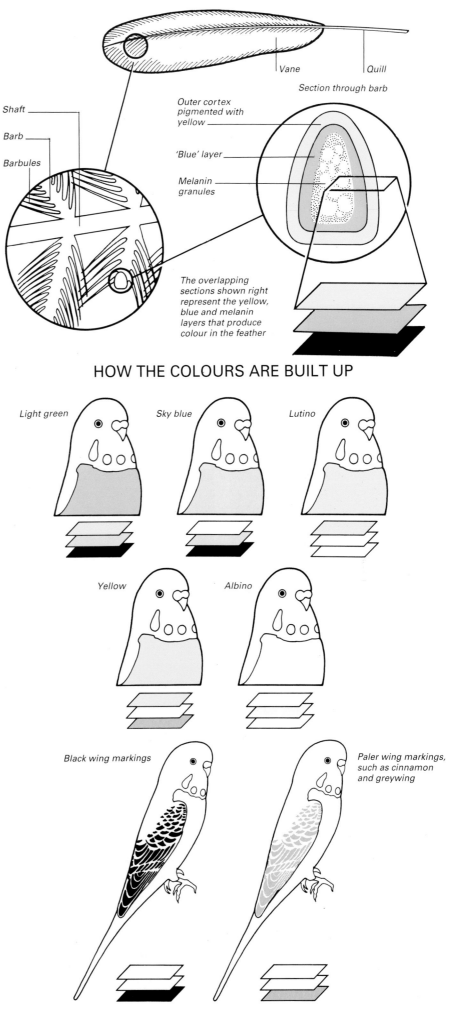

Vane   *Quill*

Section through barb

Shaft

Barb

Barbules

Outer cortex pigmented with yellow

'Blue' layer

Melanin granules

The overlapping sections shown right represent the yellow, blue and melanin layers that produce colour in the feather

HOW THE COLOURS ARE BUILT UP

Light green

Sky blue

Lutino

Yellow

Albino

Black wing markings

Paler wing markings, such as cinnamon and greywing

THE BUDGERIGAR

The budgerigar is the most popular pet bird in the world and is now found in a vast selection of different colour combinations. What is perhaps less well-known is the fact that the budgie's appearance has altered quite dramatically over the years through selective breeding; wild birds are much slimmer and smaller than their domestic counterparts. Relatively few colour mutations have arisen in recent years, but the spangle, which emerged in the 1970s, has excited considerable attention among budgerigar fanciers around the world. As new colours have emerged, however, some have also been lost.

Green

Light green is the normal coloration of the budgerigar. This has been so widely used in the development of other mutations that it can be difficult to obtain pure light greens. Indeed, the mating of two light green budgerigars usually gives rise to various other colours in the chicks. The emergence of the dark factor (a gene that literally 'darkens' the colour of the budgerigar) in 1915 meant that it was then possible to obtain greens of three shades: light green, dark green and olive green. Pairing dark greens together is the most versatile option in terms of colour production since, in theory, all three shades of green should be represented among the offspring.

Combining olive and yellow features has given rise to budgerigars with a body coloration of an overall mustard shade. Cere coloration is normal and the feet are greyish in colour. The popularity of some varieties, including the olive yellow, has declined over recent years.

Below left: **Normal light green**
This is the natural colour form of the budgerigar, but it is now quite difficult to obtain pure light greens. Wild individuals tend to be much smaller than their domestic counterparts.

Below: **Normal olive green**
This colour variety represents a darkening of the normal light green shade. This particular bird is showing early signs of scaly face; note the whitish areas on the upper bill.

Below: **Normal dark green**
These budgies are of a laurel shade, between the light and olive green in colour. There is also a violet form of the dark green.

Grey

Two forms of grey mutation have been recorded: the recessive form, which was evolved in England, and the now widely kept Australian grey, which proved to be a dominant mutation and rapidly became established after first appearing during the 1930s. The English variety declined once the dominant greys became available in 1937, and it appears to have become extinct during the Second World War, although it could re-emerge in the future. Combining the dominant grey and light green has made it possible to evolve the grey green, which shows some similarity to an olive, although it is paler and tends to have a more even coloration.

Below left: **Normal grey green**
Budgerigars of this colour are similar to the olive green but can be easily distinguished from the latter by their jet black rather than deep blue tails.

Above: **Normal grey**
Two varieties used to exist, but it now appears that all greys are dominant. Slight differences in the depth of coloration may be noted between individual birds.

Below: **Cinnamon grey green**
Other mutations can be superimposed on changes to body coloration. The cinnamon grey green has deep brown tail feathers.

Blue

Blue budgerigars have always been popular, since the first examples were exhibited during 1910 in London. The sky blue arose just over 30 years earlier, in Belgium. The stock available to British breeders found a ready market, but because they were apparently reluctant to pair these birds with any other colour, the fertility of the blue budgerigar appears to have declined until the mid 1920s. Once the effects of the dark factor were appreciated, however, it was possible to develop cobalts (with one dark factor present) and mauves, which are darker in colour and possess two dark factors in their genetic make-up.

At this stage, the coloration of the facial area was white. The yellow-faced characteristic did not emerge until the late 1930s, although it may well have existed before this time. Two distinctive forms developed, often described as yellow-faced blue types I and II, with the former variety having lighter coloration than the latter. The deepest coloured individuals are now sometimes described as being golden-faced.

*Below: **Normal cobalt***
This form is bred by combining the dark factor and blue mutations and is one of the most popular colours.

Above: **Yellow-faced cobalt**
It used to be thought impossible to combine yellow and blue on one bird, but the yellow-faced cobalt is now a popular variety.

Below: **Yellow-faced sky blue**
The yellow-faced characteristic has proved to be dominant. Originally, several different forms of this variety could be recognized.

Above: **Normal sky blue**
Blue budgerigars have always been popular, since the sky blue mutation first appeared in Belgium in 1882, but it was only developed slowly.

Violet

Although this is accepted as a colour in its own right, ideally a deep purplish shade, the violet mutation is a separate dominant character. Violet budgerigars only result when this mutation is combined with both blue and dark factor characteristics. When combined with green series budgerigars, it will give rise to violet dark greens. These are distinguishable from the normal variety by their darker, and often more yellowish, coloration. Violet greens, although nowhere near as popular as the visual violet, can be of great value in improving the overall depth of coloration of violet chicks when crossed with blue series stock. Visual violet coloration can also be featured on both dominant and recessive pieds and in combination with many different forms of markings.

Right: **Normal (visual) violet**
The deep violet coloration of these budgies makes them one of the most popular colour forms. They were first bred in the late 1920s.

Below: **Yellow-faced mauve**
Mauve budgerigars, first developed in about 1924, are the blue series equivalent of the olive green; both are double dark factor.

Lutino

This is one of the most popular colours, being an attractive rich shade of yellow, with red eyes. Its cere, beak and leg coloration match that of the albino. Lutinos were bred on several occasions during the last century, but this mutation was not finally established until the 1930s, in the aviaries of German breeders. Although there was an autosomal recessive form of the lutino, all birds now in existence are of the sex-linked recessive variety. The lutino is the green series counterpart of the albino, and thus some birds may show a faint green tinge to their plumage, which is considered a show fault.

Below: **Lutinos**
The cere of the adult cock of this pair is purplish rather than the more normal blue. The hen's cere is the usual brownish colour, so it is still possible to sex lutinos easily.

Albino

This is the red-eyed white, which first emerged in Austria during 1931. Albino budgerigars are pure white in colour, with pink legs, reddish eyes and a pale yellowish beak. They should show as little trace of blue suffusion in their plumage as possible. Adult cocks have purplish, rather than blue, ceres; hens have brown ceres.

Exhibition albinos still tend to be relatively small, and are less common than the lutino, which is dominant in terms of inheritance when these two mutations are paired. The albino characteristic in budgerigars is sex-linked, although for a period there was said to be an autosomal recessive form, which could emerge again in the future.

White

This mutation, white with black eyes, has a similar history to that of the lutino, but did not emerge until 1920. It is smaller than its yellow counterparts and has never achieved the same popularity.

Yellow

The black-eyed variety of the yellow was certainly in existence before the end of the last century, but has faded in popularity with the rise of the lutino. Such birds can be easily distinguished by their black eyes and dark feet, as well

as by the normal blue cere of the cock birds. Throat spots are absent, with the coloration of the cheek patches being mauve, rather than white as in a lutino.

Dark-eyed clears

These 'clear' yellow or 'clear' white budgerigars originated in Europe towards the end of the 1940s, and were first described as lutinos and albinos with black eyes. This information proved incorrect, however, since they had plum-coloured eyes, reflecting the role of the Danish recessive pied in their ancestry. It is possible to breed dark-eyed clears by pairing these pieds with dominant continental clear-flights in the first generation, then mating the clear-flighted offspring back to the recessive pieds. These birds have not become very popular, partly because it has proved difficult to increase their size because of the Danish recessive pied stock used in their development.

Right: **Dark-eyed clear yellow**
These budgerigars, developed using Danish recessive pieds, are distinguishable from the lutino by their plum rather than red eyes.

Below: **Albino**
This pure white budgerigar should show as little blue as possible in its plumage.

Pied (dominant)

Pied budgerigars show a combination of coloured and clear areas in their plumage, and it is possible to distinguish between dominant and recessive forms visually as well as genetically. The Australian dominant pied was first bred near Sydney in 1935, and became available in Europe during the late 1950s. These birds resembled normals, in terms of their black eye coloration and white irides, with throat spots and cheek flashes present. In some cases, the clear area of plumage forms a distinctive band across the front of the body, with the wings being clear from this point downwards. These birds are described as banded pieds, in contrast to those in which the patterning is more random.

As a dominant mutation, these pieds rapidly increased in numbers, but crossings with the Danish recessive pied left an indelible mark, which has still not been fully eliminated even today. These crossings have affected the head markings, specifically the mask, with the loss of throat spots and some variation in cere coloration also being apparent.

Left: **Dark green dominant pied**
Green of any shade can be combined with yellow. The extent of the pied markings can be quite variable, even between nestmates.

Below: **Sky blue dominant pied**
Any shade of blue coloration can be offset against areas of white plumage. Yellow-faced blue and grey pieds can also be bred.

Pied (recessive)

This mutation had arisen by 1932, when a pied budgerigar of this variety was exhibited at a show in Copenhagen, Denmark. As a result, they became known as Danish recessive pieds. This being an autosomal recessive mutation, breeders at first tended to pair their birds together rather than outcrossing them to normals, the latter yielding no pied offspring in the first generation. Danish recessive pieds were much more slender than their dominant counterparts, and this trend is still apparent today.

They have plum-coloured eyes with no apparent irides, even when adult, and cocks have purplish mauve, rather than blue, ceres. The number of spots present in the mask is a variable feature. They can be bred in the full range of colours, including dark factor combinations, such as the olive green recessive pied, where the clear yellow body plumage and darker markings are offset against olive green areas. (The depth of yellow coloration is not influenced by the shade of green, being a rich canary yellow in all cases.)

Right: **Grey green recessive pied**
The wings should be mainly free from black markings in these pieds, ideally extending over less than 20 percent of the wing area.

Below: **Dark green recessive pied**
These pieds can be bred in all the usual colour combinations. They tend to be more nervous than their dominant counterparts.

Right: **Cobalt recessive pied**
The number of throat spots present in these recessive pieds is a variable feature, ranging from one to a full complement of six.

Cinnamon

This mutation is a sex-linked recessive characteristic and first arose in 1931. It alters the markings, causing them to be brown, rather than black, and the chicks' eye coloration becomes a deep shade of plum red. Although at first known as the cinnamonwing, this became shortened just to cinnamon. This feature can be combined with both blue and green series birds. Various forms of the cinnamon mutation have arisen in different parts of the world, from Australia to the USA.

The characteristic plum-coloured eyes can be seen in chicks as soon as they hatch and using this facet of the cinnamon mutation can be a very valuable way of sexing the chicks of certain pairings. Pairing a cinnamon cock with a normal hen is a good example, since the cinnamons (i.e. with plum-coloured eyes) in the resulting nest must be hens and all the remaining birds must be cocks.

Below: **Cinnamon light green**
The cinnamon mutation reduces the concentration of melanin, changing black markings to brown.

Above: **Cinnamon sky blue**
The modified wing and tail coloration, with the characteristic brown tinge, is clearly shown here.

Below: **Cinnamon yellow-faced sky blue**
Note the cinnamon-brown throat spots, matching the wing markings.

Pied (clear-flighted)

In this variety the flight feathers are clear (i.e. yellow in green series and white in blue series birds). There appear to be distinctive continental and Australian strains, but they are not especially popular.

Right: **Opaline cinnamon grey**
It has proved possible to combine more than one mutation affecting the wing markings on a single bird, as shown by this example.

Far right:
Opaline cinnamon yellow-faced grey
An attractive colour combination, underlining the wide diversity of varieties that can now be bred.

Below:
Clear-flighted sky blue dominant pied
Clear-flighted budgerigars of all the normal colours can be bred. Green series birds have yellow flight and tail feathers, whereas those of blue or grey budgies are white, as here.

start

Left: **Greywing cobalt** (left) and **greywing light green** (right)
The overall coloration of these budgerigars is paler than normal. The greywing light green was first bred in 1925, when it was known as the apple green. The blue form appeared three years later.

Below: **Greywing sky blue**
In this mutation, the black markings on the wings and body are reduced to grey, and the body coloration is lightened.

Greywing
As their name suggests, here the black markings of the normal budgerigar are diluted to grey, with the body coloration tending to be relatively unaffected. It is possible that this mutation may have arisen as long ago as 1918.

Whitewing
A member of the so-called clearwing group, this mutation alters the coloration on the wings, so that they become virtually white, with very little trace of melanin apparent. Again, the body coloration is essentially unaffected. By combining the yellow-face characteristic with opaline and clearwing features, it has proved possible to produce the striking and much sought-after rainbow budgerigar.

Below: **Whitewing sky blue**
The wing markings of the whitewing are paler than those of the greywing. The body coloration of this bird is that of the normal sky blue.

Yellow-wing

Here, the yellow wing markings (virtually free of melanin) create an attractive contrast with the green body coloration, especially in dark factor birds. This mutation can also be combined with the opaline characteristic, yielding opaline yellow-wing dark greens and other colours. The yellow-wing characteristic is recessive to the ordinary green, so all offspring from a pairing of this kind will be split for the yellow-wing markings (i.e. they appear light green but carry the recessive gene for yellow-wing). Yellow-wing budgerigars will be produced if these chicks in turn are paired with yellow-wing stock.

As with mating green and blue budgerigars together, so the yellow-wing mutation is dominant to the whitewing, with all offspring of a yellow-wing × whitewing pairing being yellow-wing/whitewing (split). (You can work out the possible combinations by substituting these features for green and blue in the table on page 73.)

*Right: **Lacewing yellow** (left); **yellow-wing dark green** (right)*
The yellow-wing characteristic can be combined with any shade of green; this variety is one of the most striking. The lacewing was first bred in 1946.

Lacewing

This is one of the few budgerigar mutations to have emerged since the Second World War. The lacewing has proved to be sex-linked characteristic affecting red-eyed budgerigars, creating a lace-like pattern of pale brown markings on their wings, with throat spots and coloured cheek patches also being present. Lacewings are not presently among the most common varieties. Although at first they were believed to be the result of the introduction of cinnamon blood, this has now been disproved and lacewings are accepted as a separate variety.

Opaline

This pattern of markings is very common, with the mutation arising in both Australia and Europe during the early 1930s. In opalines the barring on the head is less prominent, and in a well-marked individual there is a V-shaped area on the back free of markings. The darker plumage is thus confined solely to the wings and does not extend from the base of the neck downwards, as is the case in normally marked budgerigars.

The appearance of some opalines is spoilt by the presence of excess barring or flecking on the forehead, which should be clear. This fault is most common in grey budgerigars, with or without yellow faces, but can be seen in other colour varieties as well.

The opaline is a sex-linked characteristic and can be combined with many other mutations, even pieds. In this case, the markings may be further broken down, noticeably over the wings.

*Above: **Yellow-wing light green***
This is a young cock. Pairing yellow-wings with whitewings can improve their coloration. Both mutations are known as clearwings.

*Below: **Opaline dark green***
The three original forms of the opaline mutation all appeared in the early 1930s, in Scotland, Belgium and Australia. This has proved to be a sex-linked mutation.

Above: **Opaline (visual) violet**
Scottish opalines often show an excess of barring, especially at the back of the neck, where a clear V-shaped area is desirable in exhibition birds.

Right: **Opaline yellow-faced cobalt**
The opaline characteristic can be combined with any colour. It is often difficult to produce opalines with the clear V shape, however.

Above: **Opaline sky blue dominant pied**
Even when combined with a dominant mutation, the opaline markings still remain a sex-linked recessive feature.

Right: **Opaline yellow-faced sky blue dominant pied**
The normally white areas of plumage have a pale lemon coloration on this cock budgerigar. This is a feature shared with all yellow-faced blue pied mutations. Note the less prominent barring on the head of both this bird and the opaline sky blue dominant pied.

Fallow

Green series fallows can be especially striking in coloration, with their dark red eyes and golden yellow body plumage contrasting with greenish brown markings and throat spots. Three different forms of this mutation are known to have occurred, firstly in the United States during 1931. This line appears not to have been established, however, and it is the German strain that is best known. These budgerigars were bred at about the same time as those in the United States, and descriptions suggest that they were similar in appearance. Slightly later, in 1933, the Australian fallow mutation was reported. Since then fallows have tended to decline in numbers in Europe, although they are still common in Australia.

Below: **Cinnamon English fallow light green** (bottom) **and cinnamon English fallow sky blue** (top)

Left: **English fallow light green**
Below: **English fallow dark green**
The distinction between English fallows and the German form is seen in the eyes; these birds lack irises.

Above: **German fallow sky blue**
English and German fallows are now better known than other fallow varieties. The German form can be distinguished from the English by the iris.

Spangle

The latest budgerigar mutation to be recorded, the spangle has become very widely known since it was first reported from Australia during 1978. This mutation appears to exert a similar effect to that of the pearl recognized in cockatiels (see page 101). The plumage over the wings is light in the centre, with attractive dark edging around the individual feathers. The flight feathers and tail are similar, while even the throat spots have pale centres.

As a dominant mutation, it has proved possible to build up the number of spangle budgerigars rapidly. Dark factor spangles are most impressive in terms of their markings, and doubtless this mutation will continue to attract considerable interest. A specialist society devoted to these budgerigars was formed during 1987 in the UK.

*Left: **Spangle grey***
The striking spangle is the latest budgerigar mutation and has become widely available.

*Above: **Spangle sky blue***
The keen interest shown in this new mutation has enabled it to be combined with a wide range of colour varieties.

*Overleaf: **Spangle mauve** (top) and **Spangle cobalt** (bottom).*

Crested

Three distinctive forms of crested budgerigar can be produced. The full-circular has an even crest positioned centrally on the head, reaching down to, but not obscuring, the eyes or the cere. The effect resembles that of a Corona Gloster Canary. The half-circular is similar in appearance, but the crest extends only forwards from a point above the eyes towards the beak. The third form of crest is the tufted, where the plumage above the cere is raised to form a tuft.

Although crested budgerigars have been known since the 1920s in Australia, there has been relatively little interest shown in them and they remain quite scarce. Nevertheless, these crested characteristics can be combined with any chosen colour or variety, which offers considerable scope for the dedicated breeder. Crested budgerigars should not be paired together.

Above: **Half-circular crested sky blue**
One of three distinctive types of crest recognized in budgerigars.

Right: **Tufted grey green**
Tufted budgerigars, first bred in Australia, are the most common form of the crested varieties. The tuft should be well shaped.

Below: **Full-circular crested opaline**
An even, well-positioned crest is required in this, the rarest, form.

THE COCKATIEL

Cockatiels were first seen in Europe during the 1830s, some 40 years after their discovery, but it was not until the 1950s that cockatiel mutations first started to appear. During recent years, cockatiels have built up a strong international following, with numerous colours now established and new colour combinations continually being developed. Their appeal is not hard to understand, as they are neither noisy nor destructive, and breed readily. Cockatiels can be housed together or in the company of other gentle birds. As pets, they will soon learn to talk and can become very tame.

Cinnamon

This mutation was established in Belgium by the late 1960s, and breeders in Europe (but not in the UK) still sometimes refer to it as the Isabelle. Cinnamons can vary quite widely in depth of coloration, with adult cocks being darker because of the presence of more melanin in their plumage.

A warm, even shade of cinnamon is usually preferred. Both the legs and eyes are lighter in coloration than those of normal cockatiels. Sexing birds is simple after the first moult, with cocks acquiring dark rather than barred undersides to their tail feathers.

Below: **Normal greys**
An adult pair. The cock on the right can be easily distinguished from the hen by its bright yellow facial markings.

Above: **Cinnamon hen**
These birds have a warm, brownish tinge to their plumage. Adult hens retain their barred tail feathers.

Left: **Cinnamon cock**
Some cinnamon cockatiels are much paler than others. This is a sex-linked mutation.

Above:
Primrose pearl (lacewing) cinnamon
Attractive coloration combines with delicate markings in this hen bird.

Above: **Dilute cinnamon pied hen**
Here, the cinnamon coloration is reduced in intensity, producing an elegant 'creamy' coloured bird.

Above: **Pearl (lacewing) cinnamon**
Sexing may be more difficult in pearl forms because of the partial absence of melanin. This is a hen.

Above:
Double-factor dominant silver cock
Lighter in coloration than the single-factor dominant silver, this is an increasingly popular mutation.

Dominant silver

The most recent cockatiel mutation, the dominant silver, is also the only one to date to have emerged in the UK. It was discovered by chance in a pet shop during 1979, by a keen breeder. He was able to trace the original pair that had produced this unusual cockatiel, only to discover that the cock had died. But pairing the young cock back to its mother yielded three further silver offspring in 1980. All proved to be cocks. Then, by a careful process of inbreeding (pairing closely related birds together) and outcrossing (introducing unrelated cockatiels to the breeding stock), the mutation was successfully developed.

Dominant silver cockatiels are likely to become increasingly common in the near future. Their silver coloration is darkish around the base of the neck, extending up onto the head, whereas their yellow and orange markings are unaffected. They cannot be separated from normals in the nest until they start to feather up. Silvers then appear paler, with a brownish tinge to their plumage, while their eyes and legs are black. Adult coloration is assumed at the first moult, although some hens may remain slightly darker than cocks. Selective breeding may lead to paler strains.

Single- and double-factor dominant silver cockatiels can be separated by their coloration. Double-factor birds are

Left: **Single-factor dominant silver cock**
This single factor form is more common and darker in coloration than the double-factor. Facial markings are retained.

significantly lighter than single-factor birds, being similar to a lutino, but with a grey overlay. They retain the darker head markings, and the black coloration of the eyes and feet.

Mating dominant silvers with other mutations will, in the first instance, produce splits that can then be used to develop other colour varieties. One of the most striking created to date has been the white-faced dominant silver, in which all trace of yellow and orange plumage is absent. This has been named

platinum, in view of its metallic coloration. It is likely to become increasingly common in the future.

Below left:
Single-factor dominant silver hen
This single-factor hen bird is recognizable by its greyish face.

Below right:
White-faced dominant silver cock
A recent mutation with metallic coloration, also known as the platinum.

Fallow

Since its first appearance in 1971, in the collection of a Florida breeder, this mutation has tended to remain better known in the United States than in Europe. Fallow cockatiels have red eyes and a greyish yellow body coloration that distinguishes them from cinnamons. The mode of inheritance is also different because this is an autosomal recessive, rather than a sex-linked recessive mutation. Coloration varies: cocks are generally darker.

Lutino

Undoubtedly, the most popular cockatiel mutation, the lutino also originated in the United States. It arose in the aviaries of a Florida breeder in 1958 and the strain was then developed successfully by another breeder, Mrs Moon.
Although these early 'moonbeams' sold for vast sums of money, lutinos are now available at low cost, having been bred in vast numbers around the world.

Until the emergence of the genuine albino, breeders often used to describe lutinos incorrectly under this name, or sometimes as whites. Because they lack just the melanin pigment, however, these birds are, by definition, lutinos. Part of the reason for the confusion stemmed from the pale coloration, bordering on white, of many lutinos. Those that show the darkest shade of yellow are usually preferred.

It is possible to influence the depth of coloration to some extent by choosing the best-coloured individuals and pairing these together. In order to indicate the depth of coloration, breeders sometimes use 'primrose' and 'buttercup' as prefixes, and describe the darker coloured cockatiels as buttercup lutinos. A truly rich yellow colour is, however, rarely achieved in practice.

A genetic flaw closely associated with the lutino mutation is the presence of a bald patch on the head, immediately behind the crest. Do not pair such cockatiels together, otherwise this characteristic will soon become widespread throughout your stud.

It is also possible to create attractive pearl lutinos, which were first bred during the mid-1970s. If you buy a single pearl lutino, make sure that you obtain a cock bird. Then, when you pair this bird with a lutino hen, you will breed pearl lutino hens and lutino cocks split for pearl. No visual pearl lutinos will result from the reverse pairing.

Left: **Lutino**
Carefully studying the underside of the tails of lutinos is the only way to sex adult birds accurately. Barring is still present in hens. Rare at first, this popular form is now widely available.

Below: **Pearl lutinos**
In lutino birds, no melanin pigment is present, hence the attractive yellow coloration. The pearl mutation provides the deeper yellow markings which, here, is most apparent on the wings.

Pearl

The pearl cockatiel was first bred in 1967 in West Germany. The scalloped patterning can be very variable; it may be confined largely to the back and wings, or it can extend onto the breast as well. Where melanin is absent from the centre of the individual feathers, this area can vary in colour from white through to yellow, and the cockatiels are then described either as silver or golden pearls. There is no consistency in this regard; chicks of both types may appear in the same nest. The situation is further complicated by the use of the term 'lacewing' to describe pearl cockatiels with more elongated markings.

Until recently, it was accepted that cock pearl cockatiels lost their distinctive markings when they moulted into adult plumage, by about nine months old. However, it now appears that in the USA selective breeding has led to the development of a strain in which adult cock birds do not produce more melanin. They therefore retain their pearl markings even when mature.

The pearl form of the cinnamon is an attractive colour variant and can be bred in a similar fashion.

Above left: **Pearl hen**
The pearl markings result from a shortage of melanin in the centre of individual feathers. Hens retain their appearance, but adult pearl cocks often moult out like normals.

Above right: **Pearl silver cock**
In this cock bird, pearl markings and the silver mutation combine to produce this unusually coloured bird. Establishing new colour combinations is a relatively quick process in the case of cockatiels because they can breed at a year old. (This cockatiel is moulting.)

Pied

Pieds, the oldest of the cockatiel
mutations, were being bred in California
as long ago as 1949. Unfortunately, it is
impossible to predict the extent of the
pied markings. While some birds are
very similar to normals, others may be
recognized by the presence of just a few
grey feathers in otherwise pale yellow
plumage. The trend among birdkeepers
appears to favour pieds in which one
quarter of the plumage is dark grey and
the remainder is clear. Symmetry of the
markings is also preferred, but is difficult
to achieve.

It can also be difficult to sex pieds,
because the pied markings may obscure
the usual plumage differences.
Nevertheless, cock birds can usually be
recognized by their characteristic song.
Various colour combinations have now
been developed, with cinnamon pieds
being among the most attractive. If you
pair a pied cinnamon cock to a normal
pied hen, half the resulting offspring
should be pied cinnamon hens, which
can be sexed at this stage. The other
chicks will be normal pied cocks, all split
for the cinnamon characteristic.

Pearl pieds have also been bred, as

Above: Pearl pieds
A pair, with the adult cock on the right
showing the typical loss of pearling. This
results from the greater production of
melanin after the bird matures.

have pearl pied cinnamons, which
combine all three mutations. The latter
variety was first produced in Texas in
1980, but it has proved difficult to
balance the markings as required for
show purposes. Pairing a pearl cock split
for cinnamon to a pearl pied hen should
result in a proportion of the offspring
being of this particular variety.

Below:
Primrose pearl cinnamon pieds
An attractive pair, but their chicks may be more heavily marked.

Above: **Primrose pied cock**
The term 'primrose' is used to describe cockatiels that have a light shade of yellow coloration.

Below: **White-faced pied**
The pied markings on this cock bird show as white areas, and in this bird the beak is also affected.

Recessive silver

Silver cockatiels have a long history. They were first recorded in New Zealand at the start of the 1950s, but that strain was never established and today's recessive silvers are of European origin.

Here they were bred in the latter years of the 1960s, but the original examples were often afflicted with blindness from an early age. Their eye coloration is red, which distinguishes them visually from the dominant silver cockatiel.

The problem of blindness has been overcome, but this recessive mutation remains scarce. Its development is likely to suffer further as a result of the establishment of the dominant silver, which is genetically easier to breed.

Below: **White-faced cinnamon pied hen**
Here, the presence of scattered white feathers over the bird's wings, outside the normal white area, confirms that it is a pied. The tail barring is also white. It is impossible to estimate the extent of pied markings on resulting youngsters when pairing adults; some birds will show greater areas of white than others.

Above left: **White-faced hen**
This autosomal recessive mutation is becoming more common. Hens have greyish faces and barred tail markings.

Above right: **White-faced cock**
Yellow and orange markings are absent from the plumage in this mutation. The male is recognizable by its white face.

Below: **Albino**
This is one of the most recent and highly prized colour varieties, bred using white-faced and lutino stock. These birds are pure white, as they lack all colour pigment. Current strains appear quite prolific and, unlike some albino forms, they grow as large as normals. Their popularity seems assured.

White-faced

The development of this mutation is equivalent to the breeding of a blue budgerigar, and has paved the way for the subsequent development of the albino cockatiel. The white-faced was first recorded in Holland in about 1969. By the late 1970s it had been bred in Germany, and had also reached the UK.

Although the yellow coloration and orange cheek patches are absent in this mutation, it is still possible to sex adults easily. Most hens have barred tails and greyish rather than white faces. A possible exception may exist among white-faced pieds, where this coloration can be disrupted.

Various other combinations have been developed, including cinnamon and pearl forms. The most significant is the albino, which was probably first bred in Germany in about 1980. This variety is the result of combining white-faced and lutino cockatiels in two stages. First, mate a lutino cock to a white-faced hen, to yield lutino/white-faced hens. It is also necessary to pair a white-faced/lutino cock to a lutino hen, producing lutino/white-faced cocks. Pairing these offspring together should produce a one-in-four chance of breeding an albino in this second generation.

Because the combination of chromosomes occurs entirely by chance, you may find more than one albino in a nest or, on the other hand, you may find none. However, the likelihood of an albino chick is increased as more chicks are produced, so over a breeding season you would be unlucky not to breed at least one albino bird.

Other colours

Cockatiels showing other markings and coloration have been recorded from time to time, but none appear established. It may be that some plumage changes are the result of metabolic disturbances and are not of genetic origin, so they cannot be described as true mutations. This probably explains the occasional cockatiel with orange rather than yellow crest feathers – and there is rumoured to be a totally orange bird in Europe!

A few cockatiels with an olive greenish tinge to their plumage have also been documented. They derive from cinnamon strains of birds and it seems that an excessive degree of yellowing, in combination with cinnamon, may create this unusual appearance.

A more conventional mutation may prove to be the clear-flight, with white flight feathers, a mutation that already exists in the budgerigar. Looking to the future, a mutation may arise that darkens the melanin, so that a black cockatiel could be developed. Whatever happens in this field, however, the popularity of the cockatiel is likely to continue growing.

Right: **Pearl white-faced hen**
A striking white-faced mutation. Symmetry of markings may be desirable, but it is hard to achieve.

LOVEBIRDS

These are a group of small, short-tailed parrots occurring in Africa and on certain offshore islands. There are nine different species, and all are characterized by their unusual breeding behaviour, which is almost unparalleled among members of the parrot family. Lovebirds collect nesting material, with which they line the nest site, carrying it either in their beaks or tucked in among the feathers of the rump, depending on the species concerned. In spite of their name, lovebirds can be very aggressive, particularly when nesting, and for this reason it is best to house breeding pairs on their own.

Madagascar Lovebird
Agapornis cana

Distribution: The island of Madagascar, off the south-eastern coast of Africa, and some neighbouring smaller islands.
Size: 13cm (5in).
Sexing: Adult cocks can be recognized by their grey heads; those of hens are green.
Youngsters: Resemble adults, and can be sexed in nest feathering.

These little lovebirds often prove rather nervous, and are certainly not as prolific in collections as the Peach-faced, for example. This is partly due to their habit of preferring to nest during the winter months. If possible, house them in indoor flights during winter in temperate zones, and provide heating and lighting as necessary.

A small hollow log acts as a good nesting receptacle for a breeding pair; alternatively, you can attach cork bark around the entrance of a budgerigar nestbox to encourage a nervous pair to enter here. Although paddy rice is reputedly a favourite seed of these lovebirds, most individuals prefer sprays of millet. These can be soaked and used as a rearing food. When buying Madagascar Lovebirds, be sure to check their breathing carefully; they are prone to air-sac mite infections. These can now be cured with appropriate medication.

Fischer's Lovebird
Agapornis fischeri

Distribution: Northern Tanzania.
Size: 14cm (5½in).
Sexing: Visual distinction between the sexes is not possible.
Youngsters: Duller in coloration than adults, notably on the head, with dark markings on the bill.

Another of the members of the so-called 'white eye ring group', because of the

*Below: **Madagascar Lovebirds**
These small parrots are easy to sex: the cock is on the left of this pair. They tend to be rather shy.*

prominent area of white skin encircling the eyes, Fischer's Lovebird is also a widely kept species. As with all lovebirds, it is vital to ensure, if pairs are housed in adjoining aviaries, that the panels separating them are double-wired. Otherwise, the birds are likely to bite each other's toes through the mesh, with potentially dire consequences.

Mutations are not well known at present, though both blue and yellow forms have been recorded. There is also an intriguing report of a lutino strain, which was established in France, but then disappeared during the Second World War. Fischer's Lovebirds build a fairly bulky domed nest, like related species, and will use virtually any material that they can gather around the aviary, such as old millet sprays and even strips of paper, for this purpose, although twigs are often favoured and should be supplied to breeding pairs.

Nyasa Lovebird
Agapornis lilianae

Distribution: Southern Tanzania into Zambia.
Size: 13cm (5in).
Sexing: Visual distinction between the sexes is not possible.
Youngsters: Duller than adults, and their cheeks are often tinged with black.

These lovebirds have gained a reputation for being somewhat delicate, but pairs can prove quite prolific, rearing as many as five chicks in a clutch. They are perhaps more numerous in Australia and New Zealand than in collections elsewhere at present and it is probably unwise to expect them to overwinter outdoors in temperate climates, certainly without the provision of heating and lighting, especially as they often prefer to breed at this time of year.

The only colour mutation recorded is the lutino, which was first bred during 1930 in Adelaide, Australia, and is unusual in being an autosomal rather than a sex-linked recessive form in its mode of inheritance. Although first brought to England in 1937, birds of this colour are now very scarce, if they still exist, but there is always the possibility that this mutation could re-emerge in existing captive stocks.

Black-cheeked Lovebird
Agapornis nigrigensis

Distribution: South-western Zambia.
Size: 14cm (5½in).
Sexing: Visual distinction between the sexes is not possible.
Youngsters: Duller than adults, with an orangish bill, which is only red at its tip.

This was one of the last species of parrot to be discovered, only being described for the first time in 1906. It has a very limited area of distribution, like other white eye ring lovebirds. This has led to suggestions that all four species evolved from a common ancestor, but have since become localized because of geological

Above: **Fischer's Lovebird**
A hardy and potentially free-breeding species, once the initial problem of identifying a true pair is overcome.

Above: **Nyasa Lovebird**
This is one of the rarest white eye ringed species in aviculture. Breeding pairs can nevertheless prove prolific.

Above: **Black-cheeked Lovebird**
The Black-cheeked has a very limited distribution, but is quite well established in aviculture.

and vegetative changes in the area of southern Africa where they are found. Unfortunately, they also hybridize together quite readily, and since Black-cheeked Lovebirds are relatively scarce in aviculture, stock has occasionally been mated with other members of this group in the past. You may be able to detect individuals of hybrid ancestry by their redder head coloration.

In terms of care, the Black-cheeked has similar requirements to those of the Nyasa Lovebird. There are some thriving breeding colonies established; provided that the birds are introduced to the aviary at the same time, it is possible to breed them in small groups without any fighting occurring. Colour mutations in this species are virtually unknown, except for a blue form, which was recorded in Denmark in 1981.

Masked Lovebird
Agapornis personata

Distribution: North-eastern Tanzania, and introduced to a few localities elsewhere, such as Nairobi, Kenya.
Size: 14cm (5½in).
Sexing: Visual distinction between the sexes is not possible.
Youngsters: Duller overall than adults, with dark markings on the beak.

The first lovebird mutation ever recorded was noted in this species back in 1927, when a wild-caught blue was received by a London dealer. A dullish yellow form, which is simply a paler version of the normal, then appeared in the United States in 1934. By selective breeding, it became possible to develop the White Masked. Although confined to a small area in the wild, it is clear that some Masked Lovebirds naturally have more orangish rather than yellow breast markings, and attempts are being made to establish a strain of such birds, as has already happened with the Turquoisine Grass Parakeet (see page 149).

Like a number of other lovebirds, the Masked is generally quite hardy once acclimatized, but pairs should be encouraged to roost under cover, preferably in a nestbox located in the shelter. Here they should be relatively safe from frostbite, which may otherwise cause loss of toes during a cold winter.

Below: **Masked Lovebirds (normal)**
These colourful, popular birds are ideal for a garden aviary, although pairs are best housed on their own.

Below: **Masked Lovebird
(blue mutation)**
This mutation has become the most
common Masked form in aviculture.

Above: **Masked lovebirds
(yellow mutation)**
This dilute form of the normal has paler
plumage, most notably over the face.

Below: **Masked Lovebird
(white mutation)**
This colour is created by combining the
blue and yellow mutations.

Red-faced Lovebird
Agapornis pullaria

Distribution: Across Africa in a broad belt from the western side eastwards to Uganda and Ethiopia.
Size: 15cm (6in).
Sexing: The red plumage on the face of the hen is more orangish than on cocks.
Youngsters: Similar to hens, but with paler faces, and dark markings on the beak.

In the wild, these lovebirds nest within the confines of termite mounds, located in trees up to 12m (40ft) off the ground. Here they will receive some protection against predators, while the heat generated within the termite nest means that they are less inclined to sit tightly on their eggs. Unfortunately, this has resulted in eggs becoming chilled in aviary surroundings if a conventional nestbox is used.

When this species was first bred successfully in Britain, back in the 1950s, nesting barrels full of peat, placed on their sides, were provided. This enabled the lovebirds to excavate their own nesting chamber. In order to overcome the problem of chilling, breeders have added small heat pads to their nestboxes. One German breeder has reared over 40 Red-faced Lovebird chicks in a five-year period in this fashion, maintaining the interior of the box at a temperature of 30°C (85°F). These are not the easiest of lovebirds to breed, however, and are probably best kept by specialists. A stunning lutino colour mutation is known, but is presently very rare.

Peach-faced Lovebird
Agapornis roseicollis

Distribution: South-west Africa.
Size: 15cm (6in).
Sexing: Visual distinction between the sexes is not possible.
Youngsters: Lack the pronounced pink coloration of adults, and initially show dark markings on the beak.

By far the most popular and widely kept member of the group, the Peach-faced Lovebird is now being bred in a wide range of colours. Among the best-known are the pastel blue, which originated in Holland in about 1963, and the lutino, which is sex-linked in its mode of inheritance. These two mutations have been combined to produce the attractive lemon-coloured cremino, while other established forms include the pied, cinnamon, yellow, and dark factor. Recently, much interest has been focussed on Peach-faced Lovebirds showing variable areas of red plumage in among their normal green feathering, but it appears that this coloration is not the result of a genetic mutation; instead, it is demonstrably related to the bird's diet. Changes of this type are often transitory. The areas of abnormal red plumage may expand or contract from one moult to the next.

*Above: **Red-faced Lovebird***
This cock bird is instantly recognizable by its dark red face; that of the hen is paler in colour.

*Below: **Peach-faced Lovebird (normal)***
The Peach-faced is widely kept throughout the world, and bred in many different colour forms.

Above: **Peach-faced Lovebird (pastel blue mutation)**
Some birds have a much more greenish tinge to their plumage than others.

Below: **Peach-faced Lovebird (cremino mutation)**
The delicate lemon coloration of these lovebirds makes them much in demand.

Above: **Peach-faced Lovebird (lutino mutation)**
A popular mutation that has been used to develop other colours.

Above: **Peach-faced Lovebird (olive mutation)**
The emergence of the dark factor paved the way for this form's development.

Below: **Peach-faced Lovebird (normal yellow pied mutation)**
Dark factor forms of green combined with pieds are also popular.

Above: **Peach-faced Lovebird (jade mutation)**
This single factor form is equivalent to the dark green form of the budgerigar.

Abyssinian Lovebird
Agapornis taranta

Distribution: Central and eastern parts of Ethiopia, extending to southern Eritrea.
Size: 16.5cm (6½in).
Sexing: Cock birds have red plumage on the head; hens have green heads.
Youngsters: Similar to adults hens, but cocks can still be recognized by their black underwing coverts.

The third and final member of the sexually dimorphic sub-group of lovebirds, the Abyssinian is now relatively scarce in collections. Compatible pairs usually prove to be reliable parents; they build a less elaborate nest than other species, often comprised of just a simple pad of feathers, augmented with a little bark off a perch. The hen may even pluck her feathers or those of her mate for this purpose, but these should regrow uneventfully in due course. Up to five eggs may be laid, and as with other lovebirds, the incubation period lasts about 23 days, with the hen sitting alone. The young leave the nest at around seven weeks old. It is relatively unusual, though not unknown, for pairs to nest twice during the summer. Sweet apple is a particular favourite of Abyssinian Lovebird, while soaked figs, diced into small pieces, are also popular with many individuals.

*Below: **Abyssinian Lovebird**
These lovebirds are easy to sex and pairs will often nest quite readily, but they are not common in aviculture.*

PARROTLETS

These diminutive parrots, which originate from Central and South America, are an ideal choice for breeders with limited space as they do not require large aviaries. Parrotlets are also quite quiet, and their calls are unlikely to disturb near neighbours. Unfortunately, however, they can be quite spiteful towards each other, especially when nesting. While they are not usually kept as pet birds, hand-reared parrotlets are said to make delightful companions. Occasional blue individuals have been recorded, but at present, despite their attractive appearance, such birds are very rare.

Celestial Parrotlet
Forpus coelestis

Distribution: Ecuador and Peru.
Size: 14cm (5½in).
Sexing: Hens are mainly green, lacking the cocks' blue markings, though they may have a bluish tinge on their rumps.
Youngsters: Resemble adults, but are duller overall.

This group of small birds will often breed quite readily and will offer you an ideal opportunity to specialize in developing strains, even if your budget and surroundings are rather limited. Results tend to be better in small aviaries than in cages, as some cocks can prove very aggressive towards their offspring as the time for fledging approaches, and may even cause fatalities. Ideally, you should remove the chicks as soon as they are independent, not only to protect them, but because the adult birds may well be nesting again. The hen may lay six or seven eggs in a clutch and the chicks will be mature by the following breeding season. Offer reasonable amounts of greenfood, along with millet sprays, during the rearing period.

This species is also sometimes known as the Pacific Parrotlet.

*Below: **Celestial Parrotlets**
The bright blue markings are clearly displayed in the cock of this attractive pair. The hen, on the right-hand branch, is much duller in colour.*

Green-rumped Parrotlet

Forpus passerinus

Distribution: From Colombia and Venezuela, east to the Guianas and northern Brazil.
Size: 12.5cm (5in).
Sexing: Hens have yellowish heads and lack the blue plumage of the cock birds.
Youngsters: Similar to adults.

As with other *Forpus* species, it is much safer to house these birds in individual pairs than to attempt to keep them on a colony basis, and secure double wiring between adjoining flights is essential to minimize the risk of fighting.

Pairs will normally nest quite freely and are likely to have more than one clutch of chicks in the breeding period. The incubation period lasts about 18 days, and the chicks leave the nest approximately six weeks later. In spite of their small size, parrotlets are relatively hardy, providing they are properly acclimatized, and can have a long reproductive life of 15 years or more. They may choose to roost in a nestbox at night, rather than on a perch, and you should encourage this behaviour during cold weather.

Right: **Green-rumped Parrotlet**
An easy species to cater for. There is striking blue plumage under the wings of this cock bird.

Yellow-faced Parrotlet

Forpus xanthops

Distribution: A small area of north-western Peru.
Size: 14.5cm (5¾in).
Sexing: Hens have a pale blue rather than violet rump.
Youngsters: Duller than adults, with a dark stripe on the beak. They are usually mature by a year old.

A small number of these parrotlets were first imported from Peru in 1979 and were available for several years. Although they have since been scarce, some breeders are successfully developing their own strains from this original stock. The Yellow-faced Parrotlet is similar to the Celestial, but has lighter coloration. These birds were difficult to establish initially because of *microfilariae* (immature parasitic worms)

Above: **Yellow-faced Parrotlets**
The cock (shown left) has brighter coloration than the hen. Although still scarce, these parrotlets are now being bred in larger numbers.

present in the circulatory system and avian malaria. These parasites caused sudden losses of birds that otherwise appeared healthy. Such problems are unlikely to arise with captive-bred stock.

HANGING PARROTS

Sometimes known as 'bat parrots', because of their habit of roosting upside down, the ten species of hanging parrot are found in parts of south-east Asia, extending to the offshore islands of Indonesia and the Philippines. Although small, these parrots need spacious accommodation that can be easily cleaned because of their liquid diet, which is comprised mainly of fruit and nectar. Interestingly, like lovebirds, they will use nesting material, often carrying it to their nest site tucked in among their feathers. They are one of the very few groups of parrots that can be housed in a planted flight.

Blue-crowned Hanging Parrot
Loriculus galgulus

Distribution: The Malay Peninsula and nearby offshore islands.
Size: 12.5cm (5in).
Sexing: Hens are noticeably duller, with a less distinct blue area on the head, and most lack the scarlet throat patch.
Youngsters: Distinguishable by their pale brown rather than black beaks, and duller plumage.

This species is common in aviculture and has been bred on a number of occasions. Both sexes are involved in cutting nesting material, but usually only the hen transports the pieces, in among her feathers, to the nest site. A budgerigar nestbox may be used for this purpose. Hanging parrots produce their eggs on successive days (rather than on alternate days like most parrots), with four forming a typical clutch. Incubation lasts about 20 days and the chicks will fledge about five weeks later.

*Below: **Blue-crowned Hanging Parrots**
The narrow, curved shape of the bills of these birds is clearly seen here.*

Philippine Hanging Parrot
Loriculus philippensis

Distribution: Philippine islands, to the Sulu Archipelago.
Size: 14cm (5½in).
Sexing: Hens have no trace of red plumage on their throat or upper breast.
Youngsters: Similar to hens, but with little if any red feathering above the bill.

Occurring over a large number of islands, the Philippine Hanging Parrot has evolved into at least 11 recognizable subspecies throughout its range. While the races on Cebu and Siquijor are now believed to be extinct, these parrots remain common on most other islands. If you intend to establish a breeding group, obtain all your stock from one source if possible; this should ensure that the birds are all of the same subspecies. Some individuals are much more brightly coloured than others.

Vernal Hanging Parrot
Loriculus vernalis

Distribution: Over a wide area from south-western India eastwards to the Malay Peninsula.
Size: 14cm (5½in).
Sexing: The blue area on the throat of cocks is either reduced or absent entirely on hens, and the irises of the latter are dark rather than yellowish white.
Youngsters: Recognizable by their brown legs and lighter-coloured bills.

The Vernal Hanging Parrot does not differ from related species in terms of its care. Offer nectar fresh, in a sealed drinker, as the birds may attempt to bathe in an open container and end up with sticky, saturated plumage. The advent of 'dry diets' has helped to overcome the very fluid nature of their droppings, but the changeover to foods of this type needs to be carried out over some weeks, so as to minimize the likelihood of a digestive upset. Check the claws of these birds regularly to ensure they do not become overgrown.

*Above: **Philippine Hanging Parrots**
There may be considerable variation in the coloration of these hanging parrots, depending on which islands they originated from.*

*Below: **Vernal Hanging Parrot**
This hen lacks the blue area on the throat of cock birds and the irises of the latter are much paler.*

CONURES

The description 'conure' simply refers to a group of medium-sized parakeets found in the Americas. It is unfortunately not possible to sex these birds reliably by visual means, but with the advent of reliable sexing methods, far more are being bred, and once a true pair is established in suitable surroundings, they will usually start breeding if provided with a suitable nestbox. Conures are also generally less costly than the larger parrots, and, as pets, have trustworthy temperaments. While they can become very tame, however, their talking skills are somewhat limited.

Blue-crowned Conure
Aratinga acuticaudata

Distribution: Across much of South America, from Colombia southwards to parts of Bolivia, Paraguay, Argentina and Uruguay.
Size: 37cm (14½in).
Sexing: Visual distinction between the sexes is not possible.
Youngsters: Recognizable by their horn-coloured bills, and reduced area of blue on the head.

These conures are easy to care for, but, like other related species, their loud calls and rather destructive natures can present problems. It can take a couple of years for a pair to settle down sufficiently to nest, but, again like most conures, the Blue-crowned usually prove to be reliable parents once breeding commences. Try to avoid any

unnecessary disturbances at the start of the incubation period, when hens are most likely to be nervous, and may leave the eggs to become chilled. Incubation lasts approximately 26 days and the chicks fledge at about two months old. They are then fed for a short time by the cock, while the hen is likely to lay again.

Blue-crowned Conures can become quite tame, even in aviary surroundings.

Peach-fronted Conure
Aratinga aurea

Distribution: Central South America, extending to parts of Bolivia, Peru, Paraguay and northern Argentina.
Size: 25cm (10in).
Sexing: Visual distinction between the sexes is not possible.
Youngsters: The area of orange on the head is smaller, and yellow feathering is evident here.

*Above left: **Blue-crowned Conure**
Although not especially colourful, these conures are attractive birds.*

*Above: **Peach-fronted Conure**
Pairs are generally keen to nest; place their nestbox under cover.*

There is usually a strong bond between members of a pair, as with other *Aratinga* conures, and if you are looking at birds that are unsexed, you may be able to recognize a bonded pair by their behaviour; the birds will follow each other around their quarters, sitting close together and sometimes engaging in mutual preening. The calls of the Peach-fronted Conure are not as penetrating as those of some other members of the group, but a cat near their aviary will solicit prolonged squawking. This species is also sometimes described as the Golden-crowned Conure.

Golden-capped Conure
Aratinga auricapilla

Distribution: Eastern Brazil.
Size: 30cm (12in).
Sexing: Visual distinction between the sexes is not possible.
Youngsters: Greener than adults, and duller.

Facing widespread deforestation through its native range, the Golden-capped Conure appears to be facing an uncertain future. The development of captive stock could be very significant and, encouragingly, these attractive conures are now becoming well established in aviculture. Unfortunately, they can be rather vocal, possessing a rather high-pitched, raucous series of calls, but they are very attractive aviary occupants. Pairs usually breed readily, and are frequently double-brooded. While individual birds may vary somewhat in their coloration, this is not a reliable means of sexing them. Place a nestbox in a secluded and darkened corner of the flight to encourage a pair to commence breeding here.

Petz's Conure
Aratinga canicularis

Distribution: From Mexico to western Costa Rica in Central America.
Size: 25cm (10in).
Sexing: Visual distinction between the sexes is not possible.
Youngsters: Distinguishable by their brown irises, and reduced area of orange on the head.

Although sometimes confused with the Peach-fronted Conure (*A. aurea*), Petz's Conure is easily distinguishable by the colour of its bill, which is whitish horn, whereas that of the Peach-fronted is black. This is a relatively common species in North America, but less often seen in Europe. Hand-raised chicks should develop into delightful pets, and can prove quite talented as mimics. They are much easier to manage in the home than larger parrots, although their calls may be persistent if they feel that they are being ignored.

Below left: **Golden-capped Conure**
This colourful and prolific species is popular with many breeders; a pair may produce two clutches in succession.

Below: **Petz's Conure**
This is one of the less common Aratinga *conures, but it is easy to maintain and breeding presents no real problems.*

Red-masked Conure
Aratinga erythrogenys

Distribution: Western Ecuador and north-west Peru.
Size: 33cm (13in).
Sexing: Visual distinction between the sexes is not possible.
Youngsters: Distinguishable by their green head and thighs.

There are a number of predominantly green conures, with variable amounts of red on the head and body, and this species is undoubtedly the most colourful, with an entirely red head. A regular spray should help to keep the plumage in good condition. A pair will show to good effect in a reasonably large aviary, which needs to be well built to resist the attention of their powerful bills. Red-masked Conures breed quite readily, especially when provided with a fairly deep nestbox; if frustrated in their desire to nest, a pair may resort to feather-plucking, so watch for such behaviour with birds housed indoors on their own. These conures are hardy birds once established in their quarters, and can safely overwinter outside, providing that they have a nestbox for roosting purposes.

Right: **Red-masked Conure**
These conures need secure housing, and perches will need replacing regularly, as they have powerful beaks.

Golden Conure
Aratinga guarouba

Distribution: Confined to a relatively small area of north-eastern Brazil.
Size: 36cm (14in).
Sexing: Visual distinction between the sexes is not possible.
Youngsters: Have green feathering over much of their bodies, mingled with yellow.

The most spectacular member of this group of parrots, the Golden or Queen of Bavaria's Conure is the only one to be considered endangered at present; the region where it lives is the subject of increasing development, and habitat destruction is widespread. Several aviculturists have established stocks of these beautiful conures, but this is a very costly species to acquire, and not to be recommended for beginners. They can prove very noisy, and are prone to feather-plucking, even in aviary surroundings. Providing a varied diet and plenty of perches for gnawing should help to prevent this problem.

Jendaya Conure
Aratinga jandaya

Distribution: North-eastern Brazil.
Size: 30cm (12in).
Sexing: Visual distinction between the sexes is not possible.
Youngsters: Significantly paler than adults. It may be two years before youngsters start to nest.

This species has proved more adaptable than the Golden Conure, and may even be increasing in some parts of its range. All stock available is likely to be captive-bred, and these conures can be prolific, laying up to six eggs in a clutch and often nesting twice a year. Breeding details for this species do not otherwise differ from those of other *Aratinga* conures, the incubation period lasting about 26 days. They have been hybridized with Sun Conures, from which they can be easily distinguished by their green wings. Such pairings are

Above left: **Golden Conure**
Rare and highly prized, this conure has been bred sucessfully, so its future in aviculture seems reasonably assured.

Above: **Jendaya Conure**
This Brazilian species, well established in aviculture, differs from related species by its yellow head and green wings.

not to be encouraged, however, as they harm the development of pure strains, which may in the future be used in re-introduction programmes.

Above: **White-eyed Conure**
The red feathering of these conures is concealed under the wings, with variable amounts elsewhere on the body.

Right: **Mitred Conure**
Another species with a variable amount of red plumage on the head. These conures can be rather raucous.

White-eyed Conure
Aratinga leucophthalmus

Distribution: Over much of northern South America, apart from the far west, southwards to northern Argentina and Paraguay.
Size: 33cm (13in).
Sexing: Visual distinction between the sexes is not possible.
Youngsters: Have yellowish green rather than red markings on the edge of the wings.

The prominent area of white skin encircling the eyes is responsible for the common name of these conures, although it occurs in other members of this genus as well. White-eyed Conures are undemanding birds in aviary surroundings, but have attracted little interest from aviculturists, possibly because of their mainly green plumage. The extent and distribution of scattered red feathering on the body differs according to individuals, some being more colourful than others. It has been suggested that these conures will add fragments of wood gnawed from their surroundings to line the nestbox; you can reduce their destructive urges when they are breeding by supplying them with lengths of suitable softwood on the floor of their chosen nest site.

Mitred Conure
Aratinga mitrata

Distribution: From Peru to Bolivia and Argentina.
Size: 38cm (15in).
Sexing: Visual distinction between the sexes is not possible.
Youngsters: Entirely green.

The amount of red feathering on the head of Mitred Conures varies between individuals, but is never as extensive as in the Red-masked. Red plumage usually extends from the forehead and encircles the eyes, merging with a scattering of green feathers on top of the head and on the sides of the face. As one of the larger conures, the Mitred proves quite vocal and destructive, especially when the birds are in breeding condition. This species has become more common in aviculture during recent years, and is easy to maintain with a diet of seeds supplemented with fruit and greenstuff on a regular basis. Pairs will nest without much persuasion, but breeding results are not widely recorded.

Aztec Conure
Aratinga nana

Distribution: From Mexico southwards to Panama, Central America, and on the Caribbean island of Jamaica.
Size: 26cm (10½in).
Sexing: Visual distinction between the sexes is not possible.
Youngsters: Duller in coloration with brown irises.

While the Jamaican race (*A. n. nana*) is virtually unknown in aviculture, small numbers of Aztec Conures of Central-American origin are being bred in several collections, and a few of these conures have become available to aviculturists during recent years. Although not the most colourful species, the Aztec or Olive-throated Conure is nevertheless an attractive, personable bird. It can be distinguished from the Jamaican race by its smaller size, relatively yellowish green plumage, and lighter-brown underparts.

Brown-throated Conure
Aratinga pertinax

Distribution: From Panama in Central America down to Venezuela and offshore islands.
Size: 25cm (10in).
Sexing: Visual distinction between the sexes is not possible.
Youngsters: Duller than adults, with a pale upper bill.

There are 14 different forms of this conure recognized through its range, some of which are considerably brighter than others. Birds of the Guianan races, notably the Guianan Brown-throated

Conure (*A. p. chrysophrys*), are most common in aviculture. This is a relatively dark form, but individual birds may vary in coloration, some having more orange on the sides of the face than others. In the wild, these conures nest in termite mounds, but appear to adapt to a conventional nestbox quite readily. To create a more natural habitat for these birds you can nail some cork bark, available from florists, around the entrance hole. (Avoid glue, which could potentially be toxic if ingested by the conures.)

Above: **Aztec Conure**
Still fairly rare in aviculture.

Below: **Brown-throated Conure**
Individuals differ in coloration.

Sun Conure
Aratinga solstitialis

Distribution: The north-eastern part of South America, including the Guianas, and may extend westwards to Venezuela.
Size: 30cm (12in).
Sexing: Visual distinction between the sexes is not possible.
Youngsters: Less colourful, with more green evident in their plumage.

This species was rare in aviculture until the 1970s, but since then has proved very prolific. The only drawback of these beautiful conures is their calls, which can be rather harsh. Sun Conures will agree well together in groups, although any newcomers are likely to be persecuted and breeding pairs are best housed on their own. The plumage of young birds is very variable; some chicks may be mainly yellow on fledging, whereas others are much greener. Hand-reared offspring will develop into lively, playful companions, but are susceptible to feather-plucking if kept indoors without bathing facilities.

Red-fronted Conure
Aratinga wagleri

Distribution: On the western side of South America, from Venezuela down to Peru.
Size: 36cm (14in).
Sexing: Visual distinction between the sexes is not possible.
Youngsters: Have little if any red plumage on the head.

Wagler's Conure, another of the larger species, is not well represented in aviculture, although it is not difficult to cater for. It can be difficult to distinguish Wagler's Conure from the Mitred, but the red plumage tends to be more restricted in its distribution on the former, being confined essentially to the area immediately above the beak, extending to the eyes and onto the forehead. (Some races also display red feathering at the bend of the wing and at the top of the thigh.) Red-fronted Conures have been bred quite successfully on the colony system at Chester Zoo in the UK.

Left: **Sun Conure**
One of the most colourful conures; some birds are more orangish.

Below: **Red-fronted Conure**
The Red-fronted – another predominantly green species with red markings – is not particularly well known in aviculture.

Dusky-headed Conure
Aratinga weddellii

Distribution: A wide area of South America, southwards to Bolivia and western Brazil.
Size: 28cm (11in)
Sexing: Visual distinction between the sexes is not possible.
Youngsters: Similar to adults but with dark irises.

Sometimes known as Weddell's Conure, this is an attractive species, in spite of its rather dull coloration. It has never been especially common in aviculture but pairs are available from time to time. Adults may be rather nervous at first, but will soon settle in their quarters, and may have two clutches of chicks during the summer. Breeding would appear to present no particular problems, and pairs will take a wide variety of fruit, including blackcurrants, as well as soaked seed, at this stage.

Right: **Dusky-headed Conures**
These conures are among the smaller and quieter members of the group. Young birds can develop into tame pets.

Patagonian Conure
Cyanoliseus patagonus

Distribution: Argentina, as well as Chile and possibly Uruguay.
Size: 46cm (18in).
Sexing: Visual distinction between the sexes is not possible.
Youngsters: Have whitish rather than black upper bills.

These are the largest of the conures, although it is the Lesser form (*C. p. patagonus*) that is represented in collections. (The larger Chilean race is protected in its native habitat and is rare.) Aside from its size, it can be distinguished by the much more prominent area of white plumage across the upper chest.) In the wild, Patagonian Conures nest communally in tunnels that they excavate in sandstone cliffs. They often show a greater tendency to breed in aviaries if more than one pair are housed together, but they will use a standard nestbox without any problems. Immediately before the egg-laying period, they can become very noisy. Do not add new individuals to an established colony – they are likely to fight. Pagatonian Conures are fond of apple and the stalks of spinach; you should also provide them with cuttlefish bone throughout the year.

Below: **Lesser Patagonian Conure**
These large conures can be housed together in groups, but often only the dominant pair will breed in these surroundings. A rare yellow mutation of this species has been recorded in the UK, but is not yet established.

Magellan Conure
Enicognathus ferruginea

Distribution: Chile and Argentina, south to Tierra del Fuego.
Size: 35cm (14in).
Sexing: Visual distinction between the sexes is not possible.
Youngsters: Recognizable by the smaller area of maroon feathering on the abdomen.

Sometimes also described as Chilean or Austral Conures, these birds have become well known in aviculture only during the 1980s. They have proved easy to care for, and also prolific – several breeders have achieved repeated successes. Pairs may produce up to six eggs, and lay two or three times a year. Being found further south than any other neo-tropical parrot, it is perhaps not surprising that Magellan Conures are hardy birds; indeed they appear to dislike very hot weather, and so have adapted well to life in northern Europe.

*Right: **Magellan Conure***
Established pairs of this species will breed without difficulty.

Slender-billed Conure
Enicognathus leptorhynchus

Distribution: Central and southern parts of Chile.
Size: 41cm (16in).
Sexing: Visual distinction between the sexes is not possible.
Youngsters: Have shorter bills, and white rather than grey skin surrounding the eyes.

The unusual bills of these conures allows them to extract the seeds of the Monkey Puzzle Tree from the cones. (In an aviary with a grass floor, they may also use their long bills to dig up turf, presumably searching for roots.) Slender-billed Conures will consume a wide variety of foods; blackberries in season are often a favourite item, but they will also take other fruit and greenstuff readily. They are social birds and can be kept and bred in a colony. Their avicultural history is similar to that of the Magellan Conure, and they are equally prolific. Young birds can become very tame, and often develop into delightful companions.

Nanday Conure
Nandayus nenday

Distribution: Southern South America, in parts of Brazil, Bolivia, Paraguay and Argentina.
Size: 30cm (12in).
Sexing: Visual distinction between the sexes is not possible.
Youngsters: Have a reduced area of blue on the breast.

These unmistakable conures with their black heads are very similar in their requirements – and in their noise level – to the *Aratinga* species, and have

*Above: **Slender-billed Conure***
These unusual conures are attractive aviary occupants, although their calls can sometimes be rather loud.

hybridized with some of these in the past. They may produce up to five chicks at a time, which they incubate for 26 days, the youngsters leaving the nest around two months later. Even at this stage, they are similar in appearance to the adults, and will soon be

*Above: **Nanday Conure***
This rather noisy species has often been overlooked by breeders to date. Once acclimatized, these birds are hardy.

indistinguishable from them. You can keep these conures on the colony system, provided that you have no close neighbours, who may be upset by their regular squawking. Nanday Conures are also sometimes described as Black-headed or Black-masked Conures.

Maroon-bellied Conure
Pyrrhura frontalis

Distribution: South-eastern South America, in parts of Brazil, Paraguay, Argentina and Uruguay.
Size: 25cm (10in).
Sexing: Visual distinction between the sexes is not possible.
Youngsters: Duller, with shorter tails.

The *Pyrrhura* conures are sometimes referred to collectively as the Scaly-breasted group, because of the pattern of markings on the breast, seen in all species to a greater or lesser extent. The Maroon or Red-bellied Conure is one of the best-known species in aviculture, and can be kept quite satisfactorily even in an urban area; its calls are reasonably pleasant, being comprised largely of clicking sounds (although it does have a harsher alarm call), and it is not a particularly destructive species. These birds are hardy once properly acclimatized, but a nestbox should be available for roosting purposes throughout the year.

Below: **Maroon-bellied Conure**
One of the most readily available species, these conures become very tame, even in aviary surroundings.

Black-tailed Conure
Pyrrhura melanura

Distribution: North-western South America, from Colombia and Venezuela to Peru.
Size: 25cm (10in).
Sexing: Visual distinction between the sexes is not possible.
Youngsters: Distinguishable by their fainter breast markings.

Somewhat confusingly, you may also see this species described as the Maroon-tailed Conure; this is not as strange as it may appear, because while the upper surfaces of the tail feathers are black, the lower surfaces are maroon. There are several races, which may be difficult to distinguish; none is especially common, but small numbers are represented in various collections, and like other *Pyrrhura*, pairs generally prove prolific. Incubation lasts about 24 days, and the chicks will leave the nestbox for the first time at about five weeks old. These young bids can be breeding themselves at one year old.

Below: **Black-tailed Conure**
This species, like most other Pyrrhura *conures is prolific; pairs may produce two clutches in rapid succession.*

Molina's Conure
Pyrrhura molinae

Distribution: Brazil, Bolivia and north-west Argentina.
Size: 25cm (10in).
Sexing: Visual distinction between the sexes is not possible.
Youngsters: Duller than adults, with shorter tails for a period after fledging.

At first glance Molina's Conure is sometimes confused with the Maroon-bellied, but the head coloration serves to distinguish them; the cheeks of Molina's Conure are green, (its alternative name is Green-cheeked Conure), the ear coverts are a more greyish brown and it has a black area on the head. In terms of care, their requirements are identical; Molina's Conure also becomes tame and confiding, even in aviary surroundings. A standard mixture of seeds suits these conures well and they particularly appreciate groats, carrot and apple. Like other *Pyrrhura* species, they tend to prefer fruit to green food; grapes and pomegranate seeds are favourites.

Below: **Molina's Conures**
The typical scaly-breasted markings, which characterize this group of conures, are clearly evident here.

Above: **Pearly Conure**
Although its distribution in the wild is fairly limited, this species is quite well represented in aviculture.

Pearly Conure
Pyrrhura perlata

Distribution: North-eastern Brazil.
Size: 25cm (10in).
Sexing: Visual distinction between the sexes is not possible.
Youngsters: Recognizable by their paler bills.

This is one of the species of *Pyrrhura* conure where captive-bred stocks are quite well established; although there are 19 different species in the genus, there are actually no avicultural records for about half of these. Interestingly, one new species, called the El Oro Conure (*P. orcesi*) has recently been recorded from Ecuador, where it occurs in a very small area. Most of the other *Pyrrhura* conures also have restricted ranges, but it is unlikely that their requirements would differ significantly from those already recorded in aviculture, should any become available in the future. The Pearly Conure has proved to be as prolific as its relatives; hens may lay up to three clutches comprised of four eggs or more during the breeding period.

Painted Conure
Pyrrhura picta

Distribution: Central and South America, southwards to parts of Ecuador, Peru and Bolivia.
Size: 22cm (8½in).
Sexing: Visual distinction between the sexes is not possible.
Youngsters: Have mainly green plumage at the bend of the wings.

The different races of this species vary somewhat in appearance, two subspecies displaying areas of red plumage on their heads. Painted conures do not prove quite so confiding as others in aviary surroundings, although they will display in a similar fashion, stalking up and down the perch in a deliberate fashion, and raising the

Above: **Painted Conure**
This Pyrrhura *conure is slightly smaller than the other species featured here. It has become more common in aviculture during recent years.*

plumage on the sides of their head. When mating, they adopt the typical neo-tropical posture, with cocks using one foot to grip the perch, while holding on to their mate's back with the other. They require a varied diet, and must have a nestbox for roosting purposes.

127

LORIES AND LORIKEETS

These colourful parrots have a lively, jaunty, almost playful manner. They are also quite vocal; many species have high-pitched calls, which, though not as disturbing as those of the larger parrots, can carry over some distance. The description of 'lorikeet' is applied to species with long tails, whereas the short-tailed forms are known as 'lories'.
The feeding habits of these birds are unusual in that they rely on nectar and pollen as a major part of their diet. Their tongues are specially adapted with small brushes, called papillae, which enable them to collect the microscopic pollen granules.

Black Lory
Chalcopsitta atra

Distribution: Western New Guinea and nearby offshore islands.
Size: 32cm (13in).
Sexing: Visual distinction between the sexes is not possible.
Youngsters: Have brown irises, and white skin encircling the eyes and bill.

Although less colourful than many of the lories and lorikeets, Black Lories are great characters. Unfortunately, their calls are loud and harsh and they become especially noisy just prior to the breeding period, when cock birds may also become quite aggressive. The incubation period lasts about 25 days, and the chicks leave the nest when they are about 10 weeks old. There is a distinctive subspecies, also described as the Red-quilled Lory, sometimes known as the Rajah Lory (*C. a. insignis*), which is strikingly marked, with red rather than black feathering, most noticeably over part of the head and the thighs.

Duivenbode's Lory
Chalcopsitta duivenbodei

Distribution: Northern New Guinea
Size: 32cm (12½in).
Sexing: Visual distinction between the sexes is not possible.
Youngsters: Duller, with white skin encircling the eyes.

During recent years, this unusually coloured lory (the combination of brown and yellow is rare in parrots) has become more common in aviculture.

Caring for these birds is relatively straightforward, and pairs prove quite hardy once they are acclimatized, although you may need to bring birds indoors for their first winter, especially if their feathering is not in good condition. Like other lories and lorikeets, they require a diet comprised largely of nectar, fruit and greenstuff. Breeding details are the same as for the Black Lory, two eggs forming the usual clutch.

*Below left: **Black Lory***
These birds are hardly the archetypal parrots, with their black coloration, but they make interesting aviary occupants.

*Below: **Duivenbode's Lory***
The major drawback of these lories is their loud calls, which are most persistent prior to the breeding season.

Yellow-streaked Lory
Chalcopsitta sintillata

Distribution: Southern part of New Guinea. Also present on the nearby Aru islands.
Size: 30cm (12in).
Sexing: Visual distinction between the sexes is not possible.
Youngsters: Duller in overall coloration.

This species has become more widely known in aviculture over recent years, but unfortunately, like other members of the genus, it can prove rather noisy. It is characterized by the streaking on the plumage, which is most noticeable on the breast. In some cases, this may be almost orangish-brown rather than the normal yellow in colour. Pairs do not always prove reliable parents, and may neglect their chicks after they hatch, so you may need to hand rear them. Two eggs form the typical clutch, with incubation and fledging periods being as for the other *Chalcopsitta* lories. Repeated breeding may occur if eggs are removed for artificial incubation.

Papuan Lorikeet
Charmosyna papou

Distribution: The central region of New Guinea, in mountainous regions.
Size: 38cm (15in).
Sexing: Hens can be distinguished by the yellow area on the sides of the rump.
Youngsters: Recognizable by their shorter central tail feathers, the brownish bill and legs.

It is the race known as Stella's Lorikeet (*C. p. stellae*) that is best-known in aviculture. In this instance, no yellow is present on the thighs. There is also a naturally occurring melanistic form of Stella's Lorikeet, where the red plumage is largely replaced by black. Pairing red birds together will only yield similarly coloured offspring, but melanistic birds can produce both red and black chicks. The melanistic offspring can also be sexed visually, while still in the nest, just like red individuals. Hens in this case have dark rumps, whereas the flanks of cocks are dull red. Incubation lasts about 27 days, and chicks fledge around eight weeks later. These birds will breed in small colonies in spacious aviaries.

Above: **Yellow-streaked Lory**
The characteristic streaks on the predominantly green plumage are clearly apparent in the bird shown here.

Below left: **Stella's Lorikeet**
The stunning beauty of these colourful birds – the best-known race of the Papuan Lorikeet – has made them popular avicultural subjects.

Below: **Melanistic Stella's Lorikeet**
This is the dark form of Stella's Lorikeet. Melanistic birds can produce both red and black offspring.

Above: **Fairy Lorikeets**
This is one of the smaller lorikeet species, which is most suitable for the specialist; despite originating from a mountainous area, it is not hardy.

Right: **Moluccan Lory**
An ideal introduction to this group of parrots, the Moluccan can be kept and – once the birds have been sexed – bred without undue difficulty.

Fairy Lorikeet
Charmosyna pulchella

Distribution: Mountainous areas of New Guinea.
Size: 18cm (7in).
Sexing: Hens usually show traces of yellow on the sides of their rump.
Youngsters: Have brown bills and little if any yellow streaking.

In spite of being found at high altitudes in the wild, these beautiful little birds are rather delicate, especially when first obtained; they are sensitive to low temperatures, and only appear to thrive in indoor accommodation, which needs to be heated through the winter months. Another difficulty is their apparent susceptibility to candidiasis; infections may prove hard to eradicate in this species. Established pairs will nest quite readily, and are likely to breed at almost any stage during the year if conditions are favourable. The hen normally lays two eggs, and apparently shares their incubation with her mate. The chicks should hatch after a period of 25 days.

Moluccan Lory
Eos bornea

Distribution: Indonesia, on various islands.
Size: 25cm (10in).
Sexing: Visual distinction between the sexes is not possible.
Youngsters: Have black beaks and dark irises.

Because it occurs on a number of islands, localized forms of the Moluccan Lory have evolved; some are bigger than others, and slight variations in coloration are also apparent. The species is quite commonly available, is easy to care for, and pairs breed readily (although the birds will need to be sexed). Chicks should hatch after a period of 24 days, and then leave the nest for the first time about nine weeks later. They may live for 20 years or more. Provide plenty of fresh perches in order to prevent their bills from becoming overgrown – a problem that is common to all other lories as well. Regular bathing is vital.

Black-winged Lory
Eos cyanogenia

Distribution: Islands off the north-west coast of New Guinea.
Size: 30cm (12in).
Sexing: Visual distinction between the sexes is not possible.
Youngsters: Recognizable by their black bills and brown irises.

The prominent areas of black on the wing serve to distinguish this species from other similar lories. It has become better known in aviculture during recent years and breeding results have become increasingly common. If you keep this species indoors you will probably notice that it has a strong, rather musky scent; this appears to be most apparent when the birds are in top condition. Outside in an aviary, it will be far less obvious, and, provided that they are acclimatized properly, these lories can live outside throughout the year. Young birds can become talented mimics.

*Right: **Black-winged Lory**
This species has become better known in aviculture during recent years.*

Blue-streaked Lory
Eos reticulata

Distribution: Tenimbar islands of Indonesia.
Size: 30cm (12in).
Sexing: Visual distinction between the sexes is not possible.
Youngsters: Have greyish bills and are usually duller in overall coloration than adults.

The characteristic feature of this lory is the blue streaking evident on the mantle at the base of the neck, which extends to the sides of the face in some cases. This species was rare in aviculture until the 1970s, when forest clearance of its native islands began in earnest. This meant there was less habitat available and so these birds were caught in growing numbers. Unless this habitat loss can be stopped their future may in fact depend on aviculture. Fortunately, pairs nest quite readily in aviary surroundings and can be quite prolific. They can nest at almost any time, although they should not be encouraged to breed during the winter, and will eat a very wide range of foods when they are rearing young.

*Below: **Blue-streaked Lory**
The future of this species may depend on aviculture; pairs nest quite readily.*

Violet-necked Lory
Eos squamata

Distribution: Western Papuan and other nearby islands, extending to the northern Moluccas.
Size: 25cm (10in).
Sexing: Visual distinction between the sexes is not possible.
Youngsters: Have brown rather than reddish irises.

One of the smallest members of the genus, the Violet-necked, sometimes also known as the Violet-naped, is a good choice if you are starting with this group of parrots. It is easy to manage, and pairs do not become aggressive, even when breeding. The typical clutch is comprised of two eggs, and incubation lasts about 26 days. When rearing chicks, these lories will consume large amounts of greenfood.

Right: **Violet-necked Lory**
These colourful lories present no particular problems in terms of care; they are one of the smallest members of the genus and not aggressive. All in all an ideal choice for anyone beginning with this group of parrots.

Chattering Lory
Lorius garrulus

Distribution: Moluccan Islands, Indonesia.
Size: 30cm (12in).
Sexing: Visual distinction between the sexes is not possible.
Youngsters: Recognizable by their dark brown irises and bill.

Few lories are more attractive than the Chattering, but unfortunately the loud calls of these birds preclude them from being suitable for most outside aviaries in urban areas; unusually for parrots, they sometimes even call after dark. Chattering Lories are bold, inquisitive birds, and pairs should definitely be kept apart for breeding purposes. They nest quite readily, producing two eggs in a clutch. It takes 26 days for the chicks to hatch and they leave the nest about ten weeks later. A distinctive race of the Chattering Lory, sometimes seen in aviculture, is the Yellow-backed (*L. g. flavopalliatus*), which is found on the islands of Obi, Morotai and Batjan, and has a broad area of yellow plumage on the mantle.

It is unfortunate that this group of parrots is so messy, as this rather precludes them from being kept as pets in the home. Even in large quarters they will climb onto the sides of the flight, and it is difficult to protect furniture from their droppings.

Right: **Chattering Lory**
This is another of the predominantly red species, but with a distinctly scarlet hue. It is important to design accommodation for these birds so that it can be easily cleaned, in view of their rather fluid diet and messy habits.

Above: **Yellow-backed Chattering Lory**
This is a very distinctive race, with the yellow patch between the wings clearly visible here. This is not, however, a sign of sexual dimorphism.

Black-capped Lory
Lorius lory

Distribution: New Guinea and offshore islands.
Size: 30cm (12in).
Sexing: Visual distinction between the sexes is not possible.
Youngsters: Have horn-coloured bills.

All the *Lorius* lories have green wings, and this species also has a prominent area of black feathering on the head, and violet plumage around the nape of the neck. They are robust birds, and lively by nature. Even in aviary surroundings, a pair is likely to become quite tame, while hand-reared birds can become very talented mimics. Unfortunately, their messy habits in the home can be a significant drawback; lories generally benefit from bathing, but they will spread water over a wide area, and surrounding furniture needs to be adequately protected.

Right: **Black-capped Lory**
This is another species likely to prove prolific in aviary surroundings. Ensure that the nestbox has an absorbent lining.

Musschenbroek's Lorikeet
Neopsittacus musschenbroeki

Distribution: Vogelkop region of New Guinea.
Size: 23cm (9in).
Sexing: Visual distinction between the sexes is not possible.
Youngsters: Lack the red plumage seen on the underparts of adults.

An avicultural rarity until the early 1980s, these attractive small lorikeets proved no less ready to nest than their larger relatives. They are unusual in that seed forms a significant part of their diet; offer them a mixture of smaller cereal seeds, such as millets and plain canary seed, and provide soaked millet sprays as a rearing food. Two eggs are normally laid, and hatch after a period of 26 days. Some imported birds have been found to be infected with gapeworms – parasites that anchor typically at the entrance to the respiratory tract and interfere with the bird's breathing. If you find that these lorikeets are losing condition, these parasites may be responsible, and you should obtain appropriate treatment from your veterinarian. Handle affected birds with great care, because the stress of being caught and examined could prove fatal.

Below: **Musschenbroek's Lorikeet**
These birds differ somewhat from other lorikeets in terms of dietary needs. They are fairly hardy once acclimatized.

Dusky Lory
Pseudeos fuscata

Distribution: Most of New Guinea.
Size: 25cm (10in).
Sexing: Visual distinction between the sexes is not possible, though some hens may be distinguishable by their silvery white rump coloration.
Youngsters: Have a darker, brownish black bill.

The Dusky Lory is another lory in which the depth of coloration may differ between individuals; some birds are a much brighter, fiery shade of orange than others. Since becoming more common in aviculture during the 1970s, Dusky Lories have proved to be both hardy and free-breeding, and captive-bred stock is now readily available. Keep a check on the progress of nestlings; one chick may receive more than its fair share of food and you may need to supplement the diet of the other (usually the youngest).

Above: **Dusky Lory**
There is a natural variation in the coloration of these lories, which make attractive aviary occupants.

Below: **Meyer's Lorikeet**
This is one of the less common species in aviculture, but these relatively small lorikeets can prove prolific.

Meyer's Lorikeet
Trichoglossus flavoviridis meyeri

Distribution: The Indonesian island of Sulawesi (formerly Celebes).
Size: 17cm (7in).
Sexing: Visual distinction between the sexes is not possible, though cock birds may have a deeper shade of golden plumage on their heads.
Youngsters: Both the bill and irises are brown.

This is the better-known race of the Yellow and Green Lorikeet (*T. f. flavoviridis*), and the smallest of the *Trichoglossus* species. Although these birds can be kept in groups, breeding pairs should be housed on their own to prevent fighting. They may breed throughout much of the year and for over a decade. Incubation of the two eggs lasts about 24 days, and the young are probably mature by a year old. A diet similar to that recommended for the Iris Lorikeet suits them well. They are quite hardy once established.

Goldie's Lorikeet
Trichoglossus goldiei

Distribution: The central, mountainous region of New Guinea.
Size: 19cm (7in).
Sexing: Visual distinction between the sexes is not usually possible, though hens often have less colourful heads.
Youngsters: Have paler, browner bills and plumage streaking is less evident.

First introduced to aviculture at the end of the 1970s, Goldie's Lorikeet has since attracted a strong following. The species is an ideal choice for a garden aviary, being quiet and quite inoffensive. These lorikeets are quite prolific and you should be able to purchase youngsters without too much difficulty. If sexed birds are not available, choose the most brightly coloured and dullest individuals available (assuming, of course, that they are in good condition). Two eggs form the clutch, and in some cases, it is believed that the cock shares the task of incubation, which lasts a minimum of 22 days, the chicks fledging around two months later.

*Below: **Goldie's Lorikeets**
These delightful little birds are now quite well-established in aviculture and pairs usually nest without difficulty.*

*Above: **Green-naped Lorikeet**
One of the most widely kept species, in all its various forms. Try to ensure that your birds are all of the same race.*

Green-naped Lorikeet
Trichoglossus haematodus

Distribution: In parts of Indonesia, New Guinea and neighbouring islands, south to Australia.
Size: 26cm (11in).
Sexing: Visual distinction between the sexes is not possible.
Youngsters: Duller in coloration, with brown beaks and irises.

It is not entirely surprising that 21 distinctive races of this lorikeet have been recognized by taxonomists, given that this is the most widely distributed member of this entire group of parrots. The main variations relate to the coloration of the breast, which ranges from greenish yellow in the case of Weber's Lorikeet (*T. h. weberi*) through to red in Mitchell's Lorikeet (*T.h. mitchellii*). View them before you obtain them to ensure that they are of the same race. Green-naped Lorikeets are very adaptable birds, and easy to maintain; they are not especially destructive or noisy, although they do have quite a loud call.

Iris Lorikeet
Trichoglossus iris

Distribution: The islands of Timor and Wetar, Indonesia.
Size: 18cm (7in).
Sexing: Visual distinction between the sexes is not possible.
Youngsters: Duller overall, especially on the head, with brownish bills.

Another of the smaller lorikeets that adapts well to aviary life, the Iris has not achieved the popularity of Goldie's Lorikeet, largely because of its duller coloration. It benefits from a wide diet and will often eat more seed, a fact that is perhaps accounted for by its stocky bill. It will also consume green food and fruit avidly, especially when there are chicks in the nest. As with other lorikeets, adults may pluck their offspring when they start to feather up, but this need not be a cause for undue concern; the plumage should regrow quite quickly after the chicks fledge, and you should simply ensure that the young birds do not become chilled during this period.

*Below: **Iris Lorikeet**
Although shown here on vegetation, these and other lorikeets are likely to destroy any plants in their quarters.*

Ornate Lorikeet
Trichoglossus ornatus

Distribution: Sulawesi and other nearby Indonesian islands.
Size: 25cm (10in).
Sexing: Visual distinction between the sexes is not possible.
Youngsters: Have dark brown bills.

One of the most colourful members of this genus, the Ornate Lorikeet has unfortunately become scarcer in collections during recent years. These are long-lived and prolific birds, however, as shown by a pair nesting in South Africa, which produced over 20 youngsters and were believed to be 18 years old. As with all lories, keep a watch on the nestbox lining once the chicks have hatched; under normal circumstances, the floor covering should prove sufficiently absorbent, but on occasions, the base may be saturated by their fluid droppings and you will need to remove the chicks and clean the box as well as possible, before replacing them. Hopefully, this will not have disturbed the adult birds too much, but you will need to ensure that they do not subsequently neglect their chicks.

*Below: **Ornate Lorikeet**
Despite its recent decline in popularity, the Ornate presents no particular problems in terms of care or breeding.*

PARAKEETS

The description of 'parakeet' basically means a parrot with a long tail. The following section features a wide variety of the most popular and colourful parakeets from around the world. As a general rule, those that originate from Australia are likely to prove among the most free-breeding, and also the quietest in aviary surroundings. Parakeets are essentially aviary rather than pet birds, although the Brotogeris species from Central and South America, in particular, will settle well in the home if you obtain them young. Colour mutations of many parakeets are now becoming more common.

Amboina King Parakeet
Alisterus amboinensis

Distribution: From the Sula Islands to western New Guinea.
Size: 36cm (14in).

Sexing: Males tend to have red upper beaks, whereas those of hens are tinged with black markings.
Youngsters: Distinguishable from adults by their green mantles and dark brown irises.

These spectacular parakeets are not common in European or North American collections, although the closely related Australian King Parakeet (*A. scapularis*) is quite widely kept in its native country. A third species, the Green-winged King Parakeet (*A. chloropterus*), may be seen occasionally, but, like other king parakeets, is expensive. Differences in markings of Amboina King Parakeets result from their island distribution; six races are recognized by taxonomists.

King parakeets show to best effect in a long flight. Compatible pairs will nest satisfactorily, although sometimes cock birds can behave very aggressively towards their intended mates. The typical clutch of up to five eggs is incubated by the hen alone for about three weeks and the chicks fledge at two months old.

If you have the opportunity to purchase recently imported stock, remember that these birds need careful acclimatization.

*Left: **Australian King Parakeet**
This species is easy to sex; cocks have red heads, whereas those of hens are green. A deep nestbox encourages breeding activity.*

Crimson-winged Parakeet
Aprosmictus erythropterus

Distribution: North-eastern and northern Australia, and southern New Guinea.
Size: 33cm (13in).
Sexing: Hens are duller than cocks, with no black mantle and a smaller area of red on the wings.
Youngsters: Resemble hens, but have a yellowish bill at fledging.

This species, also known as the Red-winged Parakeet, prefers a deep nestbox. You can build this as a free-standing structure, but as an added precaution, you may decide to bolt it to the side of the aviary. Some cocks are aggressive and, if possible, you should make up pairs before the birds reach maturity, by three years of age. These parakeets prove reliable breeders; one pair on record produced 26 chicks over a nine-year period. Other breeding details are similar to those of the king parakeets, although youngsters may fledge at a slightly earlier age. They can live for over 20 years.

In the past, imported Crimson-wings have been badly infested with tapeworms, so it is advisable to administer appropriate treatment to newly purchased birds.

Another species of Crimson-wing, the Timor form, is found on some of the Lesser Sunda islands but is rarely seen in avicultural collections at present. Cocks of this form can easily be distinguished from hens by the absence of black feathering on their wings.

Below left: **Crimson-winged Parakeet**
The spectacular markings of this species can be clearly seen here. Hens are less colourful than this cock.

Below: **Crimson-winged Parakeet**
These attractive parakeets may live for 20 years, and have a correspondingly long reproductive life.

Barnard's Parakeet
Barnardius barnardi

Distribution: Interior parts of eastern Australia.
Size: 33cm (13in).
Sexing: Cocks generally have more colourful plumage than hens, particularly on their backs and abdomens.
Youngsters: The crown and the nape of the neck are brownish.

The two members of this genus tend to rank amongst the least common and more expensive of the Australian parakeets in aviculture. Three separate races of Barnard's Parakeet are recognized. The Cloncurry (*B. b. macgillivrayi*) is the one you are most likely to encounter and this is also the most colourful form, with a prominent area of yellow plumage present on its underparts. Discovered as recently as 1900, this race occurs as an isolated population, found in northwestern Queensland and an adjoining part of the Northern Territory. It remains most common in continental Europe. Pairs have double-brooded (bred twice in a season), producing as many as nine youngsters.

Right: **Barnard's Parakeet**
A cock may prove aggressive if you venture too close to its nestbox. Mealworms are popular with these birds during the rearing period.

Port Lincoln Parakeet

Barnardius zonarius

Distribution: Over a wide area of western and central Australia.
Size: 38cm (15in).
Sexing: Hens usually have a more brownish head than cocks.
Youngsters: Duller in colour than adults.

Both races of this species have become more common in aviculture during recent years, although they remain relatively expensive. The Twenty-eight Parakeet (*B. z. semitorquatus*) can be easily distinguished from the nominate race by its green rather than yellow abdomen and the red band usually present above the beak, surrounding the cere. Blue mutations of both have been recorded in the past and are said to be currently represented in European collections, although they are scarce.

As with Barnard's Parakeet, the incubation period lasts approximately 19 days, and the chicks fledge at around five weeks old. A few cocks are egg-eaters, and so you may need to remove cocks from the aviary as soon as mating has taken place.

Right: **Port Lincoln Parakeet**
Like other Australian parakeets, these birds will often feed on the ground.

Sierra Parakeet

Bolborhynchus aymara

Distribution: Eastern Andes, from Bolivia to north-western Argentina.
Size: 20cm (8in).
Sexing: It is generally difficult to distinguish between the sexes, but some cocks have dark grey heads and more silvery breasts.
Youngsters: Similar to adults, but with shorter tails.

You may also find these delightful parakeets advertised under a variety of other names, such as the Aymara or the Andean Parakeet. They were first brought to Europe by Gerald Durrell, the famous naturalist, in 1959. Since then, there have been a number of further importations, but stock is now scarce. Nevertheless, they are prolific birds – they may rear up to seven chicks in one nest, and it is possible to breed them on a colony system, provided that you supply them with an adequate choice of nestboxes and do not add new individuals to the group. At present, however, reasonably large numbers are produced only by Danish breeders.

Like other members of its genus, the Sierra Parakeet is quiet, with a high-pitched and not unattractive call. A further advantage of this species is that it is not very destructive.

Right: **Sierra Parakeets**
Sierra Parakeets breed well in the aviary and will use a conventional nestbox. (In the wild, they may nest in holes in prickly cacti, where they are out of reach of predators.)

Golden-fronted Parakeet
Bolborhynchus aurifrons

Distribution: In isolated populations along the eastern side of South America, from Peru southwards to Chile.
Size: 18cm (7in).
Sexing: In some cases, males are more colourful than females.
Youngsters: Similar to the hen.

Four separate populations of the Golden-fronted Parakeet have given rise to an equivalent number of races, so that birds purchased from different sources could turn out to be different sub-species.

Although doubts have been expressed about how well these parakeets travel, the few recent importations have had a very low level of mortality. Golden-fronted Parakeets do require a reasonable acclimatization period, but they are not delicate birds, and their poor survival rate in the past is more likely to have been caused by an unsuitable diet than by stress. Ensure that they receive a mixed diet of smaller cereal seeds, including millet sprays, greenfood, and regular supplies of fruit, such as apple and blackberries in season. Avoid excessive amounts of sunflower seeds.

Lineolated Parakeet
Bolborhynchus lineola

Distribution: Central and South America, ranging from Mexico to Panama and from western Venezuela to central Peru.
Size: 16cm (6in).
Sexing: The barring on the rump and tail feathers is more prominent on cocks than on hens. These markings have given rise to the species' other name of Barred Parakeet.

Youngsters: The bluish tinge on their heads is usually more pronounced than on adults.

This species is probably the most commonly available member of its genus in the UK at present. Its habits do not differ markedly from those of related parakeets. Breeding on the colony system is quite feasible; indeed, you are likely to achieve better results if you can keep these birds in a group, rather than as individual pairs. Incubation lasts

about 18 days and the chicks fledge at about five weeks old. The average clutch size varies from three to six eggs.

Above: **Golden-fronted Parakeet**
These parakeets are variable in coloration; some cocks are more yellow than the one shown here.

Below: **Lineolated Parakeet**
Quiet, attractive and free-breeding when kept in small groups, these birds are also less destructive than most species.

Cobalt-winged Parakeet
Brotogeris cyanoptera

Distribution: Western Amazonian region, including parts of Colombia, Venezuela, Peru, Ecuador and Bolivia.
Size: 18cm (7in).
Sexing: Not visually possible.
Youngsters: Duller overall in colour than adults, with a dark grey, rather than brown, upper mandible.

This is presently one of the less common members of the genus in avicultural circles. It can be distinguished from similar species by its violet-blue wing colour.

House these parakeets, and other *Brotogeris* species, in small groups if you want to breed them successfully. To minimize the risk of aggressive behaviour, position the nestboxes at the same height.

You may encounter problems if you have to remove one member from an established group of Cobaltwings; it will lose its place in the flock hierarchy, and when you try to return it, even just a few days later, it will be treated as a newcomer, and may be attacked. Ideally, if you do need to remove or add one bird, you should transfer all the parakeets to temporary accommodation for up to a week, before reintroducing them all to the original flight. They should then accept one another more readily. Do not mix different *Brotogeris* species together, however, as hybridization can occur.

*Right: **Cobalt-winged Parakeet***
These lively parakeets must have natural wood perches to gnaw in order to prevent their beaks becoming overgrown like this.

Tovi Parakeet
Brotogeris jugularis

Distribution: South-western parts of Mexico, and northern parts of Colombia and Venezuela.
Size: 18cm (7cm).
Sexing: Not visually possible.
Youngsters: Resemble adults.

This is another species that is known under a variety of common names, including Bee-Bee Parrot and, more accurately, the Orange-chinned Parakeet. This characteristic and the dark, olive-brown wing markings of these parakeets are both identifying features. In the wild, Tovis remain in flocks at all times of the year and may use the nests of termites, located in trees. In captivity, significant breeding results have been obtained only when these parakeets have been housed in colonies. As many as eight young have been reared by a single pair, and are mature at one year old.

*Left: **Tovi Parakeet***
Like all Brotogeris *parakeets, Tovis nest more readily if they are kept as a group, and are hardy once acclimatized.*

Grey-cheeked Parakeet
Brotogeris pyrrhopterus

Distribution: South America, in coastal areas of western Ecuador and north-western Peru.
Size: 20cm (8in).
Sexing: Not visually possible.
Youngsters: Their green heads lack the bluish markings of adults.

These birds, also called Orange-flanked or Orange-winged Parakeets because of the prominent orange area on the undersides of the wings, used to be freely available but are now scarce. Like all *Brotogeris*, tame youngsters were once very popular pets, but few were kept by serious breeders. They have quite a loud call, which can become persistent if the parakeet is upset. Youngsters often form a strong bond with their owners, and may become jealous of other pets.

Assorted fruits need to form a significant part of the diet of this group of parakeets. Banana is a favourite food, although it can be messy, sticking to

perches and the sides of the cage, and sweet apple is also very popular. You can also feed soaked dried fruits occasionally, and drained canned fruits, that been mixed with natural juice rather than syrup, are also suitable.

Above: **Grey-cheeked Parakeet**
Also known as the Orange-flanked Parakeet because of the colourful orange plumage hidden under its wings, this bird is highly gregarious by nature and can be destructive.

Canary-winged Parakeet
Brotogeris versicolorus

Distribution: Over a wide area of the Amazon Basin, and further south, across Brazil, to Bolivia, Paraguay and Argentina.
Size: 23cm (9in).
Sexing: Not visually possible.
Youngsters: Usually duller in colour than adults.

Two very distinct forms of this parakeet are recognized: the White-winged race (*B. v. versicolorus*) is much darker in colour and has paler yellow wing markings than the Canary-winged, which is the most commonly available member of the genus.

Once acclimatized, these parakeets are quite hardy, but you should encourage them to roost in the shelter if they will not use a nestbox. Records of successful

Above: **Canary-winged Parakeets**
Young birds can develop into very tame pets. Fruit is a favourite of these and all Brotogeris species. Offer some every day as an important item in their diet.

breeding are scarce, but four eggs appear to form the typical clutch, and these hatch after about 26 days. The chicks fledge at approximately seven weeks old.

Yellow-fronted Kakariki
Cyanoramphus auriceps

Distribution: New Zealand and neighbouring islands.
Size: 23cm (9in).
Sexing: Males are larger then females, with bolder coloration.
Youngsters: Recognizable by their shorter tails and brown irises.

This species is slightly smaller than the better-known Red-fronted Kakariki. The unusual name of these parakeets is said to describe their call, and originates from a Maori word. They make ideal occupants for a garden aviary, as they are quiet and usually keen to breed. Pairs normally nest twice in a season, laying between five and nine eggs, which hatch after a period of 19 days. The hen will usually lay again before her first chicks have left the nest, at about six weeks old, and the cock will then feed them for a few more days until they are able to eat on their own. You should then remove the young birds before the cock becomes aggressive towards them.

Right: **Yellow-fronted Kakariki**
These New Zealand parakeets are becoming increasingly popular. Pairs nest readily and mature quickly, but don't breed birds less than a year old.

Below: **Yellow-fronted Kakariki (yellow mutation)**
This is a very rare mutation.

Red-fronted Kakariki
Cyanoramphus novaezelandiae

Distribution: New Zealand and neighbouring islands.
Size: 28cm (11in).
Sexing: Hens are usually slightly smaller than cocks.
Youngsters: The area of red on the head is smaller, and the tail shorter than that of adults.

Both these species of kakariki are unusual aviary birds, scratching around on the floor with their feet, and capable of running straight up the mesh to a perch without using their beaks. If you have adjoining aviaries, it is vital, therefore, that you install double-wiring to protect them from other parakeets in neighbouring flights.
   Kakarikis will benefit from a very varied diet, which can include softbill food and livefood, such as mealworms. They also enjoy greenfood and various berries. Unfortunately, because they often spend time on the ground looking for food, they are susceptible to intestinal parasitic worms.
   Mutations have been recorded in these prolific birds, including a lutino and a pied form, which is at present being developed in the UK.

*Right: **Red-fronted Kakariki***
This is a prolific and popular aviary species but has a maximum lifespan of about five years.

Swift Parakeet
Lathamus discolor

Distribution: South-eastern Australia.
Size: 25cm (10in).
Sexing: Hens may be duller than cocks.
Youngsters: Recognizable by their brown irises.

These parakeets resemble lories, certainly in terms of their diet – they have even evolved the latter's characteristic papillae on the tongue, used to collect pollen. But they should also be offered seed (especially millet and plain canary seed) as a regular part of their diet, as well as fruit and greenstuff. Pairs do not show the same close inter-relationships as lories, and so display some similarity also to Australian Parakeets.
   Swift Parakeets are attractive and quiet birds but are not especially common in aviculture (they are most often seen in collections on the European mainland). They are fast fliers, migrating in the wild across the Bass Strait to Tasmania each year, and benefit from being kept in a spacious aviary. Hens typically lay up to five eggs in a clutch. These should hatch after about 18 days, with the chicks fledging around six weeks later.

*Left: **Swift Parakeets***
Despite their attractive appearance and quite nature, these birds are not particularly common in aviculture.

Quaker Parakeet
Myiopsitta monachus

Distribution: Bolivia and parts of Brazil and Argentina.
Size: 29cm (11½in).
Sexing: Not visually possible.
Youngsters: Recognizable by the green tinge to their foreheads.

The breeding habits of these interesting but rather noisy parakeets are unique. Although they will use a nestbox, they often prefer to build a nest of twigs in the aviary, as they do in the wild. These nests can become very large and will be difficult to look into, which is a disadvantage. If you do decide to try this method of breeding, therefore, provide the birds with a stout horizontal mesh support, fixed onto the side of the flight, and a supply of twigs. (Even in a nestbox, Quakers will include pieces of wood taken from perches if they do not have access to twigs.) You are likely to obtain the best results by keeping these birds in a colony. Up to seven eggs form the usual clutch.
  Colour mutations are known, the blue form being the most common. It is usual to pair a blue with a normal because of a lethal factor, which prevents some of the embryos from hatching if two blues are paired together. A rarer yellow mutant has also been bred.

Right: **Quaker Parakeet**
These fascinating, though noisy, birds live in colonies in the wild and build large bulky nests of sticks.

Bourke's Grass Parakeet
Neophema bourkii

Distribution: The interior of southern and central Australia.
Size: 19cm (7½in).
Sexing: Hens have a mainly white forehead, whereas that of males is entirely blue.
Youngsters: Resemble hens, but have paler pink abdomens. Young hens have a well-developed wing stripe.

These highly popular parakeets are the only grass parakeets that show no green coloration in their plumage. Their eyes are relatively large, confirming that they become more active towards dusk.
  Pairs will usually breed readily in aviary surroundings, with the hen laying up to five eggs. She incubates these alone for about 19 days, and the chicks leave the nest for the first time when they are just over a month old. Once they become independent, shortly after this, you should remove them so that the adult pair can continue breeding without interference.
  During recent years, the rosa mutation, also known in continental Europe as the opaline, has become quite

Left: **Bourke's Grass Parakeet (normal)**
This small attractive parakeet is widely available. Pairs will often nest twice during the summer.

Below: **Bourke's Grass Parakeet (yellow rosa mutation)**
A number of such attractive colour mutations have now been developed.

Above: **Bourke's Grass Parakeet (cinnamon mutation)**
The normal form's dark markings are modified to a paler brown here.

Below: **Bourke's Grass Parakeet (rosa mutation)**
This is the most widely kept mutation by virtue of its strong pink coloration.

common. The effect of this mutation is to increase and intensify the soft reddish coloration most noticeable on the belly of the normal-coloured bird. You can distinguish young Bourke's of this form from normals while they are still in the nest; by ten days of age, the feet of normals have darkened in colour, whereas rosa Bourke's retain pinkish feet throughout their lives. Other rarer mutations include a yellow, which has a pinkish head and breast, and a cinnamon. Apart from its reddish eyes, this cinnamon form closely resembles a normal in appearance. Pied Bourke's have also been recorded, and colour combinations are now being produced, though as yet they are not common.

Left: **Blue-winged Grass Parakeet**
This species is less common than other grass parakeets, but is as easy to care for as its relatives.

Below: **Elegant Grass Parakeet**
The beautiful appearance of this species can be clearly seen here. Like other Neophema *species, these parakeets may live for 10 years.*

Bottom: **Elegant Grass Parakeet (lutino mutation)**
This rare form was first bred during 1972 in Belgium. Initially the strain was weak, but such birds are now much stronger.

Blue-winged Grass Parakeet
Neophema chrysostomus

Distribution: South-eastern Australia, including Tasmania.
Size: 20cm (8in).
Sexing: Hens have olive-green crowns and duller blue wings, whereas cocks are more colourful, with black, rather than brownish black, primary flight feathers.
Youngsters: Wing stripes are always present in young hens, but not always in cocks. Juveniles of both sexes lack the blue frontal band of adult birds.

This species has never achieved the popularity of other grass parakeets, possibly because it is less colourful. In its favour, it lays its first clutch of eggs slightly later in the year than other parakeets so that the likelihood of egg-binding is greatly reduced. Bluewings can be prolific breeders and often double-brood; one pair are on record as having produced 68 chicks to fledging over a nine-year period. A further advantage of Blue-winged Grass Parakeets is that the fledglings are rarely as nervous as those of other related species, such as Turquoisines.

Elegant Grass Parakeet
Neophema elegans

Distribution: South-west and south-east Australia.
Size: 23cm (9in).
Sexing: Hens tend to be duller in colour than the cocks, without any orange visible on the abdomen.
Youngsters: Similar to hens, but lacking the frontal band.

These parakeets are well established in aviculture and will nest readily in the aviary. Breeding details are similar to those of Bourke's Parakeet (and some other members of the genus).
   A beautiful, bright yellow lutino form, with red eyes and white head and wing markings, was produced in Belgium during the 1970s. The loss of surrounding pigment emphasizes the orange between the legs of cock birds of this mutation. Unfortunately, the first chick died at a few months old, and the strain proved to have poor fertility. Interestingly, this is one of the very few lutino mutations known in parrots to be of the autosomal recessive form, rather than having a sex-linked mode of inheritance.

Turquoisine Grass Parakeet
Neophema pulchella

Distribution: South-eastern Australia.
Size: 20cm (8in).
Sexing: Hens are duller than cocks, and lack the red wing patches of the latter.
Youngsters: Similar to hens. A slight outline of the wing patches may be visible on young cocks.

The Turquoisine Grass Parakeet is a very common species in aviculture, but its status in the wild is unclear and it may be becoming increasingly rare in its natural habitat. There is an orange-bellied form of the Turquoisine, which is very popular, and birds with this distinctive coloration are known to occur in the wild. Among the mutations bred

in collections are yellow, pied and olive forms. The pied mutation of this parakeet is a sex-linked recessive character, rather than the autosomal recessive type (see pages 73-74).

As aviary subjects, these parakeets are rather more aggressive than related species. If possible, avoid keeping pairs in adjoining aviaries, since cocks, especially, will bicker through the mesh. They will also attack their youngsters soon after fledging. Young Turquoisines are probably the most nervous of all the grass parakeets. Screening the end of the flight with climbing plants, such as nasturtiums, may help to reduce the risk of injuries. Take particular care when catching young birds; try to shut them in the shelter, where they will be less likely to injure themselves.

Top left: **Turquoisine Grass Parakeet**
A colourful and popular species. Hens lack the distinctive deep red wing patches of this cock bird.

Top right: Two mutations of the Turquoisine Grass Parakeet; a red-fronted cock and a yellow hen.

Above left: It has proved possible to combine various mutations of the Turquoisine. These parakeets, the result of combining the red-bellied form with the yellow mutation, are strikingly colourful birds.

Above right: These orange-bellied Turquoisines are identical to the more common yellow-bellied form, apart from the coloration of their belly.

Splendid Parakeet
Neophema splendida

Distribution: The interior of southern Australia.
Size: 19cm (7½in).
Sexing: Cocks are instantly recognized by their scarlet chests.
Youngsters: Similar to hens, but cocks may have bluer faces. Young cocks start to show red feathers on their breasts from about two months after fledging.

These stunningly beautiful parakeets used to be very scarce, but aviary stock is now well established. This species provides an excellent introduction to the hobby of breeding parakeets, since pairs are relatively inexpensive and usually become quite tame in aviary surroundings.

Several mutations have been bred, of which the most common is currently the blue form. However, as with the Quaker Parakeet, blue stock should not be paired together because of the lethal factor. These particular birds are not pure blue in coloration, but have a greenish tinge to their plumage. Yellow, cinnamon and fallow forms are also recognized.

Right: **Splendid Parakeet**
This beautiful species has proved extremely prolific in aviaries.

Below left: **Splendid Parakeet**
(cinnamon mutation)
This is a hen bird, lacking the bright chest marking of the cock. Such birds are somewhat paler than the normals.

Below right: **Splendid Parakeet**
(blue mutation)
This is not a pure blue; the outline of the red breast of the normal cock is still visible as a pale shade of orange.

Mealy Rosella
Platycercus adscitus

Distribution: North-eastern Australia.
Size: 30cm (12in).
Sexing: Cocks lack the wing stripe of hens.
Youngsters: Duller in coloration than the hen, juveniles may also have red or grey markings on their heads.

The rosellas, or broadtails, as they are otherwise known, are a group of eight Australian species, which are generally well represented in aviculture. There are two distinctive sub-species of this particular rosella in the wild; the

*Below: **Mealy Rosella***
These attractive rosellas are larger than the grass parakeets, and need aviaries with plenty of flying space as they are lively by nature.

nominate race is the Blue-cheeked (*P. a. adscitus*), while the Mealy itself (*P. a. palliceps*) has pure white, rather than blue, feathering surrounding the lower beak. Unfortunately, indiscriminate pairings in the past have obscured these features in aviary-bred stock, although well-marked Mealy Rosellas can occasionally be seen. Careful selective breeding should refine the markings.

Green Rosella
Platycercus caledonicus

Distribution: Tasmania and some neighbouring islands.
Size: 36cm (14in).
Sexing: Hens tend to be smaller than cocks and may have orange-red markings on the throat.
Youngsters: Duller in colour than adults with blue cheek patches and a wing stripe.

These parakeets, sometimes also known as Tasmanian Rosellas, have tended to be less popular than their more colourful counterparts, although increasing numbers are being bred in Europe.

These rosellas eat greenfood eagerly; if possible, provide fresh supplies each day, but remember that excessive amounts may lead to scouring. A standard seed diet, comprised of cereals with some sunflower and pine nuts, suits all rosellas well and they may also take fruit in their diet.

A related species, the Yellow Rosella (*P. flaveolus*), is similar in appearance and requirements to the Green Rosella, but is relatively uncommon.

*Below: **Yellow Rosella***
This species is often confused with its relative, the Green Rosella, but is slightly smaller, more brightly coloured, and rarer than the latter.

Crimson Rosella
Platycercus elegans

Distribution: Eastern and south-eastern parts of Australia.
Size: 36cm (14in).
Sexing: Visual sexing is difficult, although hens may have smaller heads than cocks.
Youngsters: Juveniles vary in appearance; some are mainly green, whereas others are predominantly reddish, more closely resembling adults.

Also known as Pennant's Parakeet, this is one of the most widely kept rosellas, and a blue mutation is also now established. Although hardy and easy to keep, some individuals are prone to feather-plucking and will pull out their feathers until their body is covered only in grey down. This is a difficult problem to overcome, but such birds will breed normally.

Established pairs can be very prolific, rearing as many as seven chicks or more, although some hens will eat the eggs or refuse to incubate properly. As a consequence, it is best to start with young birds, rather than attempt to breed adults, which may have these vices. The birds will be mature by one year old.

Rosellas will hybridize with each other and, in the wild, this tendency appears to have given rise to the Adelaide Rosella. This population is thought to result from Crimson and Yellow Rosellas breeding together in two small areas of Southern Australia. Trial matings in aviary surroundings have confirmed the appearance of such offspring and, unusually, these hybrids are fertile.

Above: **Crimson Rosella**
Among the most striking and popular of all rosellas, these birds can prove very prolific breeders in aviary surroundings.

Below: **Adelaide Rosella**
This species could be a natural hybrid, resulting from matings of Crimson and Yellow Rosellas.

Eastern Rosella
Platycercus eximius

Distribution: South-eastern Australia and Tasmania.
Size: 30cm (12in).
Sexing: Hens are duller than cocks, with a reduced area of red on the head and breast.
Youngsters: Distinguishable by their green napes and hind crown.

These rosellas usually prove reliable breeders, laying on average six or seven eggs. As with other species, the incubation period lasts about three weeks. Chicks leave the nest when approximately six weeks old, and can breed during their second year, before they have moulted into full adult plumage. (This normally occurs by the age of 15 months.) All rosellas have a potentially long lifespan and are quite capable of breeding into their twenties.

Right: **Eastern Rosella (pastel mutation)**
This rare form shows the characteristic paling of the normal dark markings.

Below: **Eastern Rosellas**
These parakeets, often known as Golden-mantled Rosellas, are very popular as aviary birds.

Western Rosella
Platycercus icterotis

Distribution: South-western Australia.
Size: 25cm (10in).
Sexing: Clearly dimorphic, hens are much duller than cocks, with a greenish head and underparts.
Youngsters: Almost entirely green at fledging.

This species, which is perhaps more often called the Stanley Parakeet, is the smallest member of the *Platycercus* genus (see pages 151-153).
  Western Rosellas are less common, and consequently more costly, than other rosellas. This is probably because they will rarely have more than one round of chicks in a season. However, as a prolific pair can lay as many as eight eggs in a clutch, you may still be able to achieve good breeding results.
  Colours mutations of this parakeet are unknown, and remain very rare in other rosellas, too.

Right: **Western Rosella**
Less common than its larger relatives, this species is easy to sex: the cock, shown here, with a red head and underparts, is more colourful than the predominantly green hen.

Princess of Wales' Parakeet
Polytelis alexandrae

Distribution: The interior of western and central Australia.
Size: 45cm (18in).
Sexing: Hens have greyish rather than light blue crowns, and a greyer rump than cocks.
Youngsters: Similar to the hen.

The attractive pastel coloration of these parakeets has ensured their popularity, and they have been bred in increasing numbers during recent years. At least two colour mutations have appeared; the blue form was first bred in Australia in 1951 and, more recently, a lutino mutation was developed by an East German breeder in 1975.

One of the most desirable features of the Princess of Wales' Parakeet, besides its coloration, is the fact that it will become very tame in aviary surroundings with little persuasion. Unfortunately, the penetrating calls of adult birds may cause problems, particularly in an urban environment. Breeding details are similar to those of other members of the genus.

Right: **Princess of Wales' Parakeet**
A colourful species that is easy to tame.

Below: **Princess of Wales' Parakeet (blue mutation)**
This autosomal recessive mutation is becoming increasingly common.

Rock Pebbler (Peplar)
Polytelis anthopeplus

Distribution: South-western Australia, and in an inland area of south-eastern Australia.
Size: 40cm (16in).
Sexing: Hens, which are predominantly olive-yellow in colour, are much duller than cocks.
Youngsters: Similar to hens.

These parakeets are also called Regent Parrots. Some pairs prefer to nest close to the ground, especially in flights containing ample vegetation. Do not encourage this behaviour, however, especially if the area is exposed to the elements. The red markings on the cock's wings feature prominently in its mating display. The hen lays about five eggs, which she incubates for about 19 days. The young parakeets will emerge into the aviary about six weeks later, but may not breed themselves until they are two years old.

When buying any *Polytelis* species, check that the nostrils are clear, and that there is no swelling around the eye, as they are prone to sub-clinical *Mycoplasma* infections, which can be difficult to eliminate, though they cause the bird no serious distress.

Right: **Rock Pebbler**
Like other larger Australian species, youngsters usually start breeding during their second year.

Barraband Parakeet
Polytelis swainsonii

Distribution: Interior of south-eastern Australia.
Size: 40cm (16in).
Sexing: Hens can be easily recognized by the lack of yellow plumage on their heads.
Youngsters: Resemble hens, but have dark brown irises.

This species, the third and final member of the *Polytelis* genus, is also known as the Superb Parrot. Like all the larger Australian species, this very majestic bird needs a long flight, both for its comfort, and for its beauty to be seen to advantage. These parakeets are quite gentle by nature and pairs do best when housed in close proximity to each other, as they are naturally social. It has even proved possible to breed more than one pair in a large aviary, although some cocks may be aggressive. Young males are still at risk from their paternal parent when they emerge from the nest, and so, as always, you should remove the chicks as soon as they are feeding independently. Try to pair up young birds as soon as possible; this should help to ensure successful breeding results later.

Right: **Barraband Parakeet**
Note the distinctive yellow head of this adult cock. Immature males are recognizable by their song.

155

Red-rumped Parakeet
Psephotus haematonotus

Distribution: South-eastern Australia.
Size: 27cm (11in).
Sexing: Cocks are far more colourful than the greyish green hens.
Youngsters: Young hens have yellower beaks than adults, while those of cocks are grey rather than black.

The Red-rumped Parakeet is by far the best-known member of its genus, of which five species are found in aviculture, and pairs make attractive aviary occupants. The cocks have a very appealing musical song, but they can be savage, especially towards male offspring, which they may attack even while they are still in the nestbox. Five eggs form a typical clutch, and incubation lasts around 19 days. The chicks will be ready to leave the nest by the time they are six weeks old.

A dull yellow form has been developed and used to be the most commonly bred Australian parakeet mutation. A blue form, which emerged during 1968 in Australia, is presently being developed, along with a lutino mutation. In time, by careful pairings, it should be possible to produce an albino form using these two primary mutations.

Other members of this genus that you may occasionally encounter are the Many-coloured or Mulga Parakeet (*P.

varius), which tends to be somewhat more delicate than the hardy Redrump, the Blue-bonnet Parakeet (*Psephotus haematogaster*), of which Red- and Yellow-vented races are known, and the striking Hooded Parakeet (*Psephotus chryospterygius*).

Above: **Red-rumped Parakeets**
These popular parakeets are easy to sex and usually breed well.

Below: **Red-rumped Parakeet (yellow mutation)**
Hens are duller than this cock.

Moustached Parakeet
Psittacula alexandri

Distribution: From the Himalayas of northern India, eastwards across south-east Asia, to offshore islands, including Java and Bali.
Size: 33cm (13in).
Sexing: In most cases, hens have black beaks, whereas those of cocks are red.
Youngsters: Duller overall in colour than adults, juveniles also have shorter tails.

The 12 species of psittaculid parakeet are found mainly in Asia and on a number of the offshore islands in this region. The Moustached Parakeet has a wide distribution, and up to eight different races can be identified. Both sexes of the Javan sub-species (*P. a. alexandri*), have a reddish bill, but the distinctions are more marked between other races.

Moustached Parakeets are attractive, although rather noisy birds. Once imported in large numbers, they are now quite scarce. Few breeding results have been recorded, but this would appear to be due largely to a lack of interest on the part of birdkeepers, rather than to intrinsic difficulties in persuading these birds to nest. Incubation lasts about 28 days, two or three eggs form the usual clutch and chicks fledge when they are just over seven weeks.

Right: **Moustached Parakeet**
An attractive species. Established pairs breed quite readily, but need to be carefully acclimatized first.

Plum-headed Parakeet
Psittacula cyanocephala

Distribution: Sri Lanka and most of India.
Size: 33cm (13in).
Sexing: Adult cocks have plum-coloured heads, whereas those of hens are greyish.
Youngsters: Resemble hens, although they initially fledge with green heads.

These highly attractive parakeets are ideal members of this genus to keep in an urbanized setting, since they are not noisy; indeed, their calls are actually quite melodious.

It can be difficult to obtain pairs, as a relatively high proportion of youngsters appear to moult out as cocks. The earliest traces of plum-coloured feathering can be seen close to the cere. Plumheads nest quite early in the year if allowed to do so, and unfortunately, they will stop brooding their chicks at an early stage, which can prove fatal. In cold climates, they will breed quite satisfactorily in an indoor flight, provided that you keep the temperature reasonably high. Like other psittaculids, they are at risk from frostbite, and need adequate protection in cold weather.

A similar parakeet, the Blossom-headed, occurs further east than the Plumhead. It is a slightly smaller form, and hens can be distinguished from Plumhead hens by their red wing patches. Most taxonomists now see these as being related sub-species rather than separate species.

Above: **Plum-headed Parakeet**
This is a mature cock. These birds are quieter and less destructive than other psittaculid species.

Alexandrine Parakeet
Psittacula eupatria

Distribution: From eastern Afghanistan through India to Indo-China. Also present in Sri Lanka.
Size: 58cm (23in).
Sexing: Adult hens lack the neck ring of cocks.
Youngsters: Resemble hens, but have shorter tails.

These large, spectacular parakeets are mature, in most cases, during their third year and, once established, pairs will nest consistently for up to two decades. Two or three eggs form the usual clutch and should hatch after an incubation period of 28 days.

Young hand-reared Alexandrines can develop into lively, trusting companions, although they are not great mimics and may be destructive towards any exposed woodwork in their aviary. Pine nuts, peanuts and sweet apple are favoured food items. Never be tempted to buy an Alexandrine (or indeed a Ring-necked Parakeet) with a pink neck collar if you are seeking a youngster, as such birds will be at least two years old.

Slaty headed Parakeet
Psittacula himalayana

Distribution: In a band stretching from eastern Afghanistan to India and Nepal, south-eastwards into Indo-China.
Size: 40cm (16in).
Sexing: Hens either lack the deep maroon wing patch of cocks, or it is only faintly visible.
Youngsters: Recognizable by their green heads and cheeks.

The Slaty headed Parakeet is similar to, though less commonly available than, the Plum-headed Parakeet. Hybridization between these two species has been reported, and in the wild may have given rise to the so-called Intermediate Parakeet (*P. intermedia*), which shares the characteristics of both species. This very rare Intermediate Parakeet is thought to occur in the region of Uttar Pradesh in India.

Up to five eggs appear to form the usual clutch, and these hatch after about 26 days.

*Below left: **Alexandrine Parakeet***
Genuine blue and lutino colour forms of this species are known, but matings with mutation Ringnecks have also been used to create such colours artificially.

*Below: **Slaty headed Parakeet***
Both sexes are characterized by their slaty grey head, but hens lack the cock's maroon wing patch.

Below: **Indian Ring-necked Parakeet**
Only mature cocks have this neck collar. Juvenile males resemble adult hens.

Right: *This stunning blue mutation of the Ring-necked Parakeet is becoming increasingly widespread.*

Ring-necked Parakeet
Psittacula krameri

Distribution: Occurs naturally across a wide belt of northern Africa, and also in India and adjoining areas.
Size: 40cm (16in).
Sexing: Hens lack the nuchal collars of cocks.
Youngsters: Resemble hens, but have shorter tail feathers.

This is the most widely distributed of all parakeet species. The Indian race (*P. k. manillensis*) is slightly larger than the African (*P. k. krameri*), and the pink collar of the cock bird is often rather more pronounced on the former. The African Ringneck has a much darker beak, with black markings on the upper mandible. Both forms have long been popular avicultural subjects.

Ringnecks may occasionally breed when two years old, but it is usually three years before they are fully mature. In northern climates mating takes place early in the year and Ringnecks are often one of the first species to start nesting. The hen may lay up to six eggs and these will hatch after a period of about 24 days. The chicks fledge when they are around 50 days old and it is unusual, though not unknown, for the adults to nest again that season unless the first round of eggs fail to hatch or the chicks die at an early age.

Many colour mutations have been established, some of which, such as the blue, are known to have originated in the wild. The lutino is presently the most common mutation and when this is combined with the blue, pure albino Ringnecks, which lack any colour pigment and so have no neck collar, result. Other mutations include cinnamons, greys and a greenish blue form, sometimes called the Pastel Blue. Sometimes pied markings may be due to nutritional factors rather than of genetic origin, in which case they will disappear after a moult (or may sometimes become extensive, if the cause of the problem is not recognized).

Above: **Ring-necked Parakeet (albino mutation)**
With no colour pigment present, both sexes appear identical.

Left: **Ring-necked Parakeet (lutino mutation)**
This is now the most common Ring-necked mutation. These two young chicks are 16 weeks old.

Below: **Ring-necked Parakeet (grey mutation)**
This is usually a dominant mutation, but a recessive form is being developed.

Long-tailed Parakeet
Psittacula longicauda

Distribution: Malay peninsula, and offshore islands, such as the Andamans, Borneo and Sumatra.
Size: 42cm (17in).
Sexing: Hens have brown upper beaks, whereas those of cocks are reddish in colour.
Youngsters: Mainly green, with short tail feathers. Young cocks moult into adult plumage for the first time at about 18 months old.

There are few of these attractive members of the psittaculid group in collections today. Long-tailed Parakeets originate from further south than related species, and this may partly explain why they are so vulnerable to frostbite. Certainly, they need to be kept in warm accommodation over the winter months. Post-mortem studies have revealed that they are also prone to blood parasites, notably *microfilariae*, which can form knots in their circulatory system, with a fatal outcome. In view of their susceptibility to circulatory disease, including fatty deposits in their blood vessels, you should give them a low-fat diet and plenty of fruit. However, these are really parakeets for the dedicated specialist only.

Long-tailed Parakeets lay two or three eggs, which the hen incubates alone for about 25 days. The young fledge after approximately six weeks.

Below: **Long-tailed Parakeet**
Regular spraying with tepid water will improve the feathering of such birds while kept indoors.

POICEPHALUS PARROTS

A group of nine medium-sized species from Africa, the Poicephalus parrots – three of which are featured here – offer plenty of scope for the specialist. They are relatively easy to care for, but breeding results are not especially common at present. This may be linked to a noticeable preference on their part to breed during the winter months in temperate areas, when the likelihood of losses of both eggs and chicks because of chilling is greatly increased. They prefer a nestbox sited in a fairly dark, covered corner of their quarters. While adult birds tend to prove shy, youngsters can develop into delightful pets.

Jardine's Parrot
Poicephalus gulielmi

Distribution: Western and central Africa.
Size: 28cm (11in).
Sexing: Hens may have brown irises; whereas those of cocks are reddish brown in colour.

Youngsters: Much duller, lacking the orange markings of adult birds.

This is one of the larger *Poicephalus* species and is less regularly available than either the Senegal or Meyer's. Birds from the Cameroon tend to be a deeper orange than those found further east.

The breeding display of these birds includes tail-flaring. The hen usually lays four eggs, which she incubates alone for about 26 days.

*Below: **Jardine's Parrot**
The depth and extent of the orange markings vary between individuals.*

Meyer's Parrot
Poicephalus meyeri

Distribution: Central and eastern parts of Africa.
Size: 20cm (8in).
Sexing: Visual distinction between the sexes is not possible.
Youngsters: Generally duller in coloration than adults.

Although Meyer's Parrots may vary noticeably in their markings, this is not a sign of sexual dimorphism; because the species occurs over such a wide area, at least six distinctive races have evolved. These parrots are attractive aviary birds, although they may prove rather shy. Unlike many other parrots, they are not noisy, and are therefore ideal occupants for an aviary in fairly urbanized surroundings. Hand-reared chicks can develop into very tame pets, and may learn to say a few words. Adult birds are more likely to remain shy, however, and should be kept in aviary surroundings rather than as pets.

Right: **Meyer's Parrot**
These colourful parrots are quite hardy once properly acclimatized.

Senegal Parrot
Poicephalus senegalus

Distribution: Western and central Africa, further north than Jardine's Parrot.
Size: 23cm (9in).
Sexing: Visual distinction between the sexes is not possible.
Youngsters: Duller (and greener) than adults with dark irises and less prominent silvery ear coverts.

The most commonly seen of the *Poicephalus* parrots, the Senegal is an easy species to maintain in good health. Its call is inoffensive, but its powerful beak needs an adequate supply of perches to divert its attention from the aviary woodwork, especially at the onset of the breeding period.

Breeding details are similar to those of Jardine's Parrot, with the chicks fledging at just over nine weeks old. However, breeding results tend to be harder to obtain than for other members of the genus. Pairs often nest quite early in the year, which reduces the likelihood of successful breeding in cold weather. Place their nestbox in a dark locality.

Below: **Senegal Parrot**
These parrots are ideal for the smaller garden aviary. Their calls are comprised largely of whistles.

PIONUS PARROTS

Members of this genus are found from Central America southwards down to Argentina. They have become better-known in aviculture during recent years; they can develop into highly attractive pets, and prove not untalented mimics, with a quieter voice than Amazons. Some pairs prove quite prolific, but avoid any unnecessary disturbances close to the nest site, particularly once the chicks have hatched, because Pionus *often prove to be rather nervous parents; there have been cases of pairs mutilating and even killing their offspring. Youngsters are considerably duller in appearance than adults.*

Bronze-winged Pionus
Pionus chalcopterus

Distribution: Mountainous parts of Venezuela, Colombia, Ecuador and Peru.
Size: 28cm (11in).
Sexing: Visual distinction between the sexes is not possible.
Youngsters: Juveniles have yellowish rather than grey skin around the eyes.

The pionus are a group of seven medium-sized parrots that, although not brightly coloured, have attractive hues in their plumage. Bronzewings show to best effect in an outside aviary where the bright blue coloration under the wings will be visible when the birds are in flight.

The pair bond tends to be quite strong, and over-enthusiastic preening

may result in the birds plucking each other around the back of the neck. Because *Pionus* parrots are rather nervous, breeding can be difficult.

Dusky Pionus
Pionus fuscus

Distribution: From Colombia through Venezuela, the Guianas and Brazil, north of the Amazon.
Size: 24cm (9½in).
Sexing: Visual distinction between the sexes is not possible.
Youngsters: Juveniles have a greenish tinge over their wings.

This is one of the less commonly available *Pionus* species, and shows considerable variation in its coloration. If possible, try to obtain young birds,

*Above left: **Bronze-winged Pionus**
The subtle coloration of this species is best seen when the birds are housed in an outdoor aviary.*

*Above: **Dusky Pionus**
Individuals of this unusually coloured species may vary slightly in their markings, but this is not a reliable sign of sexual dimorphism.*

which will settle well and should prove less nervous than adults. Unfortunately, there seems to be a preponderance of hens in this species, and you may have difficulty in obtaining a cock bird. Although they have been hybridized with other *Pionus* species, this practice is not recommended, and any offspring resulting from hybridization should be sold as pets.

Maximilian's Parrot
Pionus maximiliana

Distribution: Over much of eastern South America, from northern Brazil to Bolivia, Paraguay and Argentina.
Size: 30cm (11¾in).
Sexing: Visual distinction between the sexes is not possible.
Youngsters: May have less blue in their upper breasts than adults.

Also known as the Scaly headed Parrot, this species is one of the most widely kept members of the genus and has now been bred on a number of occasions. Pairs may take mealworms when they have chicks in the nest and greenfood is also a popular rearing food. The hen lays up to five eggs, which she incubates for 26 days, and the young leave the nest by the time they are eight weeks old. Offer plenty of fruit to *Pionus* species to help prevent obesity.

Right: **Maximilian's Parrot**
Reasonably quiet and easy to maintain in an aviary, this species is becoming increasingly popular.

Blue-headed Pionus
Pionus menstruus

Distribution: From southern Costa Rica in Central America, through South America to parts of Bolivia and central Brazil.
Size: 28cm (11in).
Sexing: Visual distinction between the sexes is not possible.
Youngsters: Mainly green in colour and duller than adults.

The coloration of these *Pionus* parrots is quite variable, some birds having a darker shade of blue on their heads than others. The amount of pink under the chin also varies.

Hand-raised chicks of this species should develop into delightful pets, and are far less noisy than most amazons.

Adult birds, once properly acclimatized, can be kept in outside aviaries throughout the year. Position a nestbox in a darkened area to encourage breeding activity. Reproductive details are similar to those of Maximilian's.

White-crowned Pionus
Pionus senilis

Distribution: Central America, from south-western Mexico to western Panama.
Size: 24cm (9½in).
Sexing: Visual distinction between the sexes is not possible.
Youngsters: The area around the eyes is grey rather than red.

These parrots are becoming more easily obtainable, and successful breeding results are recorded with increasing frequency. Corn-on-the-cob is a favoured rearing food and is easy to grow in your garden if you have space.

When purchasing *Pionus* parrots, pay particular attention to their breathing. Although they may breathe noisily when you approach them – a normal reaction to stress – they also seem more vulnerable to aspergillosis than some other species.

Below left: **Blue-headed Pionus**
If you obtain a juvenile of this attractive species, it may become quite tame and even learn to talk.

Above: **White-crowned Pionus**
Like other Pionus *parrots, this species (also sometimes known as the White-capped Parrot) is not very noisy.*

AMAZONS

This genus consists of some 27 species that are found both in Central and South America, as well as on some Caribbean islands. The mainland species, which predominate in aviculture, are mostly green, and for this reason Aamazons are sometimes described as 'Green Parrots'. Amazons were first brought to Europe by Columbus when he returned from his voyage of discovery to the New World in 1492, and they have been popular as pet birds ever since. During recent years, they have been bred regularly, so that it is now quite easy to obtain hand-reared chicks, which should develop into tame pets.

Blue-fronted Amazon
Amazona aestiva

Distribution: Bolivia, Brazil and northern Argentina.
Size: 36cm (14in).
Sexing: Visual distinction between the sexes is not possible.
Youngsters: Duller than adults, with less yellow and blue on the head.

One of the most widely kept amazons, the Blue-fronted is now becoming even more popular as an aviary bird than it has long been as a pet. It is known to be one of the longest lived of all parrot species, with a potential lifespan of nearly a century in captivity.

Although colour mutations are rare in New World parrots at present, several brilliant lutino examples of this species have been documented. Such birds are bright yellow, with white markings replacing the usual blue ones.

White-fronted Amazon
Amazona albifrons

Distribution: From Mexico to Costa Rica in Central America.
Size: 25cm (10in).
Sexing: Hens usually have green rather than red wing coverts.
Youngsters: Juveniles have less red plumage than adults and a yellowish rather than white area on the head.

This parrot, which is the smallest of the 27 different species of amazon, and less raucous than its larger relatives, is becoming a more common sight in collections than it has been in the past. White-fronted Amazons are easy to sex visually and breeding results are now fairly frequently reported. Three or four eggs form the usual clutch, and the incubation period lasts around 25 days. The chicks fledge at about seven weeks old and can be removed once they are feeding independently.

*Below left: **Blue-fronted Amazon**
The attractive red wing speculum, shown here, helps to distinguish this species from the Orangewing.*

*Below: **White-fronted Amazon**
This attractive and relatively quiet amazon is the only member of the genus that can be easily sexed by sight.*

Orange-winged Amazon
Amazona amazonica

Distribution: Over much of northern South America, as well as Trinidad and Tobago.
Size: 30cm (11¾in).
Sexing: Visual distinction between the sexes is not possible.
Youngsters: Resemble adults but with dark brown rather than orange irises.

This species may be confused with the Blue-fronted Amazon, but is distinguishable from the latter by its smaller size and paler beak. As its name suggests, it also has an orange rather than red wing speculum, and similar orange markings at the base of its tail.

Orangewings are talented mimics, but are also rather noisy. Breeding details are similar to those of the White-fronted Amazon, but there are likely to be only three eggs in an average clutch.

Red-lored Amazon
Amazona autumnalis

Distribution: Central America, from eastern Mexico down to western Ecuador, with an isolated population in north-western Brazil.
Size: 34cm (13½in).
Sexing: Visual distinction between the sexes is not possible.
Youngsters: Juveniles have dark irises and their head markings are less colourful than those of adults.

Of the four distinct races recognized, you are likely to see only the two Central American forms; the nominate form and Salvin's Amazon (*A. a. salvini*). Salvin's Amazon is larger than the nominate race, and lacks the yellow cheek markings of the latter.

More of these amazons have become available to aviculturists in recent years, as export quotas have been established, and breeding results have become more common during the 1980s. They can be kept without difficulty in an outside aviary once acclimatized, although they are likely to prove rather noisy.

*Above left: **Orange-winged Amazon**
A popular pet bird, this species is now being bred increasingly in collections. Head markings vary.*

Mealy Amazon
Amazona farinosa

Distribution: East of the Andes, from southern Mexico, south as far as Bolivia and eastern Brazil.
Size: 38cm (15in).
Sexing: Visual distinction between the sexes is not possible.
Youngsters: Significantly duller than adults, with dark brown irises.

Mealies are large amazons, and rank among the most raucous members of a noisy group. However, they are long

*Above: **Red-lored Amazon**
This species is also known as the Primrose-cheeked Amazon. It has been more common in recent years.*

lived and, if you buy young birds, they will normally become very tame.

The Central American race (*A. f. guatemalae*) is the most colourful, with an area of blue extending from the top of the head to the nape of the neck, and yellow cheek patches. The nominate race, *A. f. farinosa*, is easily distinguishable, being largely green with an area of yellow plumage on the crown of the head.

*Below: **Mealy Amazon**
These large amazons are intelligent, and have lively, if somewhat noisy, natures.*

Lilac-crowned Amazon
Amazona finschi

Distribution: Western Mexico.
Size: 33cm (13in).
Sexing: Visual distinction between the sexes is not possible.
Youngsters: Recognizable by their dark irises.

These amazons tend to be more widely kept in North American than in European collections. They are similar in appearance to the Green-cheeked (*A. viridigenalis*), but the area of red on their head is smaller and does not extend over the eyes.

Pairs have nested on various occasions. In common with other amazons, they will rarely start breeding in an outdoor aviary before May in northern temperate regions. Three eggs form the usual clutch and incubation lasts about 26 days. The chicks fledge approximately eight weeks later.

*Right: **Lilac-crowned Amazon**
Also sometimes called Finsch's Amazon, this species is not widely available in Europe, although small numbers are bred each year.*

Yellow-fronted Amazon
Amazona ochrocephala

Distribution: From Central Mexico to Peru and the Amazon Basin.
Size: 35cm (13¾in).
Sexing: Visual distinction between the sexes is not possible.
Youngsters: Irises are dark and yellow markings are less extensive than those of the adult birds.

There is often confusion over this species, as many different races are recognized, varying largely in the amount of yellow plumage on their

*Above left: **Yellow-fronted Amazon**
Various races of the Yellow-fronted Amazon are found over a wide area, from Central America to Colombia and parts of Brazil. This is the most commonly seen form.*

heads. The most colourful are the so-called Double yellowhead and its related forms, of which there are four in all. The completely yellow head of mature birds develops with successive moults, taking place over a period of about four years. You are most likely to encounter the yellow-fronted race from Guyana, although the yellow-naped (*A. o.*

*Above: **Double Yellow-headed Amazon**
The more colourful forms of the Yellow-fronted, such as this double yellowhead, are relatively scarce in aviculture, but more are now being bred in collections worldwide.*

auropalliata), with yellow plumage on the nape of the neck, has become more commonly available. This yellow-naped form of the species is currently being exported under a quota system, like other Central American amazons, but appears more reluctant to breed in captive collections than other forms of the Yellow-fronted.

Tucuman Amazon
Amazona tucumana

Distribution: Eastern Andes, in southeastern Bolivia and Argentina.
Size: 30cm (11¾in).
Sexing: Visual distinction between the sexes is not possible.
Youngsters: Yellow or orange markings in the red patch above the nostrils, and green thighs.

It appears that this species differs somewhat from other amazons in its lifestyle; it inhabits Alder trees (from which it takes its alternative common name) in the wild. Its beak is relatively thin and pointed, and may be used for extracting seeds – pine nuts are a favourite food. This lively species has been available to aviculturists only for a short period since the mid 1980s; successful breeding results are starting to become more widely reported but it is now prohibited from export.

*Right: **Tucuman Amazon***
This attractive species has been available only since the mid 1980s. Like other amazons, it needs a regular spray, and will enjoy bathing in a rain shower.

Green-cheeked Amazon
Amazona viridigenalis

Distribution: North-eastern Mexico.
Size: 33cm (13in).
Sexing: Visual distinction between the sexes is not possible.
Youngsters: The red area on the forehead is smaller than on adults, and young birds have dark irises.

Sometimes known as Mexican Red-headed Amazons, these parrots were quite often available during the 1970s, and a number of pairs are now established in collections. Like other amazons, they will frequently flare their tails feathers when in breeding condition, creating a momentary fanlike effect. The pupils of their eyes may also constrict, causing the eye to appear more colourful. This is sometimes described as 'eye blazing'.

Breeding details do not differ significantly from those of other members of the genus. The hen stays in the nestbox for at least three weeks after the chicks hatch. She will then begin to leave the nest for progressively longer periods during the day, but will return to brood the chicks at night until they are about five or six weeks old. It is likely to be four or five years before the chicks are sufficiently mature to start breeding themselves. However, like other larger parrots, their lifespan can usually be measured in decades, and pairs will normally nest consistently once they have commenced breeding.

*Right: **Green-cheeked Amazon***
A species more commonly kept in North America than in Europe. Pairs will usually nest quite readily once they are established.

MACAWS

The characteristic feature of the Ara macaws is the large area of essentially unfeathered facial skin on either side of the head, extending from the lower beak up to and around the eyes. This is usually whitish or yellowish in coloration. While the macaws include the largest of all parrots, tame individuals are normally very gentle with people they know well. They are not particularly talented as mimics, but will learn to repeat a few words. While housing one of the bigger species in the home can be a daunting task, dwarf macaws will settle well as pets. Like other larger parrots, they have a long lifespan.

Blue and Gold Macaw
Ara ararauna

Distribution: From eastern Panama across most of northern South America, except western coastal areas, extending to Bolivia, Paraguay and Brazil.
Size: 86cm (34in).
Sexing: Visual distinction between the sexes is not normally possible, but hens may have narrower heads than cocks.
Youngsters: Have dark irises.

In spite of their large beaks, these birds can be extremely gentle once tame. Nevertheless, be cautious when handling an unfamiliar macaw, as these birds can inflict a very painful bite. An aviary for these macaws needs to be suitably robust, and will be expensive to construct. Bear in mind, too, that macaws can be noisy, especially when in breeding condition. The usual clutch consists of two or three eggs, which hatch after about 28 days. The young macaws then spend a further three months or so in the nest. A rare mutation of this species, in which the yellow pigment is absent, creating a blue and white bird, has been reported.

Yellow-collared Macaw
Ara auricollis

Distribution: From Matto Grosso, Brazil, to Bolivia, Paraguay and parts of north-western Argentina.
Size: 38cm (15in).
Sexing: Visual distinction between the sexes is not possible.
Youngsters: Easily recognizable by their grey rather than pink feet.

This is one of the smaller, predominantly green species, sometimes referred to collectively as the dwarf macaws. These birds are usually easier to house and maintain, especially in an urban locality, than the larger

*Left: **Blue and Gold Macaw**
An impressive, but rather noisy species. Providing accommodation for these large birds is costly.*

multi-coloured species. Pairs will normally nest quite readily, with the hen laying up to three eggs in a clutch. Incubation lasts 25 days, and the chicks fledge at about nine weeks old. Hand-raised birds of this species make very tame pets, and often start talking soon after they become independent.

Green-winged Macaw
Ara chloroptera

Distribution: From eastern Panama in Central America, south across most of northern South America, east of the Andes, to Bolivia, Brazil and Paraguay.
Size: 90cm (35½in).
Sexing: Visual distinction between the sexes is not normally possible, but cocks may have broader heads than the hens.
Youngsters: Recognizable by their dark irises.

These majestic birds are very similar to Blue and Gold Macaws in their requirements. Pairs can usually be persuaded to nest, but young birds breeding for the first time may prove unreliable parents when feeding their chicks. Avoid disturbing the birds if all appears to be progressing well, and provide plenty of greenfood, such as spinach beet, vegetables, such as corn-on-the-cob and carrot, and fruit laced with a food supplement as rearing foods. This will help to ensure that the chicks do not develop any skeletal abnormalities during the relatively long period they spend in the nestbox before they emerge at about 13 weeks old.

Left: **Yellow-collared Macaw**
Hand-raised birds of this species (one of the so-called dwarf macaws) make very tame pets and will often learn to talk.

Above: **Green-winged Macaw**
This large species needs plenty of space, but tame birds can become very devoted to their owners.

Scarlet Macaw

Ara macao

Distribution: From eastern Panama in Central America, south across most of northern South America, east of the Andes, as far as parts of Bolivia, Paraguay and Brazil.
Size: 85cm (33½in).
Sexing: Visual distinction between the sexes is not normally possible, but cocks may have broader heads than the hens.
Youngsters: Have brown irises.

This species, also known as the Red and Gold Macaw, can be easily recognized by the characteristic area of yellow plumage on its wings, which helps to distinguish it from the Greenwing (also known as the Red and Green Macaw). The Scarlet Macaw has declined in numbers in the northern part of its very wide range because of deforestation. As a result, it has been listed as an endangered species, which means that you may need to apply for a permit when selling, purchasing or moving these macaws. Contact your national CITES Management Authority for advice about the current position.

Red-bellied Macaw

Ara manilata

Distribution: Over much of northern South America to Peru and parts of Brazil.
Size: 48cm (19in).
Sexing: Visual distinction between the sexes is not possible.
Youngsters: Have dark irises.

The management of this species has proved rather difficult in the past. The Red-bellied is less hardy than other macaws after being acclimatized, and may need to be transferred indoors for the winter period. It has also acquired a reputation for having a nervous disposition, and birds sometimes die unexpectedly. Further study has shown that these macaws rapidly become obese, and this, apparently, has been responsible for the premature death of individuals. You can prevent obesity by ensuring that a high proportion of fruit and vegetables forms part of their regular diet, and by placing a greater emphasis on cereal seeds, such as corn-on-the-cob, maize and millet sprays in the diet, than on oil-rich sunflower seeds. In spite of their wide distribution, these macaws have been generally available to aviculturists only since the mid 1980s. Now, with better insight into the dietary needs of these birds, breeders are starting to obtain positive results with this species.

Below left: **Scarlet Macaw**
A striking, but rare, species. Keep pairs of these large macaws on their own to prevent hybridization.

Below: **Red-bellied Macaw**
Less robust than other macaws, these birds are prone to obesity. House them in secluded surroundings.

Hahn's Macaw
Ara nobilis

Distribution: North of the Amazon, from Venezuela to north-eastern Brazil.
Size: 30cm (11¾in).
Sexing: Visual distinction between the sexes is not possible.
Youngsters: Recognizable by the lack of red on their wing edges, and reduced area of blue plumage on the head.

This species is the smallest of the macaws, but is instantly recognizable as belonging to this group of parrots by the bare patches of skin on the sides of its face. As with the larger species, these may become redder if the bird becomes excited, due to increased blood flow.

Unlike many parrots, Hahn's Macaws are sociable, even when breeding. You can keep pairs together in a colony, and they will nest readily in such surroundings, without aggression in most cases. Nestboxes measuring 23cm (9in) square and 46cm (18in) deep will suit them well. They are often prolific, with hens laying a clutch of as many as five eggs, which should hatch after an incubation period of 25 days. The chicks leave the nest at two months old. Hand-reared Hahn's Macaws make ideal pets; they will become very tame and are easy to manage.

Severe Macaw
Ara severa

Distribution: From eastern Panama in Central America, south as far as Bolivia and Brazil.
Size: 51cm (20in).
Sexing: Visual distinction between the sexes is not possible.
Youngsters: Have dark irises.

Occurring over a wide area, the Severe Macaw, also known as the Chestnut-fronted, has never been very popular, possibly because of its rather plain coloration. But it is not a difficult species to cater for, provided its housing is suitably robust. Young birds will develop into affectionate birds, though they are not talented as mimics and their calls are rather harsh.

A nestbox measuring 30cm (12in) square and about 77cm (30in) high will be suitable for a breeding pair. Two or three eggs form the usual clutch, with the incubation period lasting 28 days. The young fledge at about nine weeks old. If you have a compatible pair, you should obtain consistently good results from this and other macaw species over many years.

Top left: **Hahn's Macaw**
This species is the smallest of the macaw family. Note the prominent area of bare skin on the face, which is characteristic of the group.

Left: **Severe Macaw**
The green coloration of these so-called dwarf macaws takes on an attractive sheen in the sunlight.

COCKATOOS

There are five different genera of cockatoos, but it is the members of the Cacatua *genus that are most commonly represented in collections; the various black cockatoos are all scarce in aviculture. The feature that distinguishes this group of birds is the crest on their heads, which is usually raised when they are excited or alarmed. The shape and length of this crest varies; in the case of the Goffin's Cockatoo, the crest is relatively short, whereas the feathers are long and broad in the Umbrella Cockatoo. Compatibility is very important when selecting breeding stock; try to start with proven pairs.*

Umbrella Cockatoo
Cacatua alba

Distribution: Central and northern Moluccan islands, Indonesia.
Size: 46cm (18in).
Sexing: Cocks usually have darker, blackish irises, whereas those of hens are reddish brown in colour.
Youngsters: Resemble adults in appearance, except that their irises are dark grey in colour.

Although they lack the bright colours of some species, these large white

Below: Umbrella Cockatoo
The crest feathers of this species are very broad. Spray birds housed indoors to keep their plumage in good condition.

cockatoos are very handsome birds, which take their common name from the umbrella-like shape formed by the broad feathers of their crest. Unfortunately, Umbrella Cockatoos have a reputation for being extremely destructive, and can also be very noisy birds.

As with other *Cacatua* species, the typical clutch is two eggs, and the incubation period lasts about 28 days. The chicks fledge when they are about 12 weeks old. If you have to remove chicks from the nest for hand-rearing, you may find that they are starting to talk by the time they are independent. Hand-raised youngsters will develop into great companions, but if you buy adult birds, they are likely to be nervous, and you should keep them only in aviary surroundings.

Greater Sulphur-crested Cockatoo
Cacatua galerita

Distribution: New Guinea and neighbouring islands, as well as eastern Australia. Introduced to New Zealand during the 1920s.
Size: 50cm (19¾in).
Sexing: Cocks usually have dark brown irises, whereas those of hens are reddish brown.
Youngsters: Resemble adults, but have

Below:
Greater Sulphur-crested Cockatoo
These lively cockatoos are popular in Australia as pets and aviary birds, but are not common at present in Europe or North America.

brown irises. They may also have some grey plumage present on the crown extending down to the wings.

These cockatoos are best known in Australian collections, although two of the three island races are kept and bred elsewhere in the world. These are the Triton (*C. g. triton*), distinguishable by its blue rather than whitish skin coloration around the eyes and its broader, more rounded crest feathers, and the so-called Medium Sulphur-crested (*C. g. eleonora*). This latter race, found in the Aru Islands, is similar to the Triton, but is distinguishable by its smaller size. The skin of the eye-ring is whitish, except in young birds, where it has a bluish tinge.

In all three races, incubation takes about 30 days, with the chicks emerging from the nest for the first time from 12 weeks old onwards.

Goffin's Cockatoo
Cacatua goffini

Distribution: The Tenimbar Islands of Indonesia. Introduced to Tual in the Kai Islands by native people of the area.
Size: 32cm (12.5in).
Sexing: Irises are normally dark brown in cocks, and light reddish brown in hens.
Youngsters: Similar to adults in appearance, but the periorbital skin is often bluer in juveniles.

Rare in aviculture until the 1970s, these delightful cockatoos are now threatened by deforestation in their homelands. Goffin's Cockatoos are destructive birds, in spite of their relatively small size, and must be housed in robust surroundings.

Below: **Triton Cockatoo**
The pale blue skin surrounding the eyes is a characteristic of this race. It is found on New Guinea and the western Papuan Islands, and has also been introduced to parts of Indonesia and the Palua Islands.

Unfortunately, pairs tend to be more reluctant to nest than other species. Adult pairs can prove very shy and it may be that they require more privacy; site the nestbox in a quiet, shaded part of the aviary. Two or three eggs form the typical clutch and these should hatch after an incubation period of 28 days. Provide a variety of rearing foods, such as chickweed, corn-on-the-cob and perpetual spinach, for this and other

Below:
Medium Sulphur-crested Cockatoo
Smaller than its Australian relative, this race is found further north, on the Aru Islands of Indonesia. These birds are sometimes available but not widely kept.

species. Try to monitor the progress of the chicks without disturbing their parents, in case they start to neglect one or both of their offspring. Chicks should leave the nest at about 11 weeks old.

Below: **Goffin's Cockatoos**
These shy, but often very destructive cockatoos tend to be more reluctant to nest than other species, but breeding reports are becoming more common.

Philippine Red-vented Cockatoo
Cacatua haematuropygia

Distribution: The Philippine Islands
Size: 30cm (11¾in).
Sexing: Adult cocks usually have dark brown irises, whereas those of hens are reddish brown in colour.
Youngsters: Recognizable by their grey irises.

The Philippine Red-vented Cockatoo is another species that has become better known in aviculture since the early 1980s and is now being bred in various collections. The hen normally lays two eggs, which hatch after about 24 days. The chicks will emerge from the nestbox when they are just over ten weeks old.

These cockatoos have proved rather difficult to establish in the past. They were often afflicted with heavy tapeworm infestations, which needed treatment, and aspergillosis. The latter was probably contracted from the nest litter – studies of breeding sites in the wild have revealed heavy contamination with the spores of this fungus – and usually proves fatal. Imported stock was also rather vulnerable to candidiasis, caused in part by a lack of dietary Vitamin A. Recent studies from the Philippines suggest that deforestation has had a serious impact on the number of these cockatoos, and their export is now prohibited. Although never traded in large numbers, a small established breeding population should now ensure that home-bred chicks remain available.

Leadbeater's Cockatoo
Cacatua leadbeateri

Distribution: The eastern interior of Australia.
Size: 30cm (11¾in).
Sexing: The irises are normally dark brown in cocks, and reddish brown in hens.
Youngsters: Paler than adults in coloration, with pale brown irises.

These striking birds, also known as Major Mitchell's Cockatoos, are sadly not widely available, and surplus stock inevitably commands a very high price. Coloration is variable, with the lower parts up to the breast being white rather than pale pink in some individuals.

One of the problems in establishing this species has been that cocks tend to be aggressive and will often attack, and even kill, the hens. There is consequently a shortage of hens in collections.

When they do nest, the hens will spend several weeks gnawing the woodwork of the nestbox before laying up to four eggs. The young hatch about 28 days later, and the chicks emerge from the box two months old. Leadbeater's Cockatoos have a long reproductive life; a pair obtained in 1903 successfully reared a chick 37 years later! Introduce young birds to each other to help ensure compatibility.

Above: **Philippine Red-vented Cockatoo**
This species is characterized by the red plumage under its tail. These birds should only be kept for breeding. Watch that a cock does not turn on his mate.

Below: **Leadbeater's Cockatoo**
This beautiful cockatoo is unfortunately rarely seen in collections. The depth of pink coloration varies – some birds are very pale, almost whitish in parts.

Moluccan Cockatoo
Cacatua moluccensis

Distribution: Southern Moluccan islands of Indonesia.
Size: 52cm (20½in).
Sexing: Irises are generally black in cocks and dark brown in hens.
Youngsters: Similar to adults, but with dark grey irises.

Highly variable in coloration, Moluccan or Rose-crested Cockatoos can range from shades of pink to almost white. Brighter coloured birds are believed to produce similarly coloured offspring. These cockatoos resemble the Umbrella Cockatoo, but are somewhat larger in size and have a rose-coloured crest.

Hand-raised chicks may develop into marvellous pets, forming a strong bond with their owners and proving very responsive. But, like other cockatoos, they can be very demanding, and their loud calls and destructive natures can create problems in the home.

When breeding, hens lay two eggs, which should hatch after a period of about 28 days. The chicks develop slowly, only leaving the nest for the first time when they are about 15 weeks old. Hand-raising Moluccan chicks is therefore a lengthy process compared with hand-rearing other species.

Blue-eyed Cockatoo
Cacatua ophthalmica

Distribution: Islands of New Britain and New Ireland in the Bismarck Archipelago.
Size: 50cm (19¾in).
Sexing: Irises are generally dark brown in cock birds and more reddish in hens.
Youngsters: Resemble adults.

Closely related to the Greater Sulphur-crested Cockatoo, this species has darker blue skin around the eyes, and a much broader crest than the Triton race (*C. g. triton*). The Blue-eyed is relatively uncommon in aviculture, and you are more likely to see it in zoos and bird gardens than in private collections.

Like other cockatoos, these birds are quite hardy once acclimatized, but you should not transfer recently imported stock outside during the colder months of the year, even if the birds were captive bred. Breeding details are similar to those of the Greater Sulphur-crested Cockatoo (see page 175).

Bare-eyed Cockatoo
Cacatua sanguinea

Distribution: North and central-eastern parts of Australia, with a separate population also present in southern New Guinea.
Size: 38cm (15in).
Sexing: Visual distinction between the sexes is not possible.
Youngsters: Resemble adults, but have a shorter upper mandible and a reduced area of greyish rather than bluish periorbital skin beneath the eyes.

*Below: **Moluccan Cockatoo**
The broad pink crest of this species is always distinctive, but the body coloration can vary noticeably – some individuals, like this bird, are virtually white, others are pale pink. The skin around the eyes has a creamy tinge until the bird is a year old.*

Although not widely kept outside Australia, these cockatoos, also called Little Corellas, are occasionally bred in captivity. Potentially, they are quite prolific; a pair kept at San Diego Zoo had 103 chicks between 1929 and 1970, the young birds being reared by hand.

Bare-eyed Cockatoos are quite pugnacious, however, especially when they are breeding, and a tame bird that has no fear of people may not hesitate to turn on its owner when he or she enters the aviary. The usual clutch is comprised of three or four eggs, and incubation lasts 27 days. The chicks normally leave the nesting site at about nine weeks old and are then fed mainly by the cock for a short period.

*Below: **Blue-eyed Cockatoo**
Chester Zoo, in the UK, has been very successful in breeding this species during recent years, but it is rare, and more often found in zoos and bird gardens than in private collections.*

*Below: **Bare-eyed Cockatoo**
These birds can prove aggressive during the breeding period. They have been hybridized successfully with Galahs (see page 182) in Australia, where they are common aviary subjects.*

Lesser Sulphur-crested Cockatoo
Cacatua sulphurea

Distribution: Sulawesi (formerly Celebes) and neighbouring islands.
Size: 30cm (11¾in).
Sexing: Cocks generally have blackish irises, whereas those of hens are reddish brown in colour.
Youngsters: Recognizable by their pale grey irises.

One of the best-known cockatoos in aviculture, and widely kept as a pet, the Lesser Sulphur-crested occurs in several forms through its range. The most distinctive subspecies is the Citron-crested (*C. s. citrinocristata*), which has an orange rather than yellow crest and ear coverts, and occurs on the island of Sumba. It is well represented in aviculture but, as with other cockatoos, compatibility can be a problem. The Timor race (*C. s. parvula*) is the smallest, at just 30cm (12in) long.

Lesser Sulphur-crested Cockatoos can be extremely nervous when first acquired, and you should only obtain genuine youngsters as pets. Two eggs form the usual clutch, and these hatch after a period of 27 days. The young cockatoos emerge from the nestbox around ten weeks later, but it will take much longer – up to eight weeks – for their beaks and feet to darken to the black coloration of those of adults.

Left: **Lesser Sulphur-crested Cockatoo**
Smaller, and with more prominent yellow ear coverts than the Greater form, this species is widely kept in Europe and North America.

Below: **Citron-crested Cockatoo**
This species, which is confined to the island of Sumba, is instantly recognizable by its more orange coloration. (Even the down of nestlings is of a deeper shade.)

Long-billed Corella
Cacatua tenuirostris

Distribution: South-eastern and south-western parts of Australia.
Size: 35cm (13¾in).
Sexing: Visual distinction between the sexes is not possible.
Youngsters: Show less orange-red plumage on the throat than adults, and also have a shorter upper mandible.

Their greatly lengthened upper mandible, which is used for digging in the ground, gives these cockatoos an unmistakable appearance. In their native Australia they are often considered a pest by farmers, as they will excavate newly sown grain.
   Also known as the Slender-billed Cockatoo, this species is very rare in aviculture collections outside Australia, and is likely to remain so, as the export of such native species is forbidden, except to zoos or scientific collections. There are probably only a dozen or so in the whole of the United States, and even fewer in Europe, although the species has bred in captivity at the extensive Loro Parque collection of parrots on the island of Tenerife, so you are unlikely to encounter this distinctive cockatoo.

Right: **Long-billed Corella**
This cockatoo uses its unusually elongated upper bill to prize roots, seeds and grubs out of the ground.

Gang-gang Cockatoo
Callocephalon fimbriatum

Distribution: South-eastern Australia.
Size: 35cm (13¾in).
Sexing: Cocks are easily recognizable by their bright red heads and crests, whereas those of hens are greyish.
Youngsters: Resemble hens, but young cocks can be recognized by the red tipping on the crest feathers, and sporadic red plumage on the head.

Gang-gang Cockatoos are rarely kept, even in their Australian homeland. They are particularly prone to feather-plucking, which appears to arise through boredom. Provide plenty of branches for them to gnaw, and give them plenty of small seeds, such as millet, as part of their regular diet, to keep them occupied. Fir cones have also been used to provide then with a source of interest as they seek to extract the nuts.
   In spite of this problem, a number of successful breeding results have been recorded. Incubation of the two eggs lasts about 25 days, and the chicks may fledge as soon as six weeks later.

Below left: **Gang-gang Cockatoo (male)**
The cock is instantly recognizable by its striking red head.

Below: **Gang-gang Cockatoo (female)**
The coloration of the female Gang-gang is more subdued.

Black Cockatoo
Calyptorhynchus funereus

Distribution: South-eastern and south-western Australia.
Size: 65cm (25½in).
Sexing: Hens have grey rather than pink periorbital skin, brighter ear coverts and horn-coloured rather than dark grey beaks.
Youngsters: Similar to hens. Young cocks have duller yellow ear coverts than juvenile hens.

There are two distinct races of this cockatoo, of which the Yellow-tailed is the most colourful. The other is the White-tailed Black Cockatoo (*C. f. baudinii*), also known as Baudin's Cockatoo, which is found in a small area of southwestern Australia. The Yellow-tailed race occurs in the southeastern part of the country. Very few of these cockatoos, of either race, are currently kept in collectons, either in their homeland or elsewhere in the world. Their export has been prohibited for many years.

Black Cockatoos are said to be very fond of greenstuff, and also regularly eat insects, such as mealworms. Their loud, penetrating calls are audible at a distance of one kilometre away. Despite their rarity in aviculture, they appear to breed without undue difficulty. Incubation is thought to last about 28 days and the chicks will normally fledge when they are about ten weeks old.

Above left:
Yellow-tailed Black Cockatoo (cock)
These cockatoos can be sexed by the colour of their periorbital skin.

Above:
Yellow-tailed Black Cockatoo (hen)
The hen's plumage is somewhat brighter than that of her mate.

Below left:
White-tailed Black Cockatoo (cock)
This race is restricted to a small area of southwestern Australia.

Below:
White-tailed Black Cockatoo (hen)
Hens differ from cocks in the colour of their beaks and periorbital skin.

Glossy Black Cockatoo
Calyptorhynchus lathami

Distribution: Eastern Australia and on Kangaroo Island.
Size: 48cm (19in).
Sexing: Hens usually sport yellow areas on the side of the head and neck and yellowish speckling on the tail band, which cocks lack.
Youngsters: Resemble hens, with spotting present on the ear and wing coverts, but lack the hen's yellow head plumage. Barring is often present on the throat, abdomen, and in the vicinity of the tail in juveniles.

There appear to be no records of these cockatoos being kept outside Australia. In the wild, they are usually found close to Casuarina trees, which provide the nuts on which they feed. In captivity, they will take sunflower seed instead,

and could probably by induced to eat pine nuts as well.

Several Australian breeders are now being successful with this species. Hens may start breeding when only two years old; relatively young for cockatoos. The incubation period is quite long – usually lasting between 29 and 32 days – and the chicks will then remain in the nest for at least eight weeks before fledging.

Right: **Glossy Black Cockatoo (hen)**
The markings on the head of the hen may vary between individuals; some have orangish markings here. There are very few records of this species in aviculture, even in its homeland.

Above: **Glossy Black Cockatoo (cock)**
The bill of this cockatoo is very powerful, reflecting its diet; in the wild it depends almost entirely on Casuarina nuts. (In captivity, it will take sunflower.)

Red-tailed Black Cockatoo
Calyptorhynchus magnificus

Distribution: Parts of north, eastern and western Australia, with a small isolated population in western Victoria and neighbouring south-eastern South Australia.
Size: 60cm (23½in).
Sexing: Hens are easily distinguishable by the prominent yellow markings over the head, and their horn-coloured beaks. The heads of cocks are black, and the beak dull grey in colour.
Youngsters: Similar to hens, but with a reduced area of spotting on the head. Young males can be recognized by their darker coloured upper mandible.

Again, stock of this species, also known as the Banksian Cockatoo, is very rare outside Australia. Cock birds are said to become very tame if they have been hand-raised, whereas hens lose their tameness soon after becoming independent. In the wild, these cockatoos rely less on insects in their diet than other related black species, feeding largely on nuts and seeds.

Red-tailed Black Cockatoos have a long reproductive life – a cock bird known to be at least 36 years old has bred successfully at Adelaide Zoo in Australia. In the wild, nests are generally found in eucalypt trees, and the hen usually lays only one egg, which hatches after a period of 30 days. (If two eggs are laid and hatch, the youngest chick is usually neglected and will die unless it is removed for hand-rearing.) The young chick will fledge at the age of about 12 weeks, but it will be a further three or four months before it is totally independent of its parents.

Above: **Red-tailed Black Cockatoo (hen)** *The barring pattern of this species varies widely between individuals. Hens are less tame than the cocks.*

Left: **Red-tailed Black Cockatoo (cock)** *The cock is larger and has a darker head than the otherwise similar Glossy Black Cockatoo (see page 181).*

Galah Cockatoo
Eolophus roseicapillus

Distribution: Throughout much of Australia, except for some coastal areas, notably the eastern and south-western seaboards.
Size: 35cm (13¾in).
Sexing: Irises are usually dark brown in cocks, whereas those of hens are pinkish red in colour.
Youngsters: Duller than adults in coloration, with a greyish tinge to the plumage of the crown and breast. Juveniles of both sexes have brown irises.

Also known as the Roseate Cockatoo, this species is quite widely kept outside its Australian homeland, although pairs are expensive. In the wild, it is often considered to be a pest, and large numbers are destroyed annually. Pressure is being put on the Australian government to allow controlled export of some of these cockatoos to aviculturists overseas, rather than annihilating whole flocks of them.

Although placed in a separate genus, the Galah is quite closely related to the *Cacatua* species. Hybrids have been produced on various occasions, although this practice is not to be encouraged.

Galahs have a number of virtues as aviary birds; they are considerably less noisy than the *Cacatua* species and often more prolific, laying up to five eggs in a clutch, and sometimes nesting twice during the course of a breeding season. Some pairs show a stronger nest-building instinct than others, filling their nestbox with items such as bark and millet sprays collected around the aviary. Development of the chicks, which hatch after a period of about 25 days, is rapid, and they leave the nest when just seven weeks old.

Ensure that they receive a balanced diet to minimize the risk of them developing fatty tumours, called lipomas. There is no effective treatment for these, apart from surgery to remove them, and they may recur.

Right: **Galah Cockatoo**
This species occurs across much of Australia. Individuals vary widely in their coloration; some even have white areas on their breasts.

Below right: **Palm Cockatoo**
Although their powerful beaks can prove very destructive, tame Palm Cockatoos are very gentle and their whistlelike call is relatively quiet.

Palm Cockatoo
Probosciger aterrimus

Distribution: Aru Islands, plus New Guinea and the Cape York Peninsula of northern Australia.
Size: 70-80cm (27½-31½in).
Sexing: Hens are smaller, with smaller upper bills than cocks.
Youngsters: Recognizable by the white edging to the beak, and pale yellow fringe on the feathers of the underparts and under the wings.

This is the largest species of cockatoo, and unmistakable in appearance. The distinctive bare reddish cheek patches are an indicator of the bird's state of health, becoming pale when the cockatoo is sick and turning redder during periods of excitement, presumably because of alterations to the blood flow to the skin.

Palm Cockatoos are not common avicultural subjects and since 1987 they have been totally protected under the international CITES agreement, for fears that they are declining in the wild. Vendors therefore now need a permit from their CITES management authority, even for captive-bred youngsters.

Breeding of the species has been problematic in the past, but now pairs are nesting more frequently in various collections worldwide. The incubation period may last up to 35 days, with the single egg being laid on a bed of sticks, up to 15cm (6in) deep, which the adult birds carry to the nestbox. It takes two weeks for the chick to gain any feathers, and as long as 14 weeks before it fledges. Raw onion is favoured by some pairs, but it may be best to withhold this when they have a chick.

OTHER PARROTS

This final section features some other parrots that may be seen in aviculture, such as the Eclectus Parrot – the most extreme example of sexual dimorphism; at first, it was thought that the cock and hen were separate species. Another parrot with striking plumage is the Hawkhead, which has a ruff of feathers when excited. There are also the strange Vasa Parrots, which are probably the dullest of all species, being predominantly greyish black in colour. But apart from the very popular Grey Parrot, none of these is really suitable for the petkeeper; they are best kept by breeders.

Lesser Vasa Parrot
Coracopsis nigra

Distribution: Madagascar and neighbouring islands.
Size: 35cm (13¾in).
Sexing: A large protuberance from the vent is clearly visible in cocks in breeding condition.
Youngsters: Similar to adults, but with a lighter bill.

Although these highly unusual parrots lack the bright coloration of some species, they make fascinating aviary occupants. Some birds are afflicted with sporadic white feathering in their plumage, which may increase or regress at subsequent moults and probably corresponds to the patchy yellow feathers that are sometimes present in Blue-fronted Amazons. A varied diet and suitable food supplements may help.

It is easy to detect the onset of the breeding period, when a large protuberance from the male's vent is clearly visible. (This prolapse is no cause for concern.) Two or three eggs form the usual clutch.

The Greater Vasa (*C. vasa*) is similar in its habits, but prefers more seeds in its diet than the Lesser Vasa – an avid fruit-eater. The Greater is also more vocal, and about 15cm (6in) larger.

Left: **Lesser Vasa Parrot**
This distinctive species was rarely seen in collections until the early 1980s, but pairs have since been bred on various occasions.

Hawk-headed Parrot
Deroptyus accipitrinus

Distribution: Northern Brazil and the Guianas to southeastern Colombia and northeastern Peru.
Size: 30cm (11¾in).
Sexing: Visual distinction between the sexes is not possible.
Youngsters: Juveniles have brown irises and a green crown.

Undoubtedly the most bizarre of all parrots, the Hawkhead has a ruff of feathers around its neck, which it raises when excited or alarmed. This behaviour is accompanied by hissing and swaying and it seems likely that it has originated as a deterrent to predators.

In some ways, the Hawkhead appears more closely related to the *Pyrrhura* conures than to other parrots of similar size. Bear in mind, however, that Hawkheads can prove exceptionally noisy birds and that they need a significant amount of fruit and other fresh foods as part of their regular diet.

Breeding is difficult, and hand-rearing, although often advised because of the nervous nature of these parrots, is itself often fraught with problems. The hen lays two or three eggs, which she incubates for about 28 days. The chicks should fledge about nine weeks later. Breeding birds can be very aggressive, so take care when entering their flight.

Eclectus Parrot
Eclectus roratus

Distribution: Islands of eastern Indonesia and New Guinea.
Size: 35cm (13¾in).
Sexing: Even chicks are dimorphic; cocks are mainly green and hens red.
Youngsters: Similar to adults, but with brown irises.

Occurring over many islands, the Eclectus Parrot has evolved into at least ten different races. Although the appearance of hens tends to be similar, cocks may vary quite widely in their markings depending on their distribution. Fruit and greenstuff are essential to keep these birds in good health. They have a long digestive tract, adapted to a fibrous diet, and if deprived of such foods, may rapidly succumb to candidiasis.

Pairs are normally keen to nest, although some hens can prove spiteful towards intended mates. Two eggs form the usual clutch, and hatch after about 28 days. You can encourage egg laying by separating a pair and then placing them, together, in breeding quarters about three weeks later. Avoid over-breeding, or soft-shelled eggs and egg-binding may result. Supplement the diet of breeding birds with plenty of cuttlefish bone, as their chicks can be prone to rickets.

Above: **Hawk-headed Parrot**
This species' magnificent ruff, displayed here, is raised when the parrot is excited or alarmed.

Below: **Desmarest's Fig Parrots**
Provide fig parrots with plenty of branches to gnaw to prevent their beaks from becoming overgrown.

Below: **Eclectus Parrot**
The main drawback of the Eclectus as an aviary bird is its loud calls, but it is well established in aviculture.

Desmarest's Fig Parrot
Psittaculirostris desmarestii

Distribution: New Guinea, in the south and west.
Size: 18cm (7½in).
Sexing: Depends on the subspecies; in some the cocks have a yellow collar; in others, the sexes appear identical.
Youngsters: Have yellowish crowns.

When they first became available to birdkeepers in the late 1970s, the fig parrots proved difficult to establish, until it was realized that they had a particular requirement for Vitamin K in their diet.

This forms a vital part of the body's blood-clotting mechanism, and the dietary deficiency was causing internal haemorrhaging, especially in laying hens. Breeding is still not straightforward, because adult birds are often reluctant to rear their chicks. These parrots are only suitable for experienced birdkeepers.

White-bellied Caique
Pionites leucogaster

Distribution: South of the Amazon, from northern Brazil to parts of Bolivia, Peru and Ecuador.
Size: 23cm (9in).
Sexing: Visual distinction between the sexes is not possible.
Youngsters: Juveniles have brown irises and some black feathers on the head.

These attractive parrots are surprisingly destructive for their size and can be quite noisy. On the positive side, however, they often become very tame, even in aviary surroundings. Caiques are highly social birds, so keep them in pairs rather than on their own. They also have a long lifespan – a number have lived for at least 40 years.

Black-headed Caique
Pionites melanocephala

Distribution: North of the Amazon, in the Guianas, and westwards to parts of Colombia, Venezuela, Ecuador and Peru.
Size: 23cm (9in).
Sexing: Visual distinction between the sexes is not possible.
Youngsters: Juveniles have brown irises and horn-coloured rather than black beaks.

This species is very similar to the White-bellied Caique in its habits. Supply these birds with plenty of fresh perches to gnaw so that their beaks do not become overgrown. You can encourage pairs to nest by providing them with a nestbox in a dark locality. The hen will lay up to four eggs and these should hatch after 25 days. Offer plenty of fruit as part of their diet, along with an occasional treat of walnuts, which are favourites of most caiques.

Grey Parrot
Psittacus erithacus

Distribution: Over a broad band of central Africa.
Size: 33cm (13in).
Sexing: Cocks sometimes have a darker back and wings then hens.
Youngsters: Recognizable by their dark irises.

These parrots have been kept as pets for centuries, but are now being bred in much greater numbers. If you want to keep them as aviary birds, you will need to take particular care with their acclimatization. The Timneh sub-species (*P. e. timneh*) – from Sierra Leone and parts of Guinea, the Ivory Coast and Liberia – can be easily distinguished from the more common nominate race by its maroon rather than scarlet tail feathers. It is also slightly smaller and invariably less costly. Both races are talented mimics. (In fact they have a reputation for their talking ability.)
   Adult Greys can prove nervous birds and may take several years to adapt to new surroundings before they start to

Above: **White-bellied Caique**
This species tends to be less often seen that its black-headed relative. The two are similar in their habits.

Above: **Black-headed Caique**
These birds are often very playful, but individuals may turn vicious when first introduced to each other.

breed. Hens generally lay three or four eggs in a clutch, and incubation lasts four weeks. Provide a good varied diet, especially during the rearing period. The chicks should leave the nest at about three months old and will soon be feeding independently. The pair bond in

Above: **Grey Parrot**
Probably the best loved of all pet parrots, the Grey is also acknowledged as a talented mimic.

this species is very strong, and the birds will show great devotion to each other.

Above: **Malay Blue-rumped Parrot**
These parrots should not be expected to overwinter outside without additional warmth. There is no strong pair bond.

Malay Blue-rumped Parrot
Psittinus cyanurus

Distribution: South-eastern Asia.
Size: 18cm (7½in).
Sexing: Hens have brown bills, and no blue on the head.
Youngsters: Have horn-coloured bills.

These small parrots are quite scarce in aviculture, but once they are established, they prove quite easy to maintain on a mixed diet containing plenty of fruit and greenstuff. They have a very attractive, almost musical range of calls. You will need to provide branches for them to gnaw to prevent their beaks becoming overgrown. Blue-rumped Parrots have been bred on a colony system, the hens usually laying two eggs, (although clutches up to five have been recorded). They may live for over a decade, but need adequate protection in cold weather as they appear to be very susceptible to frostbite.

Great-billed Parrot
Tanygnathus megalorhynchos

Distribution: Indonesia, and Balut in the Philippines.
Size: 41cm (16in).
Sexing: Difficult to sex visually, but cocks may have larger beaks and brighter coloration than hens.
Youngsters Similar to adults, but lacking black on the wings.

The requirements of these parrots are similar to those of the Eclectus but, unlike the latter, Greatbills are not continuous nesters, normally laying only two or three eggs during a breeding season. Incubation lasts about 30 days.
Great-billed Parrots can become quite tame and, although not common in aviculture, they make interesting aviary occupants. Their calls, while loud, are not normally persistent, but these birds require a solidly constructed aviary because of their destructive natures, coupled with their powerful bills.

Above: **Great-billed Parrot**
This species needs careful acclimatization, and plenty of fruit, greenstuff and carrot in its diet.

INDEX

SPECIES INDEX

190

Acknowledgments

The author, photographer and publishers wish to thank Rita Hemsley for typing the manuscript, and the following for their assistance with the photography of birds for this book: George Anderson, Charles Attard, Paul and June Bailey, Don and Irene Bardgett, Tom Bassant, Fred Barnicoat, Christine Baxter, Blean Bird Park, Trevor and Maura Buckell, Sue and Mick Cadwallader, Chester Zoo, Irene Christie, Phil and Janet Clarke, Pete Clear, Terry and Jean Cole, David Colson, Dulcie and Freddie Cooke, Fred Cooper, Roy and Debbie Coster, Marion Cripps, Ken Davies, Phil Dobinson, Alan Donnelly, Tony Durkin, Bruce Duthie, Ken and Shirley Epps, Alfred and Marguerite Essex, Ray Fisk, Ken Furssedon, Kevin Gibbs, Jim Gill, Mike Green, Geoff and Sandra Hornsby, Sue Ingall, Colin and Lesley Jackson, Tim Kemp, Barry and Kath Kyme, Alan Jones, Shirley and George Lawton, Louis and Heather Martin, Stanley Maughan, Stuart Mayer, Gerry Mills, Ian Mitchell, Judith Nicholas, Richard Nicholls, Mike and Denise O'Neill, Ron Oxley, Rosemary and Reg Parker, Janet Ralph, Stan Rook, Dave Russell, Stan Sindel, George Smith, John and Geraldine Stevens, Jack Stunnell, Nigel Taboney, Roger Wilkinson, Sue Willis, Rosemary Wiseman, Henry and Jean Wood, Andrew Woolham, Margaret Yound.

Artists

Copyright of the artwork illustrations on the pages following the artists' names is the property of Salamander Books Ltd.

Peter Bull Art Studios 21, 35
Rod Ferring 53
Bill Le Fever 23, 29, 32(T), 34, 38, 54, 63, 64
John Francis 19, 20, 30-1, 32-3, 36-7
Alan Harris 11, 12
David Noble 72, 73, 75
Guy Troughton 26, 69